Successful
Business Plans
for Architects

Successful Business Plans for Architects

Ronald A. McKenzie

Bruce H. Schoumacher

McGraw-Hill, Inc.

New York   St. Louis   San Francisco   Auckland   Bogotá
Caracas   Lisbon   London   Madrid   Mexico   Milan
Montreal   New Delhi   Paris   San Juan   São Paulo
Singapore   Sydney   Tokyo   Toronto

Library of Congress Cataloging-in-Publication Data

McKenzie, Ronald A.
    Successful business plans for architects / Ronald A. McKenzie.
Bruce H. Schoumacher.
        p.   cm.
    Includes bibliographical references (p.   ) and index.
    ISBN 0-07-045654-2
    1. Architectural practice—United States—Management.
I. Schoumacher, Bruce.   II. Title.
NA1996.M39   1992
720'.68—dc20   92-1160
                                                     CIP

1 2 3 4 5 6 7 8 9 0   DOH/DOH   9 8 7 6 5 4 3 2

ISBN   0-07-045654-2

*The sponsoring editor for this book was Joel Stein, the editing
supervisor was Kimberly A. Goff, and the production supervisor was
Suzanne W. Babeuf. This book was set in Century Schoolbook. It was
composed by McGraw-Hill's Professional Book Group composition unit.*

Printed and bound by R. R. Donnelley & Sons Company.

Contents

Preface   ix
Acknowledgments   xiii

Part 1   Business Planning   1

Chapter 1. Architectural Business Environment   3

   I Don't Want to Be in Business; I Just Want to Practice Architecture   4

Chapter 2. Business Plan Explained   17

   What Is a Business Plan?   18
   Methodology   19
   Business Plan Outlines   23

Chapter 3. Business Plan   55

   How Is a Business Plan Prepared?   55
   Annual Operating Business Plan   61
   Annual Operating Business Plan for Sample, Inc.   63
      I Executive Summary   65
      II Positioning   65
      III Opportunities and Issue Analysis   68
      IV Goals and Objectives   71
      V Marketing Strategies   74
      VI Financial Strategies   77
      VII Conclusion   79
      VIII Appendix   80
   Business Planning—The Reasons Why   86

Chapter 4. Strategy and Marketing   88

   Strategy   88
   Marketing   102
   Marketing Conclusion   117

Chapter 5. Financial Planning and Implementation   118
Financial Planning   119
Implementation   130

Chapter 6. Management Perspectives   139
Computers, CAD, and the Architect and Engineer   139
Management Perspectives   153

Part 2   Business Planning Strategies   157

Chapter 7. Selecting the Form of Doing Business   159
Forms of Doing Business   159
What Factors Should Be Considered?   160
Sole Proprietorship   165
Partnerships   166
Corporations   170
Joint Ventures   172
Terminating the Business   173

Chapter 8. Planning: Legal Strategies   175
Selecting an Attorney   175
Strategies for Collecting Accounts Receivables   177
Protecting Clients from Competitors   179
Contracting with Consultants   180
Professional Liability   181
Conclusion   189

Chapter 9. Planning for Risk   190
Insurance   191
Self-Insurance   197
Transfer Risks via Contracts   198
Controlling Litigation   203
Alternative Dispute Resolution   205
Conclusion   206

Chapter 10. Negotiating the Professional Services Agreement   207
Working with Consultants   210
Specific Contractual Provisions   211

Chapter 11. Planning for Fringe Benefits   222
Selecting Fringe Benefit Plans   223
Compensating Employees   225
Retirement Plans   226
Types of Retirement Plans   229
Selecting the Retirement Plan   233
Individual Retirement Options   234
Group Insurance Plans   235

Other Benefit Plans   236
Loss of Owner or Key Employee   237

Chapter 12. Planning for Ownership Transition   239
Conclusion   244

Appendix. Making Your Own Business Plan   245
I   Fill-in-the Blanks Business Plan   246
II   Alternative Business Plan Outlines   260

References   264

Bibliography   266

Index   267

Preface

The professions of architecture and engineering continue to experience change due to the impact on the business climate by a variety of internal and external forces and constraints relating to the demands of the changing economy. These forces are different for each office but can generally be summarized as increased competition, a slowing demand for services, and the pressure to become more productive through computerization. Tight budgets can also make the client more demanding of the services they seek and the resulting contractual arrangements. Marketing strategies, financial strategies, and overall business planning is more important than ever before in order to have the necessary controls in place to manage the cash flow coming through an office.

The architect's and engineer's commission is tied to the in-house projects, and the resulting profit is a function of how well the office and these projects are managed. In most cases, the architects and engineers allocate parts of the fee to certain phases of the design, such as schematic design, design development, construction documents, bidding and negotiations, construction, and observation, depending upon the scope of the work and the amount of additional services. Monies in each phase cover overhead, expenses, direct costs, and additional expenditures required to keep the office doors open. It is hoped that this office and project management system results in profit at the end of the project, as well as a method for evaluating the performance of different parts of the office relative to the different phases. This form of business planning is well understood and written about and practiced with great care by most engineers and architects. However, some offices never seem to get a handle on the fee as it relates to the total practice. Often, the profit that is supposed to be waiting at the end of the project is not there. There is always a risk to the bottom line.

This increased competitive environment, coupled with varying economic strengths, has accentuated a problem that has plagued architects and engineers for years. The problem is managing the architectural or engineering practice with a goal of steady projects which produces a steady cash flow that is profit oriented. This problem is accentuated by the need to make necessary capital investments. As is known, architecture and engineering have been rather inexpensive businesses to enter. A place to draw and a client are basically all that was needed. How many firms started by moonlighting work? But now, to remain competitive, architects and engineers are required to make certain capital investments. Making a capital investment is new to this world. Most businesses deal with capital investments, and/or product and material investments on a daily basis. Architects and engineers are faced with similar problems in running their practice; however, capital investment requirements and constant cash flow problems make the task more difficult, particularly in a competitive environment.

For example, architects and engineers deal with buildings and space, and what better way to impress prospective clients than to dazzle them with ambience and charm? Drafting rooms are not the 50-table layouts that used to dominate the drafting scene, but articulated alcoves with indirect lighting and music coming from someplace. The reception area is now a place which provides an opportunity to display examples of one's work in a pleasant environment. In essence, the architect's or engineer's office is now a marketing tool and is considered by many to be a required expense. Certainly there are exceptions to this rule, where a firm operates out of the same space for long periods of time due to a large customer base. But for the most part, over the course of a business life the architect's or engineer's product, as demonstrated by the interior and exterior spaces created by sensible structural themes, may have an important effect on the office's overall competitive effectiveness. It is a realistic capital expense.

Another new capital expense is the computer, which should be used in every aspect of the architect's and engineer's work. Because of the power of the computer, the private work spaces offering flexible interior landscaping systems have replaced the sea of drawing boards. One ramification of this technology is that it gives firms a competitive edge, allowing them to be more competitive by assisting architects and engineers in the development of graphic diagrams for design studies, which later evolve into well-organized construction documents. Firms can now serve their clients better by offering clear, concise documents and related databases of information that can be changed and modified relatively easily. A clever firm will market this advantage. But this advantage does mean a capital investment, which has an impact on the always variable cash flow that architects and engineers have lived with forever.

Other businesses have greater economic impacts and requirements for capital investments, and they still maintain a level business structure. Their cash flow can be just as variable. What do these corporations and a host of other small-to-medium size businesses do differently that allows them to survive? The answer is they plan their business: They establish goals, objectives, and marketing plans that provide a vehicle for accomplishing the goals; they create financial plans that provide a framework and method of evaluating the plan's progress. Business is essentially the art of planning.

Although an architect or engineer may have the artistic and structural sensitivities to be successful, many lack the business planning skills necessary to handle today's complex world of business decisions. The most common excuse is that they just don't know how to put a plan together. However, more than any other profession, they are accustomed to planning—they plan complex new structures that satisfy the goals and needs of the customer within the constraints of different planning agencies, building codes, and so on, and often within complicated construction cost requirements. The truth is that architects or engineers simply have not been exposed to the management philosophies that are necessary for economic survival—to make a profit. That is the reason for this book—to provide an overview of business planning practices that will familiarize architects and engineers with the necessary techniques and show them how to apply these techniques to a practice effectively. This knowledge can then be used as a foundation to build a practice that will grow and prosper. Specifically, the area of business plans, marketing strategies, financial planning within the context of the business plan, and implementation plans for the architect are addressed.

At the same time, *Successful Business Plans for Architects* provides a framework for when things don't go as planned or when a problem develops. In effect it provides a decision-making structure for the firm in good times and in bad times. In addition, this book offers insight into several topics critical to the development and longevity of an architectural or engineering office. Such areas as legal problems arising during practice, liability insurance, retirement, and transition are discussed. Knowledge of these areas and the understanding of how they fit into the annual business plan will serve to make an architectural or engineering practice better able to cope with the overwhelming variety of problems that face the architect and engineer. As a result, the firm will be able to face new opportunities with a confidence that will allow them to seek profitability aggressively.

Successful Business Plans for Architects is divided into two parts for purpose of clarity and convenience. The first part demonstrates how to construct a business plan and presents important elements of marketing, strategy, and implementation. A sample business plan of a mock firm in Chap. 3 shows how theory might be put to use. Architects and engineers are then given the opportunity to form their own business plans. The second part contains important business and legal issues that each firm must pay particular attention to. Issues such as liability exposure, contracts, and insurance are important considerations for any to address in its annual business plan, and so they are given ample discussion here. The intent of this book is to illustrate how important it is for the architect and engineer to pay attention to business issues facing their firm. By taking an active business planning role in all matters important to a firm, one has a better chance of continuing to do good design work in the future and making a profit while doing so. Thus, the information provided in this book serves as a sourcebook of planning and business information for the architect and engineer. Using this information will further one's efforts in practicing architecture and engineering at the highest level of professionalism.

As a starting place, the architectural and engineering business environment for developing a business plan is examined.

Ronald A. McKenzie
Bruce H. Schoumacher

Acknowledgments

We would like to thank Leo Egan; Robert H. Windeler, Jr.; Michael Yantos; Charles E. Whalen of Querrey & Harrow, Ltd.; William R. Jackson of Bradley & Jackson; and Tom Okarma of AVA Insurance Agency, Inc., for their invaluable help in reviewing this book.

Successful
Business Plans
for Architects

Business Planning

1

Architectural Business Environment

In order to properly develop a business plan, architects and engineers must first understand the environment in which they operate. Environment means the attitudes and conditions that an architect or engineer must respond to in his or her particular practice. One good way to understand that environment is to look at several problems or misconceptions that your architectural or engineering firm may have to deal with. Signs of impending economic instability within a firm could stem from a variety of problems. A good business plan, and the resulting marketing and financial plans, addresses issues which provide you with a degree of control by offering a framework for evaluating predicted and current difficulties. How you address a problem is a measure of how well your office management system works. It is this decision-making process, using your business plan, that makes the difference between one office succeeding and another one failing. By examining problems that are common in the profession, you will see how these problems can be addressed by a business plan. Business plans are real tools that can be used to address specific issues in your architectural or engineering practice environment.

One common characteristic separating the architectural profession from other professions and businesses is the idea that architects are artists who create spaces for others to enjoy. Some say that architecture is sculpture you walk through to experience different parts of the space. In fact, training an architect in the most classical sense is a combination of all art forms—from the freehand drawings when visions first take shape, to massing studies when three-dimensional complexities are explored, to the studies of color and texture when suggestions of sensitivity and scale are made. This artistic training is balanced with mechanical engineering sciences to make dreams realistic and buildable. It is the true architect who can sketch a project and at the same time see the three-dimensional forms take shape—usually to the bewilderment of the client. Not everyone can do this. You use your education to communicate visions to others, so you can sell them, and in the end, build them.

The architectural and engineering business is one of the most difficult professions to keep balanced with just the right amount of work flowing through the system complemented by the necessary amount of labor and talent to complete the projects on a timely basis. This problem is compounded by the nature of architectural and engineering projects. Timing of projects is understandably unpredictable—from bank loans to the planning commission approvals, from building permits to the environmental impact reports. Architects and engineers know how to do the work but generally lack the skills to balance the process. Understanding this is important, because although the business management tasks are not necessarily complicated, architects and engineers are not given training in management. You must rely on training from other architects or engineers, who usually want to use young architects in a different manner, mainly for production. Although this internship methodology is good, it lacks the business emphasis. It is only the larger, more sophisticated firms that can afford to train a young architect or engineer properly to take on the future responsibilities of a principal. It is necessary for the architect and engineer to develop the business skills that will help him or her cope with the complexities of surviving in today's marketplace.

I Don't Want to Be in Business; I Just Want to Practice Architecture

Generally, all architectural and engineering offices, large or small, new or old, eventually face a common problem. This problem is the realization that there is more to a balanced architectural or engineering practice than good design. It might start when the office experiences a lack of work. A short time later there is usually a cash flow problem. Then someone is let go. The cycle is typical and familiar and one reason why some architects and engineers are now contracting out so much of their work, particularly in the CAD area. Contract labor is becoming more prevalent: It is much easier to let someone go, and there are no strings attached, no vacation pay, no unemployment considerations, and so on.

An architect or engineer soon learns that architecture or engineering is first a business. Businesses strive for prosperity—to make a profit. It is the profit that allows the architect or engineer to design.

Because of the service business orientation, for a long time architects and engineers have been taught that producing a good quality design will be followed by cash flow and profit. This may be true in some cases, but it is actually the furthest from the truth in a realistic sense. Good design may or may not produce more work and may or may not be profitable. Quality design and proper business attitudes work together. A more realistic view is that quality design services coupled with quality fee structures with all contract entitlements, good management execution, and planning methodologies lead to a well-rounded profitable business.

Striving for profit is not bad. Profit (besides paying the bills) allows the practice to grow, the office to experiment with new ideas, and marketing to go after bigger and better commissions. The truth is, without profit eventually there will be no practice; there is no chance to do good quality design work—to excel. So, in the end, it is profit that wins. Gaining a basic understanding of how a business plan works can help point an office in the right direction. A business plan can offer guidelines for maintaining stability and benchmarks to measure performance in good times and in bad times. It is not a total cure but a tool if one really wants to survive to practice competitively.

The architectural and engineering problems (or misconceptions) that will be discussed in an effort to understand the environment in which architects and engineers practice will also help you understand the business planning process. These misconceptions may or may not occur in every office and are less likely to occur in an office that has some degree of management control. However, when they do occur, one problem may grow into another to the point where a project may actually impact the quality of work on other projects.

For example, the first problem or misconception is that the principal architect's time is not billable to a client—the principal's time is essentially free. Now this sounds like a rather strange concept, but it does exist. There are times when architects do not bill for their time, even if it's legitimate billable time. The argument is that the staff is responsible for creating the billable hours, leaving the principal to have a friendly detached client relationship. Or the architect's job is one of putting out the fires. Another reason is that if there is any question about a bill, the architect never has to defend personal billing time—it's always the staff's fault! This leads to the good architect/bad staff scenario.

The underlying problem, beside a poor understanding of profit management, is that the architect or engineer is not confident of his or her ability and self-worth. The client will soon sense this lack of confidence and self-worth and come to the conclusion it should use another firm. The principal architect is the one who sets an example and should radiate confidence. It is the most persuasive selling tool. A firm's personality is an advantageous marketing tool, as well as a strong negotiating tool. An architect or engineer who has no confidence will soon see the poor presumptions come true.

This is an unfortunate dilemma for the profession. If architects or engineers consider their time free, it leads to problems concerning the larger issue that architectural and engineering fees have remained basically constant for years, whereas the responsibilities, liabilities, and expenses have risen. Drawings are much more complicated to assemble than ever before. Labor rates, even though they're below that of other professionals, often create problems. Errors and omissions (E&O) insurance now takes a large portion of overhead, and many contracts require proof of coverage. Avoiding E&O insurance produces a climate of risk. On top of this, the nature of the building process suggests that the drawings engineers and architects produce will be free from error. Whereas this is always the desired objective, it is difficult to achieve no matter what effort is expended in coordination and checking. All of these factors have effectively shrunken the architect's and engineer's fee. With this perspective, the professionals who consider their time to be free are asking for problems.

The second problem, closely related to the first, is that of fee cutting. Fee cutting generally occurs in competitive situations in which engineers or architects are requested to lower their fees. It usually occurs when work is tight and something is better than nothing—the old cash flow problem. The ramifications of accepting work for less, with the same design and legal responsibilities, is frightful. Consider the architect who designed a beautiful building and, later, when someone asked where the architect was, the reply was out of business; the firm lost its shirt on the project. Sometimes an architect's best work is a financial disaster. Why?

Quite often a client turns to the architect out of habit, asks that the fees be reduced, and the architect dutifully complies. Or a client might sense the architect is having a cash flow problem and turns this to an advantage in the fee negotiation. This situation generally results in a smaller fee, with more problems and greater liability exposure. In this situation, the architect turns to the scope of work to see what can be adjusted or eliminated so the job can still be done at some profit level. But the question is, How often is the fee lowered to such a point that the same quality of design and construction documents cannot be achieved? Is the architect creating a liability? For example, one common area to cut is construction observation from the scope of work. When the architect or engineer does not have an opportunity to observe the work, however, there can be all kinds of consequences—particularly if legal issues arise. The architect or engineer may end up spending a lot of free time on the project—sometimes to avoid some form of legal entanglement. Now you are back to problem one: The architect's and engineer's time is free.

Why are architects always the first ones to be asked to lower their fees? Why are owners of projects so resentful of the architect's commission but repeatedly pay 6 percent or higher commissions to real estate agents for selling or marketing the project or similar commissions for leasing the property? The scope of liability between real estate and architecture is enormous. Why do architects have a rather unnecessary image with adjacent professionals and often with their clients? Is architecture becoming the expendable profession?

The answers are within the entire profession and how its image relates to the public. Image is one of the most serious issues the industry must face. Image is how the outside world views architects and engineers. The general consensus is that architects and engineers are more into their thing and thus tend to lack certain business disciplines. They simply don't address business problems seriously. As an example, architects don't stand up for what is rightly theirs; they seem to be the first ones to back down in a fee confrontation situation. This is certainly not all inclusive, for there are excellent businesspeople practicing architecture, both in large and small offices. But the tendency of the architecture and engineering profession dealing with business matters is to avoid the situation, to postpone it; it will be better tomorrow. Each architect and engineer needs to address his or her own image as he or she prepares a marketing plan. The architect and engineer must view themselves as businesspeople first and as architects or engineers second.

How many times has an architect or engineer sent out an invoice, only to back down when the client hits the roof, even over a small amount of money clearly covered in the contract? Architects do not send out hourly contracts charging for every minute as those in other professions do. Why? There is a clear indication that clients do not respect the architect's or engineer's time. They might in the beginning, but they don't when it comes time to write the check. Clients take advantage of the architect or engineer because of their image. They ask, How long did it take to do that sketch? They know the architect or engineer will probably bend in an effort to get some form of payment. The image of the architectural and engineering profession is the most volatile and sensitive issue the professions face. That is why issues such as fee cutting are important—it relates to how architects and engineers conduct their work. These subjects should be addressed in business plans which can lay out tighter controls and philosophies of negotiation.

As a note, the correct answer to the question How long did it take you to do that sketch? is the total number of years of education plus the number of years working in the field of architecture! So it might go something like this: It took 16 years, 5 months, and 10 days. There is always the other side of the negotiation table. Fee assessment and negotiation is an art form in itself and, as you shall see, a lot of it has to do with the policy and direction the office has chosen to take, which is reflected in the business plan.

Another example is the problem where an architect or engineer must act upon the applications for payment or similar document submitted by the contractor so the owner can release construction funds. If the owner also owes the architect or engineer for services rendered, this would seem like a logical time to address the issue of remuneration. How often has the architect or engineer gone unpaid for months while approving thousands of dollars in construction monies? If the architect or engineer, with guidance from an attorney, had set up provisions for payment in the initial owner and architect or engineer agreement, the client would understand that the architect or engineer could not be left unpaid. Taking a more aggressive businesslike approach to fee payment is easier to address when the necessary preparation has been completed. Part of this preparation is business planning, for it sets up philosophies that take a business in one pointed direction.

A third problem is the lack of marketing. Marketing is relatively new to architects and engineers, probably because the professions tended not to advertise or market themselves. There have also been stringent connotations about advertising imposed by the profession itself. In actuality, there are no restrictions regarding advertising at a national level, just as there are no fee-setting policies for member organizations such as the American Institute of Architects (AIA). The architect and engineer should, however, check at the state level for separate policies. Architecture and engineering have each been determined to be competitive professions, with all the same rights as other professions. However, these professions have always maintained a degree of aloofness when it comes to marketing. References and word of mouth seem to be the highlight of many marketing campaigns. Other efforts are sometimes feeble. A common example is when work runs out, the staff is put to work developing a company brochure. That's rather an odd time to be doing a brochure. It seems logical, when you think about it, that a spirited marketing campaign should be orchestrated well before the work runs out.

Ideas change with time, and the increased arena of competition has moved the architect and engineer to accept marketing without becoming scorned. There are many marketing and advertising efforts which an architect or engineer can do to get the word out. Many marketing programs that can be developed are reasonable in cost and can be tastefully implemented. In that architects or engineers are graphically oriented, it seems they, if any professional, would be in a good position to develop clever marketing messages.

However, to a certain extent, these antiquated marketing perceptions are still around. As an example, a Chicago firm advertised for the position of marketing director to be responsible for the development of its future client base. On inquiring about the position, it was learned that the firm was looking for a marketing director of a competing firm who could bring a strong client base. The reply was, I thought you meant the *blood and guts* type of marketing that corporations generally use to develop market niches, identify new customers, then determine the best way to close those prospects, etc.! The answer was, No, that's not what we mean in Chicago. This is a classic example of what marketing isn't and what it should not be.

Marketing, as you shall see, relates directly to the business plan. Marketing is the answer to the goals and objectives of the plan. Marketing is essentially everything it takes to get a contract and generate revenue. It is an activity that is well thought out, with its own strategies. There are no shortcuts. Creating a well laid out marketing campaign, then implementing it throughout the year should be one of the more focused business activities of the principal architects and engineers. For both large and small offices, marketing is important.

The fourth problem area is the lack of fee collection. Small- and medium-sized offices often do not have an employee responsible for account receivables and must address the issues as they arise. Too often the principal architect or engineer must call the client and ask about payment on the overdue account. Many times the principal uses the buddy technique and after some half-hearted embarrassed attempts puts it off to the following month. The architect or engineer is often baited with future projects, or the client calls attention to the problem he or she might be having with a building, even if it's unrelated to the architect's or engineer's work. It is sometimes easier to hope to get a check in the mail next month, than to be forceful and treat the situation with the business skills necessary to resolve the situation favorably.

Again, the problem snowballs. First, the client knows now he or she can buffalo this architect or engineer—that the architect or engineer does not have the confidence to demand what is his or hers. Why? Is the architect or engineer on poor financial footings? The result is a lack of respect and, most likely, continued late payments. These late payments mean an impact on the cash flow and that means financial restraints on the business. Anything financial has to do with business planning.

The fifth problem area is the inability of a firm to account for project cost overruns that occur because of the changes in the scope of work. When these changes of work are not properly accounted for, they develop into serious impacts on project cost controls. Profits go down, and breakeven situations, or worse, losses, are developed. Sometimes, the change of scope of work is well documented by the staff, but the architect or engineer is not comfortable in presenting this information to the client, even with a solid contract. Again, this is a sign of a lack of confidence by the architect or engineer and the staff. The financial stability of a business depends upon making a fair profit on each and every project.

The sixth problem area is the worst—it is when no appropriate architectural or engineering contract is used at all. The AIA has spent a lot of time and effort in developing a comprehensive set of architectural contracts that allows for a variety of methods of fee calculation, and so on. The contracts have been tested in court and are improved upon by attorneys familiar with construction law and related case decisions who advise their architect clients on a project-by-project basis. To not use one of these contracts or an attorney in today's world of liabilities and lawsuits is inexcusable. To use letter forms of agreements not approved by an attorney or, worse yet, the handshake method is simply not being responsible.

The reason why architects or engineers might not use a contract is the belief that the contract will intimidate and scare off the client. The answer is to get a legitimate client. The cost of litigation for any problem, whether real or imagined by the client, is extraordinarily expensive. Contracts offer provisions for negotiations; they offer a foundation for examining claims as well as alternatives to the courts. Contracts are there to help the architect and engineer. Why not use them?

There can be no excuse for not using a contract. Some architects or engineers feel awkward in working with attorneys. This can be illustrated by the architect who commented that an architect should never be seen walking into an attorney's office. When asked why, the reply was that the mere association with an attorney would lead to a bad public image. Furthermore, if a client saw an architect going into an attorney's office, the client would begin to suspect something was wrong. It was suggested that perhaps the client might take it to mean the architect was being responsible for the firm by reviewing relevant legal contracts and proposals. The end result is, of course, the architect or engineer loses. Sooner or later, an architect or engineer who doesn't use an effective contract will be in court. The only ones who will make money are the legal counsels. The architect or engineer will eventually receive his or her comeuppance. The subject of contracts is important as it relates to business planning and the health of the firm.

The seventh area of concern is that of insurance and liability issues. Errors and omissions insurance is very costly. However, the downside of not having it can mean the difference of an office growing or failing. It is a difficult area to deal with because of the high cost of the expense. But avoiding or ignoring this issue poses even bigger problems if something should happen, such as a client turning bad or being forced to take legal action, defensive or offensive, even if you have not done anything wrong. Are there ways of protecting yourself by contractual provisions that limit the liability on a job? Are there office practices that will, to a certain extent, help reduce or limit the liability?

The eighth area of concern is the confrontation of CAD and the use of computers in general. It has been relatively difficult for the architecture and engineering professions to welcome this high-tech advantage. The problem goes back to the training of an architect as an artist and the impression of what an architect or engineer is (or was) in society. The fact is, a structure is a complex creation, and when this is combined with the building and zoning ordinances and restrictions and construction material requirements, there should be an overwhelming acceptance of anything that will help sort out the problems and reach a solution. Computers offer marvelous opportunities in these areas. They also open up possibilities for architects and engineers to expand their service into consulting areas, such as facility management or evaluation of any number of engineering problems. To say, as an architect once did, "that CAD doesn't work" is a statement that sheds light on really how far the profession has gotten. Even though surveys suggest that from 40 to 60 percent of architects use CAD, the number of architects truly using the full power of these systems, compared to other professions, is more like 15 to 20 percent. Fortunately, schools are taking an aggressive role and training students on computer systems, but the integration is still left to the practicing architect or engineer who most likely has not been trained.

The question is raised, Why CAD and business planning? The answer is that computers are the biggest single change to come along that will continue to impact the profession in a multitude of ways for a long time. Not only has it affected the way you can analyze information, it can have a great effect on marketing and thus should become a part of every architect's and engineer's business strategy. Computers cost money, and where best to address financial requirements but in a business plan. CAD is very important to the architect's and engineer's environment, and Chap. 6 develops these ideas further.

Why plan?

Why should an architect or engineer spend valuable time developing a business plan and resulting marketing and financial plans? The American Management Association (AMA) identifies four reasons for planning:[1]

- It coordinates the company's activities.
- It motivates those involved in plan development.
- It provides a basis for measuring actual performance against expected performance.
- It acts as a vehicle for communicating to others (both within the company and outside it) the company's objectives.

Any one of these is reason enough to include an annual business plan in the firm's arsenal of business strategies. When combined, they offer an unarguable cause to plan for one's future. When used properly, a business plan gives the architect a competitive edge.

The development of a plan is a time-consuming task, particularly the first time it is done, and may have an impact on the office routine. However, the benefits derived from being forced to review the company's financial position and marketing strategies, and all the other parameters, far outweigh any downtime. For once, the charter of the office, its motivation, and its subtle relationships can be put down on paper and evaluated. A plan forces a firm to coordinate the company's activities.

It takes more than one person to author a plan. This statement should not, however, be construed that a sole practitioner is excluded from business planning. It means that when available, it is important to develop communication with other executives or managers in the firm. The result will be a better and a more widely accepted plan. For example, the architect or engineer in charge of production, as well as the project architects and engineers, must be involved in preparing and submitting information. An office manager and marketing manager, if they exist, should play a large role in the development of the plan. When the plan has been accepted as a basis for managing next year's business, those who developed the plan, to a great extent, own it. As a result, these staff members are motivated to see the plan implemented successfully.

For example, the principals working with marketing may be required to bring in and sign a specific level of business to reach the firm's annual goal of X amount of construction dollars. Production, under the project architects or engineers, will be required to produce jobs at a certain profit level avoiding the cost overruns that are common. The architects or engineers in charge of contracts will be charged with making sure they are covered from a legal point of view and are able to collect on all additional services. The architect or engineer in charge of the contracts should also ensure that the client understands his or her responsibilities and effectively manage the relationship. They all, in effect, take ownership in the plan and their own contributions and responsibilities and are inspired to see it to completion. That is not to say there will not be problems—in those cases there should be no excuses for shortfalls, only sound reasonable business discussions.

Having this information available, and hence making and approving proposals for next year's activities, provides a degree of measurability. By providing a goal to work toward and attaching a financial plan to it, one will be able to measure performance and thus have the basis for real and logical discussions about corrective measures. As additional annual plans are implemented, one truly begins to understand where the firm's strengths and weaknesses are. In turn, the firm will better be able to carry out the plan. Not achieving the goals of a plan does not mean the firm or participants are incompetent nor does it mean the plan is wrong. It may only mean the plan was too ambitious given the resources available.

Last, a business plan is a communication tool. What better way is there to communicate an idea and a strategy to another group? For example, a business plan may call for the acquisition of an architectural or engineering firm in another part of a city in an effort to grow a business and add new, specific talent to the organization. The principal in charge of this project for the year may find several firms available for a merger. This team of planners, which may consist of the principal architect or engineer, a CPA, and the firm's attorney, will prepare a business plan for the acquisition of the firm. It will generally be financial in nature and have staffing implications. If outside funds are required, a bank may have to review the plan in reference to financial aid. What better way to communicate these ideas than with a well-prepared business plan? The point is, a plan is used to communicate ideas to others so logical decisions can be made based on carefully prepared material. This process ensures a better chance of success by, one hopes, identifying some of the risk.

From this discussion you can see why you should plan and the benefits an architect or engineer derives from the process. There are also other reasons why the planning process is so important. It gives a firm a real *competitive advantage* in the marketplace and a better chance to develop opportunities that are presented.

Competitive advantage

Planning your future will provide you with a real competitive advantage. A plan, for example, might uncover a market niche not yet penetrated by other firms. Suppose a business plan, as a strategy, suggested that a market research project be undertaken by the company to determine all the areas of new work being discussed by different government agencies, from financed low-income housing projects to state and federal buildings. What if the market research study revealed that there were plans to pump money into federal projects? This information could change the entire future of an architectural or engineering firm. Even if a firm does not have the experience, it can begin to align itself with consultants and other firms that specialize in specific facilities. By carefully adopting the idea into long-range business planning strategies, the firm can be in a position to step forward some time in the future with all the proper credentials in place. It may even be able to show job references and coordinate work with its architectural or engineering alliances.

By developing a structure to address problems, a firm has a better chance to succeed. Many books and lecturers talk about the wisdom of formulating one's goals and objectives within a specific time frame.

The planning methodologies introduced here is the perfect forum for setting down these goals and objectives in writing. The process will give any firm a competitive edge because it will have a *focused direction* in its thinking.

It is important to note that there are always opportunities available for those willing to look. Planning methodologies offer an organized method to look for and evaluate personnel, current job characteristics, income levels, liability exposures, marketing trends, and a host of other factors to determine where an architectural or engineering firm might be the most competitive. Opportunities are often disguised as problems, and it is this sort of attitude that will lead to creative solutions. It is the nature of the business game.

Ultimate survival game

To review, the following are some problems an architect or engineer can encounter and general categories to which these topics relate. All of these problems may relate to more than one topic, but as a starting point consider the following:

- The architect's or engineer's time is free relates to *opportunities* and *issue analysis,* as well as *financial strategies.*
- The practice of fee cutting relates to *financial strategies.*
- Lack of marketing relates to *marketing strategies, opportunities* and *issue analysis,* and *goals and objectives.*
- Fee collection relates to *financial strategies.*
- Cost overruns relate to *financial strategies.*
- Lack of effective contracts relates to *positioning.*
- Insurance and liability issues relate to *positioning.*
- Not using CAD relates to *goals and objectives* and *marketing strategies.*

These problems are all closely related and, collectively or singularly, can be signs of impending financial problems. Financial problems are one of the first indications that a business may fail, or suffer a hardship, even though the product of that business, the architecture or engineering, may be superior in design. These are the issues that cause firms to begin to develop an understanding of the environment that surrounds the practice of architecture.

Figure 1.1 illustrates a diagram of planning categories. The development of a business plan starts with the simple outline in the figure, which sets into place a methodology that allows the identification of problems as they occur and a framework to work toward a solution. The outline consists of the following:

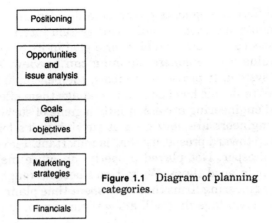

Figure 1.1 Diagram of planning categories.

Positioning, which relates to whom a firm is and what it's doing

Opportunities and issue analysis, which relates to the opportunities facing the firm, as well as the problems an office might be having, such as staffing, cost overruns, or not enough work coming to the office

Goals and objectives, which relates to what the firm is after

Marketing strategies, which relates to what a firm is going to do to achieve its goals and objectives

Financial, which relates to operational considerations

All of these topics relate to and support each other in developing a concise interrelated presentation of facts and strategies. Consequently, the diagram should actually appear as Fig. 1.2.

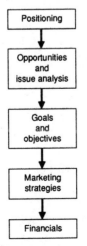

Figure 1.2 Relationship of planning categories.

As the different segments of the plan develop in conjunction with other segments, a system is built. This system interrelates the essential tools needed to view a problem or a goal in its proper perspective, then to evaluate it. Business planning can be viewed as a problem avoidance system. It provides the tools, the benchmarks, and the forum to meet problems head on and to manage them effectively. Architecture and engineering are essentially a game of survival, and architects and engineers are very good at surviving; it's learning to take the next step toward prosperity that is important. Played properly an office will prosper. Not played properly, an office may survive and even prosper in good times. When times become rough, the architectural and engineering firms that have spent time planning will have a competitive advantage that will allow them to win, to survive, and to prosper.

2

Business Plan Explained

A business plan is a set of goals and objectives that are quantified, are subject to a specific time frame, and have within it the necessary strategies to accomplish or satisfy the plan. It is the most proven method of presenting new ideas in a logical fashion and should be the starting point of any serious business endeavor.

This chapter outlines a business plan approach and methodology. Chapter 3 presents a completed business plan for an architectural or engineering office. In addition, at the end of this book is an appendix with a fill-in-the-blank outline business plan that provides the basic framework for continued development. It's meant as a starting point.

A business plan is a planning tool. As such it's meant to change over a period of time as ideas mature and opportunities present themselves. A business plan allows a firm to focus on where it wants to be and the forum to address how to get there. A business plan is meant to be flexible. Thus, if an opportunity arises that was not suggested in a plan, it does not mean the firm disregards it. It means the opportunity should be looked at in the context of the existing goals and objectives and a decision made as to its viability and fit within the firm. It may mean that another business plan may have to be written to explore the advantages and disadvantages fully. More than one business plan may exist in different stages at the same time.

Some members of the firm could, for example, be developing an annual operating plan, while other members of the firm are researching and developing a plan to acquire another architectural firm or implement a CAD system. Plans are meant to be flexible. One plan might be a few pages in length; another might be 30 pages or more. Plans tend to reflect their maker; that is to say, some plans will be optimistic, whereas other plans will be conservative. Overall, they tend to be more conservative because each step must be well substantiated with details. A plan is a fluid, dynamic reflection of the firm and its goals and objectives.

What Is a Business Plan?

The first step is to understand what a business plan is. According to the AMA, a business plan "means the development of a written document that spells out, in considerable detail, where a company's current business is and, more important, where it is headed."[2] Obviously, this is a time-consuming task and requires resources of the company. Most architectural and engineering firms use some planning process that might consist of income statements, balance sheets, and cash flow statements. The business plan requires one also to look at the services a firm offers to its customer base, how competitive the firm is, and what other service it might offer to help reach its goals, all in relationship to the financial status of the firm. The business plan also takes into account what the firm wants to be in terms of its future. Then the business plan takes this information a step further and "forces management to identify opportunities and threats, recognize both the strength and weaknesses of the company, reconcile conflicting views, and arrive at a set of agreed-upon goals, objectives, and strategies for the company in a systematic and realistic way."[2]

Business plans have many names, each indicating what the plan is addressing. Here are names of several different business plans:

19__ Second Quarter Business Plan

Five-Year Long-Range Business Plan

Five-Year Strategic Plan

19__ Fiscal Annual Operating Business Plan

19__ Marketing Plan

CAD Acquisition Business Plan

Each of these business plans addresses a specific business issue.

Many corporations have adopted specific names for their annual business plans so there is some coordination between the different types and for the different authors. Other plan titles are chosen by the author to best convey what he or she is trying to accomplish. Architectural and engineering business plans tend to be marketing related plans unless they are addressing a specific issue or business decision, such as expansion. A marketing plan may be an individual plan or part of another plan, such as an annual business plan. It depends upon the size of the firm, the specific characteristics of the organization, and the preferences of management.

A business plan also has a purpose, a reason for being. A good practice is to write a one-sentence description of the purpose of the business plan and to include it on the title page. In that way, the author of the plan sets the stage for the reader as to what problem the plan is going to address. Several purpose statements are as follows:

The purpose of this business plan is to outline the Annual Operating Plan for 19__ .

The purpose of this business plan is to analyze the opportunity for *Sample, Inc.,* to become a dominant force in the financial institution marketplace within the next 5 years.

The purpose of this business plan is to examine the merger of *Sample, Inc.,* with *Example Imaging Architects, Inc.*

The purpose of this business plan is the analysis of all opportunities facing *Sample, Inc.,* and the recommendation of a growth strategy.

The purpose of this business plan is to analyze the integration of CAD into *Sample, Inc.*

As a note, two fictitious offices named *Sample, Inc.,* and *Example Imaging Architects, Inc.,* will be used as examples to explain the business planning process. Furthermore, the pseudonyms used and discussed in this chapter are reflected in the completed business plan. This will provide a framework that is clear, since only one firm is being discussed.

As you can see, the purpose statement on the cover sheet, combined with the title of the plan, announces to the reader what the plan is going to be about. There should be no mysteries or secrets. A business plan is decision-making information that needs to be conveyed quickly, efficiently, and with as much supporting documentation as required by each situation. To do this effectively, there must be a consistent methodology used as an overall guide to organization.

Methodology

Understanding how to organize a business plan and what a business plan is trying to accomplish will go a long way in helping to understand a plan when it is read. The ultimate goal is to present a clear and precise plan. Three questions can be used to establish the purpose and direction of the entire plan, as well as individual parts of it. Understanding and using these questions will set forth a clear understanding of what is required to write the plan and what you can expect when reading one. The questions are shown in Fig. 2.1.

These three questions summarize the direction a business plan

Figure 2.1   Planning methodology.

should take. If one of the questions is left out, readers will not have sufficient information to make a decision about the plan. For example, suppose a small architectural or engineering firm has decided to start using a business plan strategy to become more competitive and to grow. That firm will want to summarize its intent before developing its plan. Remember, a business plan, whether done annually or in response to a specific need, addresses specific issues that are important at the time. Each year has different problems facing it. One year an annual business plan may focus on the problems associated with growth; the next year, the plan may address sustaining growth. The combinations are endless and all are in response to the basic charter or mission statement of the firm. The point is, each plan will have a purpose that gives it a character of its own. Thus, the three questions outline and provide direction to the plan.

Who are we?

The response to who are we relates to who the firm is, what kind of work it does, who the staff people are, what the current business situation is, and so on. The answers provide the reader with a foundation for making a proper evaluation. They are necessary since not all readers of a business plan will know about that specific firm. For example, a banker evaluating a loan application may not know the firm.

An answer to the first question might be as follows:

Sample, Inc., is a small firm that is in a specific market niche of residential and commercial projects. It has achieved an annual income level of $612,000, however. It is experiencing low growth since it is not able to get commissions on the size of commercial projects it would like to work on.

This information might be supported by financials and biographies about the principals and associates. With this brief sketch of the firm, the reader will have a sense of what might be expected, what might be realistic in relationship to subsequent goals and objectives, and essentially what drives the firm. One is also in a better position to address the rest of the plan, as the preliminary groundwork has been completed.

Where do we want to go?

The answer to the second question is straightforward: It's a statement about where the firm wants to go. Who answers the question is important. It's usually the decision of the principals, who are the owners. In some cases, it may be a decision of the board of directors or advisors. The answer is an expression of the firm's intent and deserves great discussion, reflection, and evaluation. Some may be conservative and only want to sustain income at the present level because they don't want the practice to become larger. Or a firm might make a decision to increase revenue so profits can be used as a capital expenditure for computer equipment. Answers to this question point the way for the future. A firm must be realistic in its expectations—where the firm wants to go and where the firm can go must be realistically appraised.

In our example, *Sample, Inc.,* has decided it must grow in some manner in order to gain a strategic advantage over its competition. It has also decided that the firm needs to start looking at CAD systems seriously to take advantage of increased performance, design strengths, and marketing value. *Sample, Inc.,* has determined that it wants to be a million dollar billable income firm within 5 years—that is where they want to go. The business plan in Chap. 3 will develop this scenario.

Authoring a plan is a process. It requires input, discussion of ideas, creative thinking, contemplation, and, above all, a good business sense. The final written report is a mere recording of the process. The recording of the plan introduces a form of measurement, making the plan responsive to future business decisions.

How do we get there?

To answer the question how do we get there, there are actually two approaches that must be considered. First, the principals may decide that the solution is to do some specific act or take some specific course that will lead to a specific conclusion. Actually, this type of approach is common and is similar to having a preconceived idea about a solution and writing the plan around that idea. Many business plans are written to analyze some course or action. The reason is that the business plan offers the best medium for outlining the facts, presenting options, underscoring the risks and opportunities, and, at the same time, addressing the specific issue. An example is a business plan that addresses the issue of the firm expanding by merging with another firm. Here, the results of the business plan are known, and the task at hand is to accomplish that event. In this type of approach, it is important to pay attention to the risks and threats of the proposal, as these will be critical, particularly in cases where potential profitability might be marginal. These risks must be pointed out in the conclusion to forewarn those of the parameters of executing the plan. This is particularly important information.

The second approach is a result of a planning process where a solution is derived from the facts, from meetings with the specific architects or engineers and managers, and from a myriad of other informational sources. The solution will be developed as part of and as a result of the planning process. This is an important point. If one wants to grow a firm, the business planning process might suggest several market studies to determine specific information that will help in making the decision. An annual operating business and marketing plan is a perfect example. One knows the purpose of the plan is to outline next year's budgets and operating expenses, as well as profit targets. Marketing issues will also be addressed as a way to reach the goals. Through the process of gathering information for the plan, such as the group meetings, market research activities, and old fashioned contemplation and thinking, a plan is formulated. It is made up of what the authors feel is the best scenario for the firm to follow based upon the marketing research.

This is where a trained marketing person with architectural and engineering experience is truly invaluable. This individual can help lead the way to new market niches for a firm. By determining the effective target market, growth projections, and a sense of the competition, a firm can develop a forecast after developing some market share strategies. These forecasts can become targets and serve as a form of measurement of how the firm is doing relative to its goals. The purpose of the plan, besides outlining performance guidelines and goals and objectives, is to answer this one question—How do we get there? One can only answer this question with confidence achieved after all the alternatives are explored. Eventually, the conclusions or recommendations must be supported by financial justifications.

The point of the three-question methodology is that by addressing the first two questions, the answer, that is, the third question, is put into a definite perspective with specific parameters. An answer that is developed with one set of goals and objectives would be quite different if other goals and objectives were used. Essentially, the three questions are used as a guide for developing the material in the plan. If, at the end, the three questions are not answered in the plan, something has been missed. It's a check and balance system and when used lends credibility to the report. Credibility builds upon credibility.

The conclusion from these plans may be that something else is going to have to happen for the firm to grow at the rate that is determined to be a goal. At this point, the firm will ask what its alternatives are, what options does it have, and so on. The information will be used to support the conclusions of the business plan. The work of doing the plan, the staff meetings at which alternatives are discussed, and so on, are what lead one to a conclusion.

Understanding the plan methodology gives the plan direction. The plan's format allows one to present the information in a logical order. A plan's outline can change depending upon the subject matter, and so on. Other outlines are in the appendix as examples. In examining these, you will see that the intent of the outline and methodology is preserved, that basically the words have changed. Different plans call for different material to be presented, which can also change the outline. In addition, in one plan a group of information, such as financials, might be emphasized, whereas in another plan, it is not. The author often changes the outline as he or she develops the material, but the basic outlines presented in this book can be used to start most business plans.

Business Plan Outlines

As you have seen, the business plan is based upon three basic questions or concepts the plan strives to answer. The business plan is thus a simple document which may appear complex. A plan for a major corporation may run into the hundreds of pages, with many charts and graphs used to illustrate and explain the points. These may be followed by extensive financials supporting the plan's proposals. On the other hand, many business plans may be presented in just a few pages and will have just as much meaning and use as a larger one. The difference is situational—some plans may require excessive length, whereas others don't.

Just because a plan is written does not mean it is going to be adopted. Plans must be reviewed and approved by those in the positions to do so. Just because a plan purports to grow a firm one way does not mean management is going to accept that. This adoption strategy is another check and balance system. Many business plans are first examined from the point of view of a business plan and are later set aside because the plan just doesn't seem to make sense or has too many risks.

For example, the group in charge of preparing an annual plan may come back to management with a request for specific funds to become available to support the year's efforts. Upper management might say that they think you are headed in the right direction, but your costs for marketing and computer equipment are too high. They might want you to look at a different marketing program and a different scenario for the acquisition of capital equipment. You must then go back to the drawing board. Sooner or later and generally on some timed basis, such as the end of the fiscal year, the plan is accepted.

One comment is in order: A business plan depends entirely upon the individual or group doing the work. Two people with different backgrounds, philosophies, and opinions may well come up with different plans. There is no right solution—it is a plan. For example, corporations might charter a group of people to prepare several business plans each quarter in an effort to examine all available opportunities thoroughly. The president may choose only one plan each year for implementation but can be assured of a choice, and, therefore, of improving the success ratio.

Success depends on being at the right place at the right time. Even the best business plan can fail, for part of a business plan is forecasting economic factors and future conditions—and that, in itself, is a tough assignment. The plan is only as good as the group or individual is, which means that one individual can become very important to a firm or to an industry when he or she thoroughly understands the firm, the micro and macro market conditions, and all the other plan factors. When a good match is found between a company and one who can put out realistic and sensible business plans, a valuable relationship has been formed.

In Chap. 1 various problems were identified that served to illustrate the architectural and engineering environment and some problems an office might encounter. Broader categories were then suggested that would include those types of subjects and presented as a diagram of relationships. These categories are the basis of a business plan outline and are also part of the three-question methodology previously discussed. They are as shown in Fig. 2.2.

In developing an understanding of how to construct a business plan, the outline in Fig. 2.2 will be expanded and examined in detail. As each part is looked at, it is necessary also to examine what the think-

Figure 2.2   Business plan diagram.

ing process is in developing a cohesive plan. Thus, beside the definitions of the individual parts, there are examples of how they may be applied in typical situations. It is hoped that using this technique, combined with a full written business plan presented in the next chapter, the business plan process will become familiar and meaningful to the architectural and engineering community.

The business plan presented in this book is a well-rounded plan which can be adjusted to fit the needs of different architectural firms. But, like any plan, it can be broken into segments. The key parts are listed above, but the first part of any plan is an executive summary. It is an overview that gives the reader a synopsis of the plan.

Executive summary

The *executive summary* is exactly what the name implies—a summary or overview of what is contained in the report, including the conclusion or chief recommendation. The three-question methodology can be used as an excellent guide for summarizing the information. It generally starts out with a quick sketch profile of who the company is, followed by the current position (who are we?). This current position may allude to problems the firm is experiencing and eventually to the intent of the plan (where do we want to go?). This is followed by the conclusion of the report (how do we get there?). Its purpose is to give readers an idea of why this plan was written and the proposed solution. The executive summary is a quick read, generally written last, and only one page in length.

The executive summary sets the tone of the report. Not all plans have a positive conclusion. Sometimes the facts of the situation suggest that a particular action not be taken or at least certain precautions be observed if a particular idea was implemented into an action plan. Following is an example of an executive summary with recommendations and cautions.

Executive Summary

Sample, Inc., is a design-oriented architectural service firm looking to expand its presence in its market territory. An opportunity has presented itself to relocate to a building which is centrally located, offering advantageous exposure. It is the purpose of this plan to look at the feasibility and financial requirements of acquiring, remodeling, occupying, and renting out the remainder of the space known as the Old Gobbi Building, a prominent historical classified building in the downtown commercial area.

Although the location of the proposed structure, along with its historical significance and our proposed remodel, are all positives, the conclusion of this analysis is that the actual acquisition should be tended to carefully and with much trepidation. The proposed conflict lies not with the idea, which is sound, but with the financial alternatives available to accomplish the task. Initially, the loans and construction monies are satisfactory, but a year out, when the loans' rates change, and so on, it will become extremely difficult to make payments based upon our current forecasts and budgets. We, thus, need to be forewarned that such a decision may initially sound appealing and accomplish our present goals, but in the long run, we may be asking for financial trouble.

This plan recommends the idea but also recommends a more thorough investigation of the alternatives, such as bringing in a partner or other strategic move, to ensure more stability and less demand on our monies and cash flow a year from now.

Generally speaking, understanding the parameters of the report and who authored the plan makes a big difference as to how it's read and accessed. As you can see, in the above summary the conclusion to proceed is underscored by strong warnings and impending cash flow risks. The tone has been set, the threats of any action underscored, and the point driven home. The remainder of the report will develop the conclusion with ample supporting details. This executive summary also follows the overall plan's methodology. It answers the three questions: Who are we? Where do we want to go? How do we get there?

Positioning

Following the executive summary is positioning; see Fig. 2.2. As shown in this figure, one way to think about positioning is back to the first question: Who are we? This encompasses several areas of information necessary to familiarize a reader with the environment of the office and the office itself. Generally, this section can be divided into the following categories:

- Mission statement
- Market characteristics
- Competition

Mission statement. A mission statement is the overall direction and the purpose of the company. A company may from time to time require that its business definition, or mission statement, be changed. Companies change, and as a result, the outside business environment needs to be updated as to the direction and purpose of the firm. In addition, employees lose a sense of where their company is headed. It is important for staff morale that they have a sense of direction and purpose. A mission statement should take into account where you have come from and where you want to go. Again, it's back to the basic questions. Companies spend many hours developing mission statements. It's an important part of their strategy to have a concise reflection of what their company is about. It states the purpose, offers direction, and should be a positive statement for the client, the employee, and the company.

As an example, here is a mission statement for *Sample, Inc.:*

> *Sample, Inc.,* is a design-oriented architectural services firm that is expanding to serve its clients with the highest degree of professional skill that provides an affordable quality solution. *Sample, Inc.,* strives to develop its expertise in the use of computers for management, design, and construction applications.

The mission statement carefully delineates that the company is a design-oriented firm that is growing. It clearly states that the firm uses computers and tries to pass the benefits on to its customers. It also stresses quality and a solution-oriented approach. As this example shows, the mission statement is a chance for the firm to decide specifically who it is. It does not say how it will get there, but it draws attention in a positive light to the firm and its desires.

Another mission statement is as follows:

> *Example Imaging Architects, Inc.,* is a profit-motivated architectural engineering firm that specializes in the preparation of construction documents and the representation of clients with construction management services.

This company's mission statement is entirely different. The company's expertise is in the area of construction management. In the first mission statement, *Sample, Inc.,* did not state it was profit motivated; in this mission statement the firm did. There is no general rule for this as all firms are different and have different personalities. Even if profit is not stated in the mission statement, it can be safely assumed the firm is striving to achieve certain levels of profitability. The method or path used to get there is, however, different. *Example Imaging Architects, Inc.,* will hire employees with different backgrounds than *Sample, Inc.,* as well as have different contractual agreements. It is clear by the mission statements that the product and the market are different in these two firms.

The mission statement is the first area a firm needs to address to help it understand the direction and the purpose of the firm. A mission statement waves a flag in the direction the firm is going. By indicating the product and the market, the firm points toward the competitive arena the firm operates within.

Market characteristics. The market characteristics are essentially the controlling economic and marketing parameters. These parameters may be very detailed or applicable only to a specific project or problem the plan is addressing. It is easier for some businesses to delineate what the market characteristics are, who its target market is, and what the market area is if there is a geographic limit to the territory it serves. The parameters should also be economic in an effort to explore trends or upswings in areas of the business that are indications of change in one's business.

Typical questions that a firm might ask provide information about the market characteristics are as follows:

Who are the primary clients?

What are the profit areas of the firm?

Do they match the market?

Is there a dominant market segment that the firm addresses?

That it does not address?

Are there other markets that should be developed?

What is the general economic environment in which the business operates?

Do banks have construction money available at reasonable rates?

These questions, and others that develop because of the specific content of a report, will give the plan a good look at a realistic answer. In a way, a plan writes itself since it is the product of the subject matter. It is the skill of the author combined with one's business sense that makes the plan come alive and be a meaningful contribution to the firm. The parameters set the stage for marketing strategies and the development of opportunities. The discussions that occur in putting together and approving this part of the report will go a long way toward developing a feeling of who the firm really is and what environment it is operating in.

Competition. "According to the ancients, the truly great in warfare are those who not only win but win with such ease and ingenuity that their wisdom and courage often go unrecognized."[3] Two thousand years ago, Sun Tzu in *The Art of War* knew the value of knowing your enemy. When you know the enemy, or the competition, you can be in a much better situation to outfox the competition. The essays Sun Tzu wrote formulate the basis of planning the strategy of military operations. The work has never been surpassed to this day and, surprisingly, has many practical applications for modern business strategies. Planning is planning, and *The Art of War* provides an opportunity to view the business struggle from another vantage point. It is interesting and gives you many ideas and different ways of thinking about your competition. It is simple and direct—if you truly know your enemy, or your competition, you can address your weak points and accentuate your strong points. Even though friendly competition is the rule among all professionals, by knowing who you are competing against, you increase your chance of victory.

To understand the positioning of a company, you must know who it is competing against. In the architectural and engineering marketplace, you can have any number of architects, designers, or engineers in the same block or section of a town and none of them competing against each other. But there are always a few architects or engineers who you run into on a regular basis. It is sometimes difficult to gain good information or intelligence on another firm, but over a period of time by observing the work, newspaper articles, and so on, you can establish profiles of other firms. These profiles should include the size, goals, market share, and marketing strategies of the competition, as well as an assessment of their strengths and weaknesses, which may suggest certain opportunities.

The intent is to develop a perspective of who is doing the work and what type of work it is. Essentially, you want to know who is winning and who is losing, then apply this information in a creative fashion to your own advantage. An analysis may determine, for example, that one type of work is always done by out-of-town architectural or engineering firms. It's sort of the grass is greener on the other side of the fence syndrome applied to the architectural and engineering world. The architect or engineer thus finds him or herself competing with a firm that is remote. This discovery can lead to certain conclusions.

There is a psychological attraction to choosing out-of-town firms. A good example was a selection process for rehab work in a northern California town. After an initial review of the respective firms' resumes and job histories, approximately five architectural firms were interviewed for an hour or so by five or six board members. The firm that received the highest points in the overall scoring was a small firm within the community. It was young, enthusiastic, and ambitious. The firm that was selected, however, was an out-of-town firm that had previously set up a telephone answering service in the community so it could be included in various bid situations. The firm was not the top firm in terms of selection criteria nor was it the most convenient to the job site. It won partly on the mysterious concept: That firm has to be better, it's from out of town. As a result, you might conclude that brochures showing offices located in different cities can give the additional exposure some prospective clients are looking for.

The point here is that knowing who the competition is will help in emphasizing certain features of your own service that, in the end, might help you to be selected. In the example, emphasizing at the meeting the availability for regularly scheduled and unscheduled site visits for interpretations of the drawings, required site observations, and so on, might have won the day for the young firm. That could have swung the favor to the firm physically located near the site. On the other hand, the out-of-town firm might stress that any emergency site observation would be handled by one of the principals who commutes regularly by the site and is available for unscheduled site visits. It might allude to an association with another firm that handles its site visits in that area of the county. Or it may casually mention that its drawings rarely need unscheduled interpretations since its regularly scheduled site visits review the current work and the work that is going to be done during the next several days. The point is, knowing your competition might provide an additional win percentage and might make the difference in securing more commissions.

Opportunities and issue analysis

The opportunities and issue analysis part of the plan is a realistic appraisal of the strengths, weaknesses, opportunities, threats, and issues facing an office or a specific project a business plan is examining. It is an essential part in answering the question, Who are we? A plan generally supports a specific idea and recommendation for a business decision. The decision was reached through market research and investigations into alternatives. The plan is a compilation of the details which support the conclusion—positive or negative, for or against. Part of the decision process must highlight the obstacles and risks associated with the plan. In the case of forced topic business plans, such as examining a merger with another firm, any negatives induced because the outcome has been specified will be identified in the report and in the summary as previously discussed.

Strength and weakness analysis. The strength and weakness (S/W) analysis is an observation about the firm's current position. What are its strengths and what are its weaknesses? A firm may be very strong in design, winning many awards, which gives it an advantage in promoting itself. At the same time, a firm may always lose money or break even in the overall job because of the difficulty in getting construction documents done on a timely basis. That would be considered a weakness. A firm's location might not be in the new growth areas and, hence, a weakness. A firm may have lost its top management person, which would also be considered a weakness—particularly if the person went to the competition.

The strength and weakness analysis is important because it forces one to look objectively at his or her firm and draw conclusions about its performance or lack of performance. Answering these questions honestly can be the first step to improving a firm's posture and eventual financial performance. Likewise, answering these questions yearly within the context of an annual report is the best way to review the progress of a firm in all areas of interest and importance. This also can be used as an excellent forum to getting the top management of a firm talking about what is liked and not liked. This level of participation is important in the overall implementation of a plan.

Opportunities and threats analysis. The opportunities and threats (O/T) analysis relates to outside factors influencing a company, now or in the future. An opportunity might be the indication by a major tenant that he or she would like you to become involved in services relating to the leasing of commercial spaces for a project you just completed. These additional services might be tenant improvement drawings, lease space calculations, and so on. This is a chance for the firm to increase its billable income by developing an expertise in a specific area.

Another opportunity might be the increase in institutional work predicted in the next 10 years. In this case, the opportunity might also be considered a threat. Given a large amount of institutional work forecast for a given area, a firm with no work history or exposure will certainly lose out on the available work and subsequent follow-up work. Likewise, a threat might be several key staff architects or engineers leaving the firm. This might be viewed as an opportunity to replace them with individuals who have certain job skills the firm needs, such as CAD. All opportunities are disguised as problems, and all opportunities are potential threats. It is how one views the world that is really important when it comes to interpreting information for a firm's use.

Threats can also be many shapes and sizes: A threat might be an economic report, an impending recession scaring off developers, or banking problems. A threat might be a statement by a client that the firm's lack of experience with CAD and other database management programs could affect the client's selection on future projects. Likewise, this threat might be considered a weakness.

A convenient way to present all of this information is by using a situational analysis chart that summarizes the information. This chart also lends itself to groups working on a particular plan or problem and becomes a good working tool in developing a plan. An example of this chart is included in the business plan in Chap. 3.

Issues and risks. At this point, the company continues its business plan development by drawing conclusions from the S/W and O/T analyses in terms of issues facing the firm. Decisions on these issues are parameters for the goals and objectives and resulting marketing strategies. These issues are often presented as questions that face the firm. It is interesting to note that one of the biggest differences between the Japanese and the Western method of management is the Japanese spend an inordinate amount of time, in our way of thinking, defining what the specific question is rather than worrying about the answer. This Zen-like approach suggests that if the wrong questions are asked, it doesn't matter what the answers are. Consequently, if the right questions are asked to the right people, the plan reflects a truer representation of the office and its goals and objectives.

Typical issues that might be facing *Sample, Inc.,* are as follows:

Should *Sample, Inc.,* look at the long-term strategy of developing an expertise in institutional buildings to take advantage of a developing market?

What does it take to compete in this marketplace?

Should *Sample, Inc.,* make a capital investment in CAD technology to become more competitive and be able to attract the necessary new talent coming out of school?

What does it take to implement CAD successfully into an office?

Should *Sample, Inc.,* look at expanding to another geographic location to attract new clients?

What is the easiest way to expand?

Should *Sample, Inc.,* develop additional expertise to attract new clients?

Should *Sample, Inc.,* develop new services it can offer to its existing clients?

The firm's principal architects, consultants, managers, and so on, must reflect carefully on these issues, as they are the basis of the goals and objectives of the firm. Later they will be the cornerstone of the marketing strategies which, it is hoped, offer the firm a competitive advantage.

It is important to emphasize that one cannot skip over areas which might make a plan look bad. This is a common problem with some business plans. The plan must be prepared with honesty and a clear sense of business integrity. The value of the author is that he or she interprets the facts given the business situation. One has to be honest about the evaluation and identification of potential problems and risks. Addressing all the foreseeable issues in a logical manner is the reason the final plan is so important. If an important obstacle was not addressed, the individual or group responsible for accepting the plan will point out the omission and ask that the problem be addressed. Or, worst yet, the problem may not be readily apparent and only become known during the implementation of the plan. The forum that results in discussions about the contents of the report during its preparation and its review is, in itself, as valuable as the end result. As you shall see, it is this forum where managers take ownership in the plan and become responsible for its implementation.

The issues that are a result of the evaluation of the opportunities and threats and the strength and weaknesses set the stage for the development first of the goals and objectives, then of the marketing strategies. In fact, one might say that the goals and objectives are the result of the issues, and the marketing strategies are the result of the goals and objectives. These issues have associated risks, for there is always a risk with any business venture. The marketing strategies outline what opportunities the firm is going to challenge, which is really a decision about what risks the firm is willing to take. Peter F. Drucker outlined four types of risks companies face:[4]

1. The risk one must accept; this is the risk that is built into the nature of the business.

2. The risk one can afford to take.

3. The risk one cannot afford to take.

4. The risk one cannot afford not to take.

There is a certain risk with practicing architecture or engineering, that of the liabilities of practicing. Engineers and architects are confronted with situations daily that may expose them to potential liability. This, in its simplest form, is a risk of practicing—it's a risk that goes with the territory.

The risk one can afford to take is generally business decisions such as venturing into another market niche or developing a direct mail program. Both have certain risks, generally monetary, or return on investment, but both are acceptable risks.

A risk that one cannot afford to take is generally one of common sense. You generally know it when you do it, but you do it anyway. An example is taking on a large project with payment based upon its future financial success. These offers are enticing at times, as it seems better to be doing something and have something to hope for than to be doing nothing at all. However, most of the time, payment is not forthcoming. Or payment can be made if just a little bit more work is done. The hole gets bigger until the experience is a complete write-off.

A risk that one cannot afford not to take is considered a breakthrough opportunity or an opportunity that if a firm didn't take would mean potential serious consequences to the firm. An example is the situation where a firm, undergoing hard economic times with wildly fluctuating cash flows, is approached as a takeover candidate or, in softer terms, a merger. Here is a situation that may allow the firm to exist as a branch of another firm, and the consequences for not taking advantage of the opportunity might be catastrophic. If the firm went to a competing firm, the combination might be enough to put you out of business. This is certainly a serious decision, but it might, after careful analysis, be one you have to take. You cannot afford not to do it.

All of these are examples of what risk is about. Business planning is the balancing of risks with opportunities and the resulting marketing strategies. Issues have risks, and in these risks are the rewards of prosperity.

Goals and objectives

Every architectural firm has the objective to excel in its design work; in fact, many architects want to be known as designers. To a certain extent, this desire often overshadows other objectives in the office and is one reason why business management often has been neglected by architects and engineers. But an architect and engineer should also want to generate a certain level of profit, although he or she may not think of that as a main objective.

Sometimes a goal can easily be misinterpreted by employees. For example, making a certain level of profit could inadvertently be interpreted by staff as a directive to cut back on the completeness of the construction documentation to a builders set, thereby impacting quality. This probably will lead to more time in the field, as the intent of the work may not be clear. There is even the possibility of liability situations being created. Certainly, any legal defense of a problem would be weakened if it was shown by opposing legal counsel that the architect or engineer did not clearly show intent on the construction documents. Furthermore, the architect or engineer is losing money with the additional time spent in the field. The above scenario certainly was not the intent of the objective of increasing profits.

This example shows one reason why goals and objectives need to be sharply defined. Everyone in the organization must understand what the business is trying to accomplish and what employees are responsible for. First, certain terms should be defined to understand their relationship within the context of the business plan clearly. Figure 2.3 and the following list show the relationships as a series of building blocks, as each part supports the one above it:

Objectives*:   An interpretation of the company's mission statement used to break the desired end result down into smaller groups. An objective is a broad statement of purpose that is measurable.

Goals: A subgroup of the quantified objectives that have a time limit.

Strategy: The approach used to accomplish the goals and objectives.

Actions or tactics: The specific actions by specific individuals required to accomplish the strategy and, hence, the goals and objectives.

The goal and objective approach is helpful during the implementation of the plan, as it later lends itself to division of tasks and necessary delegation of responsibilities or actions. An objective or a goal should have certain guidelines. An acronym, SMART (source un-

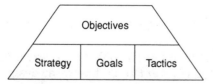

Figure 2.3   Relationships of goals and objectives.

---

*A goal is sometimes referred to as an objective. The terms are often interchanged.

known), is often used by planners as a guide for establishing individual goals and objectives:

*S*pecific

*M*easurable

*A*ction oriented

*R*elevant

*T*imely

SMART suggests that business plans must develop goals and objectives that are specific as to their intent; they must be measurable in some way; they must require action by someone; they must be relevant and contribute to the overall plan; and they must be timely, meaning they must address issues that are confronting the organization today within the context of the plan. Using the SMART concept when establishing individual goals and objectives is a check that helps ensure uniformity and continuity.

There are three different areas or categories on which businesses focus when establishing goals and objectives:

- Financial objectives
- Marketing objectives
- Human resource objectives

The goals and objectives of the plan relate to the specific strengths and weaknesses, the opportunities for and threats to the firm, and issues and risks. They are also an interpretation of the company's mission statement. Goals and objectives are different for each type of plan. That is, the goals and objectives of a 5-year strategic plan would be different from that of an annual business plan. Thus, every plan has its own S/W and O/T and issues and risks.

There will always be some overlap; however, the perspective will be different. As you shall see, goals are developed from the objectives and are part of the process used to implement the plan. Business plans develop the way they do for a reason. One firm may determine that its primary objective is to increase market share, whereas another firm determines it must diversify its business by offering additional services. An objective of a third firm might be to control expense in order to improve the bottom line.

Many offices may have the same general objectives but each has its own peculiar mix that distinguishes it from other offices. Every office is different in some way mainly due to the principals and the personality of the office projected to the public. "The most common objectives are profitability, sales growth, marketshare improvement, risk diversification, innovation, and cost control."[5] These objectives fall under the financial, marketing, and human resource objectives mentioned above.

It is the personality of the office and how the office interprets and implements a plan internally that produces offices with such varying interests. These different interests create a diversification strategy that may lead one to prosperity because of the different market niches. This diversification, or differentiation strategy, usually means a risk, and most offices are not willing to accept that price in exchange for potential profit. But some do, and those are the ones you read about.

Financial objectives. In the architectural and engineering environment where professional services are offered, fees are basically a function of construction dollars. However, with architects and engineers doing more and more planning and expanding their additional service responsibilities, the gross fees earned are not necessarily tied to the amount of construction the firm is representing. Nevertheless, as a general rule, the architect or engineer should be looking at some level of profit over and above what was done the previous year. Remember, profit is what allows the firm to grow.

Without having specific goals and objectives that look toward the future, an office is just experiencing a day-to-day existence. More important, if an architect or engineer has thought about any long-range planning ideas, such as how the firm may be passed on to others someday rather than just end, then establishing a good financial track record is very desirable. That track record is expressed best through solid evidence of growth and profitability. Thus, one of the objectives of the firm might be a strong and balanced financial statement. This objective might have been developed through the dialogue created by a firm going through the planning process.

A good starting place is to set up profit center areas within the office. These profit centers could be based upon services currently offered by the architect, as well as new services that might be offered, such as architectural programming or lease management services. CAD might become a profit center and billed to each project as required. Each of these categories should have financial objectives based on the year's plan. At the end of the year, when the numbers come in, it will be easier to see where one is making a profit and at what expense ratio. It will also be easier to plan for the following year.

Typical financial objectives are as follows:

- Produce a gross income 11 percent above last year's or $679,320.
- Produce a net profit of 10 percent.
- Develop and use a financial plan.
- Monitor and control cost.

These four objectives provide a financial direction for a firm. Each firm requires different objectives. As long as they are reasonable and within the economic structure of the micro and macro environment in which the firm practices, they are suitable as a benchmark to measure the firm's performance. Initially, when reviewing financials, two numbers become important. The first is the top line, or what is projected in revenue or gross income. This is often referred to as the *image number*. The second is what is projected in operating income, or profit—the *cash flow number* or *bottom line*. A more in-depth look at the numbers will include several financial ratios to help understand how the business compares to industry standards.

If the plan hits the numbers, or comes within 10 percent of either side, you can conclude that the plan was realistic. If the office exceeded the objectives by more than 10 percent, the plan did not take into account the potential of the firm and next year's plan should reflect this growth rate in some way—perhaps by being more aggressive. If the plan was missed on the short side substantially, the firm does not have the potential to grow that much because of the economy, or the firm did not have the necessary experience, or the plan was too ambitious, or the plan was not implemented properly. A variety of reasons might be offered, from management's failure to implement the plan, to inappropriate marketing strategies. In any event, adjustments will have to be made the second year. Working with a plan is a matter of refinement and adjustments. Nothing is perfect, and a plan is only a tool to help provide logical direction and realistic benchmarks along the way. A plan whose targets are missed should provide as much or even more information than a plan whose targets are met.

Marketing objectives. The financial objectives will be reached with the help of appropriate marketing objectives. The architect or engineer will only achieve the plan by concentrating in areas the firm knows will be profitable and/or will open new opportunities in the future. Market size and market share numbers are helpful at this point but are difficult for an architect or engineer to obtain and apply. But architects or engineers do know what percentage of work they do in residential, commercial, and so on, areas and can provide a future guide for a market niche evaluation. Typical marketing objectives are as follows:

- Achieve a total sales volume of $150,000 in residential work.
- Expand market share of commercial work by 10 percent, achieving $200,000 in sales volume.
- Continue expansion of additional services to $52,000.
- Expand the identity of *Sample, Inc.,* into additional market areas to broaden its client base by 15 percent.
- Continue to offer and emphasize quality design.

With the adoption of these objectives, there is a definite marketing direction for the firm to follow. The emphasis is in the commercial area, with a similar expansion in additional services. The objectives also recommend that the client base be expanded by 15 percent by getting *Sample, Inc.'s,* name out to new, potential clients. The idea is to develop a campaign that looks at where the new work might be coming from and to get *Sample, Inc.'s,* name in front of these prospects. The objective does not address how this will be achieved, only that it's the objective of the firm to work in these areas based upon the plan's analysis.

In addition, quality design becomes a marketing objective. It could be argued that quality design could become its own objective, and many firms may take this posture. However, design is really a marketing issue and is therefore promoted by *Sample, Inc.,* through marketing programs. Even though good design is what all architects and engineers strive to achieve, good design is not a fundamental business goal but an objective of the marketing effort.

Human resource objectives.   Here objectives concerning staffing can be addressed. This is a complicated area, and many books, seminars, and lectures are available that explore employee relationships. The point is that a plan should examine issues regarding the working environment. It has been shown time and again that providing good working conditions will do as much for increasing productivity as anything will. A good example is the architect's or engineer's work space. Many offices still provide a backless hard drafting stool for drafters, project architects, or engineers. Offices that provide modern types of furniture have gained in the rewards of productivity. The reasons are simple—people don't look forward to coming to work and sitting on a hard stool all day long.

Another aspect of this area is a clear understanding by employees on where they stand within the firm. It's important to your psychological development to have a clear idea where you are going and what you have to do to get there. Career paths are important, particularly in professions with extensive education and testing requirements. This process of communication should start when an employee is first hired, then continue as the employee is reviewed for wage increases, and so on. A sad profile of architects or engineers as managers and businesspeople is the number of firms that do not have regular review processes for wage increases or that do not provide benefits. Improving this area will help improve productivity and the stability of the firm.

Many architects and engineers use intimidation as a way to keep expenses down by preventing escalating wages. An example is the fact that it's difficult for employees to ask for raises, particularly when horror stories float around the office about someone who did and is no longer there. As a result, most people sit at their drafting station and fret about the confrontation and, as a result, productivity decreases. To overcome this, one should examine the communication process between employees and employer and work toward equitable solutions. To start, just look at what employees think their jobs are compared to what the principal thinks they are; this may develop a dialogue that serves to strengthen the communication process. This is far too complicated to analyze in depth here; but employee relations are important to companies and the reason it's treated as an objective.

Another area is the employees' knowledge that they will be treated fairly. For instance, how many times does the principal take an employee aside and tell him or her the firm has not been prospering lately, work has fallen off, and it looks like the firm will have to let the person go? Sometimes 2 weeks' notice is given, and sometimes it isn't. Although this is a difficult task for both the employee and the principal, the employee gets the short end. Even with unemployment compensation, there are times when it's difficult to secure work and make ends meet. An employee who has spent some time with a firm deserves better than to be shown to the door. Separation packages based upon length of service, and so on, as well as other benefits should be available. Hard work, responsibility, and dedication should be met with fairness and equitability. Being treated right and knowing that you will be treated right is part of the *quality of work life.*

A firm should also be able to attract new people with the degrees and caliber it wants. If the architect or engineer is moving into CAD, for example, there is probably a need to hire someone with experience in managing the CAD environment. If the architect or engineer is moving into institutional work, the staff may also be affected. Can the firm hire the proper people or do the candidates in the job pool want to work for the competition? Is there something that can be changed to improve the employee climate to make the firm more attractive? Having the proper employee environment where employees enjoy coming to work, and thus spend time working and not complaining about lack of leadership or poor working conditions, is an important objective for an architectural or engineering firm.

A list of objectives in the business plan that takes into consideration the employee might be as follows:

- Improve the quality of work life.
- Establish a review program that outlines a career path.
- Establish a compensation award program relating to the performance of all individuals.
- Establish employee benefits.

The creation of a better employee environment depends upon the size of the firm. The process can be as simple as taking an employee to lunch once in a while to as sophisticated as providing employee activity programs. Some place between this span is a happy medium for all firms. It is important to understand that large firms can show interest in the person, just as small, intimate firms can. Much of this has to do with the manager's style and ability to relate to co-workers. When one shows interest in what an employee is doing and understands the goals and objectives, then a better working relationship can be achieved.

Goals

The next step is to begin to break down the financial, marketing, and human resource objectives into goals. Goals reduce objectives to their next level of interpretation. Some refer to goals as subobjectives. Goals become *time specific measurable* items. For example, the following marketing objective can be broken down into parts, or into individual goals.

Objective. Achieve a total sales volume of $150,000 in residential work:

1. By January 15 review with marketing (or staff architect, engineer, etc.) its proposal to increase the residential client base and resulting commissions.
2. By January 15 establish a client list of prospects for residential housing.
3. By February 15 formulate a team that will be responsible for all parts of residential design.
4. By February 15 implement the marketing plan.

The purpose of breaking the objectives into goals is to begin to get a handle on what it takes to solve the problem or accomplish the task. It is well understood by architects and engineers that to solve a complicated design problem, one breaks down the problem into many parts. The architectural program is the first step in furthering the idea and delineating the constraints of a proposed project. This is augmented by building code interpretations, planning interpretations, site considerations, existing utilities, and so on. At some point, when the architect or engineer has developed the necessary information, the task is manageable. That's because the architect or engineer has broken the problem down into manageable parts that are well defined. Breaking down the objectives of a firm into goals is no different; it is part of the process that brings one closer to the answer, to the solution, and to the final plan. It's a necessary and important part of the business plan process.

Internal and external promotions. Many companies plan their campaigns around their goals and objectives to inform people what the company represents. This is a highly effective program used by the majority of large corporations. This can also be a highly effective program for architectural and engineering firms. A good example is a campaign that outlines its objectives for its prospects and clients, as well as its employees, by carefully placing the firm's goals throughout the work environment. Here is a typical set of objectives that outlines for everyone what the firm is about:

- Provide high-quality service.
- Keep and attract talented people.
- Improve the quality of work life.
- Protect the environment.

This is an excellent example, where long-range objectives have been developed into a program in which the people who do the work are kept informed on what is going on and what they are working toward. In addition, they are able to create a feeling of self-worth as they contribute in their own area.

An extension of this is the slogans companies use to distinguish themselves from other companies. Examples are as follows*:

Ford	Quality is job one
Xerox	The document company
General Motors	The heartbeat of America
AT&T	The right choice
Business Week	There is no second place
Allen-Bradley	Where the possible becomes practical
Avis	We try harder
CalComp	We draw on your imagination

Slogans are a very popular advertising and marketing technique; the slogan becomes so identified with a company that people can name the company by the slogan. Slogans also have subliminal messages that work long after the person has seen or heard the message. With

---

*Ford, Xerox, GM, AT&T, Business Week, Allen-Bradley, Avis, and CalComp and their slogans are registered trademarks of their respective companies.

the amount of advertising done by large companies, when the time comes to go hunt for a car to buy, probably the only thing you can think of is, Quality is Job One or a similar message.

Architects or engineers can also use this idea and establish for their firm a tag line that customers will relate to. These ideas grow out of the goals and objectives of a company—they are what a company is all about. The architect or engineer must look for methods to get the unique marketing message in front of prospects and clients. This unique message should serve to differentiate you from the competition. It can be incorporated into the title block of the construction documents, stationery, brochures, and so on. The places where it appears are endless. Following is a list of ideas for architects and engineers:

- Design solutions
- The planning firm
- On time and on budget
- Designs for the times
- The architectural (or engineering) planning firm
- The environmental firm
- Why second best?
- Quality spoken here
- We build America's dreams
- Engineering solutions
- Designing your future
- Your high-tech architect (or engineer)
- The wine country architect (or engineer)
- Plan on (your name here)

This list can be as long as one's imagination. The purpose is to illustrate that goals and objectives have many avenues of discovery and can be expressed in many ways. It can be done casually, or it can be done in concert with an organized plan that seeks to focus all thoughts and ideas in one direction to increase public awareness and one's chances for prosperity.

Marketing strategies

Marketing strategies is the core of any plan, as it outlines the broad approach that will be used to meet the company's sales and profitability objectives. The strategies are relative to the goals and objectives that have been set, which are reflective of the company's mission statement. This is where specific strategy statements are set down in writing. In this example, as in most architectural or engineering business plans, one is interested in the marketing strategy. This marketing strategy may be the recommendation of the marketing vice president who prepares a plan for an office to approve. Or it may be the result of a firm's upper-level managers and project architects or engineers working together. It also might be the result of the owner of the firm who maps out the strategy for the company. The marketing strategy is the most creative part of any plan, and the most debatable. For this reason it should be succinctly put, with no room for misinterpretation.

Even for the sole proprietor, it is important to develop a strategy and discuss business ideas with others. Just because a firm does not have a manager in charge of marketing, it does not eliminate one's responsibility to have a strategic plan that sets out to accomplish one's goals and objectives. It is suggested that sole proprietors develop business relationships that allow them the opportunity to develop cohesive strategies. This can be an informal process and is a big step at becoming competitive.

Marketing strategy is probably the part of the plan that receives the most attention. This should not be interpreted that the entire marketing or strategic program should change every year. Marketing programs must have time to take hold and to grow. Marketing programs are, however, refined as new information becomes available. There may be instances where an entire program may have to be scrapped because of some unforeseen reason, but it is hoped that with experience this will not be a regular event.

New opportunities exist in every business, and in the coming years there will be more opportunities for the architect and engineer than ever before to explore new areas. This is due to the changing nature of the profession and the subliminal messages by adjacent professions that perhaps architects might be excessive baggage. Architects and engineers must respond to this challenge on an individual basis, and, it is hoped, professional societies that surround the profession will also take meaningful action for all size architectural or engineering firms.

However, when opportunities do make themselves known, the discussion that should take place is how the existing business plan will be affected, particularly in the area of marketing strategy. The annual business plan is the perfect forum to orchestrate the discussion, as it offers a benchmark for the firm any place in the fiscal year. Without the benchmark, the discussion will have less meaning, as there is really nothing to compare it to. Changing a business plan because of an extraordinary opportunity is not wrong. Making a major decision without a business plan is, however, a tragedy. Businesses fail because of tragedies that can mostly be avoided with the proper decision-making techniques in place. That's not to say that a business plan will prevent a tragedy or a missed opportunity. The business plan is simply an insurance policy that might help avoid litigators as they take a position for and against.

Marketing is the process whereby the needs and wants of the individuals or groups are satisfied through the production of a product or the offering of a service. Specifically, "marketing strategy spells out the game plan for attaining the business objectives."[6] "Marketing strategy consists of making decisions on the business marketing expenditures, marketing mix, and marketing allocations in relation to expected environmental and competitive conditions."[6] This formal definition includes all the important parts of a balanced market strategy program. It is a game plan that consists of decisions based upon the parameters of the particular business in which one is involved. The plan must specify how much money is going to be spent on marketing and in what areas. This information eventually ends up as the basis of the financial plan.

The plan must also determine the marketing mix of the firm. *Marketing mix* is a term closely aligned to manufacturers who produce a product. Architects and engineers also have a marketing mix, but they don't tend to think in those terms. The basic 4 P's[7] of the marketing mix include an additional group which serves to align the concept with the service industry, and that is people. The marketing mix is as follows:

Product	What are the services that are going to be emphasized by the firm's marketing arm? Is the firm going to go after institutional work, residential work, commercial work, and so on?
Place	What is the market territory? Is the office going to expand into other locations? How is it going to do this? Does the firm want to design projects in locations in which someone else has to do the on-site observations?
Price	What price structure is going to be used? Is it a commission basis? How is the firm going to be competitive?
Promotion	How is the firm going to market itself? Is it going to follow recommended guidelines or try to use innovative techniques?
People	What are the talents and sensitivities of the people creating the product for other people to use?

Every prospect has a proposed project of some specific scope, that is to be located in some specific area, that has been attracted to an architectural or engineering firm by some promotion, and that will respond to certain costs or price structures. It's up to the architectural or engineering firm to develop a marketing strategy that attracts the prospect to that firm, puts the firm in the location to do the project, and sets up a fee structure that is commensurate with the customer for services the customer desires. All things being equal, the client will receive a project it paid for, and the architect or engineer will make a profit and be in a position to ask for a referral from the customer. The project was a success. The marketing plan was a success. The business plan was a success.

As alluded to before, just because a building was a success does not mean the architect or engineer was successful. A project may function as it was intended and be received by the community in a positive light. The project may even have received some architectural or engineering acclaim. But the architect or engineer may have been severely over budget, causing an understandable problem. This is assuming the contract documents maintain a limit of construction cost based upon the architect's or engineer's design or lack of such documents and clarifications that further cloud the issue. *The point is architects and engineers are judged by what they do. Architects and engineers should judge themselves by how they do it.* A strong bottom line is an indicator of financial success, but that is only one part of a balanced office. Remember, it is profit that allows an office the opportunity to excel in design again by keeping the office strong. There must be adequate financial controls, responsible marketing strategies that have some foresight of where the firm wants to go, strong employee identification, and goals and objectives that truly interpret the mission statement. In this light, the marketing strategy becomes a very important part of the business plan. It is where the most dialogue will occur and where the most doubts will present themselves.

Following is a marketing strategy statement that illustrates how the business plan is becoming specific about the firm's business philosophy:

Marketing Strategy Statement

Target Market: Sample, Inc., will continue to grow its commercial market, with a long-term objective of developing a presence in the institutional marketplace and a larger target market area.

Positioning: Sample, Inc., will initiate a four-step positioning strategy to enter this institutional market.

1. Establish a relationship with a consultant.
2. Establish alliances with other firms.
3. Develop acquisition targets with the experience you need.
4. Expand CAD.

In addition, *Sample, Inc.,* will strive to continue to preserve and develop its existing client relationships by overservicing its clients in proportion to its contract. This does not mean *Sample, Inc.,* will lose money on the contract but only that it will always provide more service than the client thinks it's getting. Service is still *king* and is a key positioning element.

Services Offered: The basic service will be represented to all clients as the minimum services they should do or will need. Additional services will be stressed during client presentations as an improvement on basic services and, in some cases, as a necessity due to the project's constraints.

Price Structure: The philosophy of the firm regarding price is to charge a fair and competitive amount. Each client has different needs and objectives; thus each situation will be looked at and will provide as much service as possible at a fair and equitable amount.

Marketing Research: A budget for marketing shall be established with the emphasis on long-term future markets and targeted prospects.

Contractual: An emphasis on legal ramifications of all contracts shall be reviewed by legal counsel on a regular basis, especially before any contract execution.

Promotion: There will be three on-going promotional campaigns that will serve to generate leads:

1. Develop a brochure that demonstrates the design capabilities of the firm.
2. Develop a direct mail campaign to prospects identified by market research.
3. Develop a telemarketing program.
4. Develop the people of the firm and use their talents appropriately.

This marketing strategy statement can be more specific, but this is the heart of the business plan. It is the summation of one's efforts to answer the issues the firm faces and addresses all five parts of the marketing mix in some manner. It represents the culmination of the market research and all the marketing meetings, where many ideas have been accepted or rejected. Or, in the case of a small architectural or engineering firm, it represents one's conclusions as the architect or engineer sorts out where one wants to go. In any case, the market strategy has one purpose, which is to develop a thesis in line with the mission statement and the resulting goals and objectives of the company. Architects and engineers must be diligent in their efforts to develop the correct strategy and must approach the subject with discipline.

A lot of common sense makes up a marketing strategy. For example, existing clients must be maintained as you go out after new ones. They must not be forgotten, and new services should be provided as part of an on-going strategy. Another example is that a good solid contractual philosophy must exist in the firm to protect it from unnecessary downside risks. Similarly, a firm has to be presented from the position that it's successful and on solid financial footing. The rationale is simple: No one likes to deal with a loser. If the client senses it is dealing with a firm that has financial difficulties, it will find a firm that doesn't. A business plan is a combination of common sense and foresight.

Below is a list of strategies an architect or engineer might consider. The combinations are endless and limited only by your imagination.

- Specialize in restaurant design.
- Market prototype designs for special applications.
- Specialize in golf course architecture.
- Specialize in judicial buildings.
- Plan hospitals.
- Enter design contests, then promote your achievement.
- Specialize in historic renovations.
- Specialize in seismic redesign.
- Specialize in custom residences.
- Specialize in office parks.
- Develop facility management capability.
- Analyze code compliance problems.
- Become a builder or developer.

There are other possibilities, and any one of them may be niche markets that the competition is not addressing. It's the combination of these strategies at the right time that is important, for this is what makes up a winning strategy. For example, all architects or engineers located in a ski resort area do custom projects relating to the ski industry and the snow environment. They all are experienced and produce good workable designs in their own styles. This develops an individuality and a start at differentiation and competition. The architect or engineer who can respond to this market situation with strategies that further differentiate themselves from others has a better chance to succeed over a long period of time. For example, one common occurrence in a ski town is that many clients are remotely located. Thus, an architect or engineer may develop a strategy whereby clients who are remotely located are served in a different manner, making it easier for the client to feel part of the project. This may entail traveling or using large format drawing transmissions, conference calls, televised conference calls, and so on. This effort to be different could become a critical factor for success.

Hence, through the development of market research, setting goals and objectives, and so on, and through the selection of proper strategies one has a better chance to succeed over a long period of time. It is the individual effort to succeed, the struggle for prosperity in competitive situations that separates the architect or engineer from those who just have a license and do the work that comes in the door. It's the true essence of practicing architecture or engineering—it is what allows one to do quality work again and again. In Chap. 4, specific ideas as to strategy development will be discussed to provide a foundation for analyzing your current situation.

Plan implementation

At some point after the plan has been completed, goals and objectives have to be implemented. The specifics as to how a plan is implemented are not necessarily part of the business plan, although it could be. This occurs after the plan has been adopted and put into motion. After a plan has been approved, something has to happen to get it going. What happens lies with management, who through the delegation of responsibilities can assign action items to specific individuals with a specific time frame for completion. They in turn make business judgments based upon these action items in their everyday work and, in some cases, pass portions of the responsibilities down to their subordinates.

There is an important point to be made here that should not be missed. A plan is not static—it is not shelved when it's completed. Once a plan is approved and accepted, it must be executed by its managers who use the objectives and subsequent goals as targets for their own personal performance. However, the plan is not referred to every day; it becomes dominant in the minds of the managers that this is what they are trying to accomplish. Do the decisions I make today contribute to the business plan the firm is trying to achieve? Am I doing my part? Having a working business plan is what separates firms that are seriously pursuing prosperity from those who are not.

Financial strategies

The goals and objectives lay the foundation for the plan, the opportunities analysis provides direction, and the marketing strategies outline how the plan will be achieved. What ties all of this together is the financial analysis. As a general rule, great ideas are useless unless they first make economic sense. There are exceptions, but for the most part for a plan to have merit, it must have meaningful numbers that support it, that show on paper that the strategies presented are realistic and achievable.

Business plans may be reviewed by many people, both internally and externally. For this reason, business plans include financial information appropriate to the project and to its audience. Some plans have only a general overview of the firm's current financial status; others also include a pro forma balance sheet, a 5-year income statement, a detailed budget, and a cash flow projection. If appropriate, a statement as to where additional investment money is coming from and how it is going to be used is included. If a business plan were written to explore the idea of a merger with another firm on a preliminary basis, the numbers would be a projection—sort of a model of what might happen. An actual merger situation would have its own financial plan that would be the actual analysis and evaluation of the joining of the two firms. In fact, there would most likely be two evaluations, as both sides look at the changes and financial consequences.

It is interesting to note that the techniques used in the financial analysis again go back to the basic methodology discussed, that is, Where are we? Where do we want to go? How do we get there?

Question	Answer
Where are we?	Financial overview Income statement Balance sheet
Where do we want to go?	Pro forma balance sheet Five-year income statement projection
How do we get there?	Budget Cash flow plan Financial resources

When in doubt about how to proceed to prepare any part of a plan, go back to the basic methodology. It offers the best starting point and direction to proceed.

General financial overview.   The creativity behind authoring any business plan is using the existing facts and information to produce a plan that is plausible. Hence, one business plan might be lengthy, whereas another brief. Both may serve the purpose the plan was addressing. One important part of the existing facts and information is contained in the general financial overview, which is a summary of the financial status of a firm. The financial overview might be extensive or just a brief sketch of the status of the firm.

There are two ways to prepare a general financial overview: one with specific information and one in general terms. In an ideal situation, current financial statements such as the profit and loss statement of the firm along with a balance sheet should be presented. Some plans may also require cash flow statements. There may be situations where the information is not available or the information is deemed to be highly confidential, such as with sole proprietors. These situations require a summary of the financial status or the inclusion of the restricted material in the appendix and provided only to those who have a need to know. This helps to let associates and other members of the firm participate in the process without showing them specific financial information.

Hence, whether balance sheets, income statements, and other financial information is provided or a summary is used, the intent is to provide a sense of the overall financial picture within the context of the plan. Following is an example of such a financial summary:

> *Sample, Inc.,* continues to generate fees at the $612,000 income level and is on track for the remainder of the year. Expenses are higher than previously experienced due to the replacement of interior office furniture

that makes a better use of our facility. The cash flow is stable and provides an avenue for growth through expansion or other means. Costs are at the required level but must be watched carefully in light of the current jobs that are now in the schematic design phase.

This summary indicates that the firm is making money but not how much. It indicates the firm is aware of possible increased costs due to the work on the boards. It also indicates the fee level of the firm. The gross fees of an architectural or engineering firm will most likely be known by any managers in charge of preparing a business plan. Although this might work for some firms, it is more desirable to have the business plan prepared by individuals privy to all financial information—particularly an annual operating plan. In the case of the sole proprietor who is generally completely responsible for writing the plan, it might only be read by that person. This plan is compiled for the same reasons that a large firm prepares a plan but is implemented in a different way. If the sole proprietor chooses to bring in an associate to assist in preparing the plan as a training experience, the summary method might be used.

The plan might also be reviewed by outside agencies such as bankers, accountants, and attorneys. This helps ensure that all viable financial information is used in the plan's preparation. The financial information provides a much better perspective in evaluating any proposal. It is clear that some business plans must have all the financial information; most plans will require it, but some won't.

Pro forma balance sheet. *Pro forma* in the accounting world means financial statements or conclusions based upon assumed facts. This part of the financial strategy shows *what* money is going to be spent *where*. Each architectural or engineering firm should have some method for evaluating the potential future profitability of the business. The balance sheet and income statements that are reconstructed to show a what-if situation provide valuable information as to the impact of a proposed project. With the spreadsheet software available, it is simple to develop ways of looking at proposals from several perspectives. Reviewing this information with an accountant will provide additional insight into the total financial picture. Furthermore, experience with the spreadsheets will transfer to other areas of the office such as fee compensations and projects. Experience builds upon experience.

Five-year income statement projection.   The 5-year income statement provides a picture of what is happening over a certain period of time to see how expenses relate to income or how a specific marketing strategy is doing. What is the bottom line of the investment? This is the question that is answered and is actually the focus of most business plans. The forecast takes into account all realistic economic variables that for all practical purposes is an economic model of the office. For example, expenses in relationship to profit, as well as costs, salaries, and other variables, are known. Using this information, and with the help of an accountant, assumptions are made as to inflation and increase of costs. Determinations as to salaries, lease expenses, and so on, can be forecast to develop a model of the business. A *what-if* scenario can be applied to determine what happens to the firm from a numbers point of view and what the profit may or may not be.

There are many marketing strategies available that could cause a firm to grow. Some investments may require minimal capital, whereas others take substantial funding and a considerable amount of time to be profitable. Without any organized financial evaluation, it is difficult to know which proposal to implement. Likewise, without a well thought out mission statement, followed by goals and objectives, it is impossible to make logical organized conclusions about managing an architectural or engineering firm in good times or in bad times. This is the nature of being in business, in participating in varying economies.

As the financial plan is prepared and meetings are held, often it is determined that the proposal should require less capital investment or that the cash flow will not support the proposal. The result is to take another look and revise the proposal. This is the essence of the planning process: Revise, revise, revise. Refine the plan until it is acceptable. There may also be times when one realizes that the goals and objectives have to change because of what is developed in the financial section or other parts of the plan. In those cases, it is definitely time to go back to the drawing board and discuss the reasons for making such a recommendation. This, too, is part of the planning process. It is not an empirical event working from beginning to end but an integrative process with all parts having synergy with the other parts. This process is what makes the plan work.

Detailed budget.   One of the most useful supporting documents is a detailed budget of what it's going to take to implement the proposal. Usually the proposal requires some investment, and the amounts requested must be justified. It also gives the opportunity to analyze the expenditures thoroughly as the firm generally has to pay for this in some way. This is another area where upper management might request that the sums be reduced and budgets cut in order to implement the plan.

Cash flow projections.   Hand in hand with the detailed budget are the cash flow projections. In other words, how does the proposed project influence the cash flow of the firm, given the budget and the new capital that is infused into its operation? The cash flow projection will give someone reading the plan a synopsis of what can be expected. These numbers should be reasonable and in line with the firm's operation.

Financial resources. In addition to examining the financial constraints of the project, the sources of funds and how they are used should be examined. Any project must be funded in some way, and this part of the plan explains where the money would come from and how the money would be used. In some cases, the money will come from internal cash flows or from savings the firm has accumulated. However, many firms may seek leverage by using other people's money (OPM) for the project.

There are many other factors that can be discussed about a firm's finances and how they are managed. Rather than letting cash flow problems dictate what an office does, the proper financial tools will help the architect or engineer and actually make it easier to manage a practice. For example, running an office without a budget and without financial planning constraints means that one reacts to the cash flow. When the cash flow stops, some things don't get done on a timely basis or are put off. This generally leads to more business problems—the problems seem to compound themselves.

In all of these discussions, it is important to remember that the personality of the engineer or architect will come out in the business plan. If the person is conservative, the projections will probably be conservative. The quality of the plan is based upon the quality of the information that is provided and the quality of the individuals preparing the plan. The more consistent one becomes in preparing and using plans, the better an office is able to predict with some degree of success certain financial outcomes.

Conclusion

The conclusions of a business plan are generally two different kinds: either to go ahead or to tread cautiously and even consider not going ahead. More often than not, the conclusion is a positive statement that the firm should go ahead and implement the plan. This is true for annual operating business plans and for specific project business plans that evaluate a marketing project or some key business decision. The key advantages for such implementation, along with the obvious benefits, should be outlined. In most business plans, this is no more than one page and is meant to plant the conclusion firmly in the reader's mind. Remember, any evaluator of a plan already knows the conclusion, as it is succinctly put in the executive summary. In the conclusion, key benefits and advantages can be underscored to draw attention to specific important details the writer wants to leave freshly in the reader's mind.

In the second case, the research may suggest that the proposal should not be implemented. This type of conclusion is usually found in specific project business plans. An annual business plan is a step-by-step planning process that moves toward a unanimous decision, where a specific project plan is evaluated from a go or no-go viewpoint. This does not mean the business plan failed, quite the contrary. The business plan was an overwhelming success. It simply pointed out that the idea is not feasible given the present situation. In most instances, certain information was uncovered that the firm did not know before. Now, decisions can be made with a better feeling for what might happen. Of course, one never knows until one tries, and this is where a certain sensitivity to business plan issues and a sense of timing can truly be valuable. However, this same business plan might show that there are other alternatives for achieving the same result. Business plans can have all sorts of outcomes and are really a forum for brainstorming to come up with creative working solutions.

Now, consider the situation where the decision is made not to recommend the proposal. How should a negative conclusion be presented? One should take a dissenting opinion and state firmly that based upon the information given, it does not seem economically favorable to adopt the given position. Another technique would be to approve the implementation with specific parameters and note that there may be significant risk if the parameters were not followed. This can be thought of as the buyer beware approach. If one recommends that a proposal should not be implemented, it has to be assumed that a lot of effort went into the decision and a lot of people spent time contributing thoughts and information to come up with the conclusion. A negative recommendation not to proceed doesn't mean the project will not be implemented. As a rule, there is always something happening that someone else doesn't know about. A plan may be put into effect in spite of the precautions.

Appendix

The appendix in a business plan provides a place to submit documentation that might be helpful to the reader in making a decision. For example, a full set of financial statements, market research summaries, or charts and graphs might be provided. Each plan will have different information, and it's up to the author to decide what is important. In fact, a lot is left up to the author or the person in charge of the plan. It's his or her skill that pulls the plan together on a timely basis so that a decision can be reached and the office can go on.

Summary

This chapter presented the different parts of a typical business plan that might be used by an architect or engineer for an annual operating plan or a specific business decision. The next chapter discusses how a business plan is prepared and provides a complete business plan. The remainder of the book provides information that will assist the engineer and architect in making business decisions.

Figure 2.4 represents a business plan and its basic relationships. Subtle internal relationships are not shown for clarity. Using this as a guide will provide a strong analytical business plan approach to any business decision.

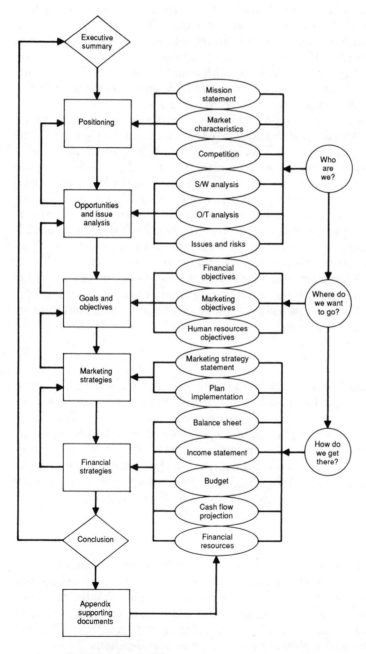

Figure 2.4   Business plan model.

3

Business Plan

Business plans should be flexible and should be able to adapt to different conditions and different sets of information. Business plan outlines can vary, as long as the essential parts of a plan are presented and the plan is satisfactory for the project being proposed. The appendix shows business plan outlines that illustrate various formats that are acceptable and that work. This chapter discusses how a business plan is prepared, and then presents a plan for discussion and review.

How Is a Business Plan Prepared?

An important question concerning how a plan is prepared is what comes first—the strategies or the goals and objectives. A usual approach is to start at the beginning and move from one section to the next, step by step, until a project is completed. This approach eliminates all preconceived ideas and assumes that at the end a perfect solution is obtained. The fact of the matter is, the preparation of the plan works quite differently. A principal engineer or architect has an idea of what the firm wants to be and how to get there. It is almost unavoidable not to have some preconceived idea of what the final outcome is supposed to look like when dealing with business planning. This is the direct opposite of what is taught in design school, where preconceived ideas were not tolerated. For example, one might have concluded that the firm should expand through alliances, then eventual mergers. Or that the firm should grow to a staff size of 25 people. These ideas are hard to put away when writing an annual operating plan.

Step-by-step process

The step-by-step method offers a logical starting point. By using this method and including one's ideas about what the solution might be, the writer creates opportunities for creativity and pulls together everyone's ideas in an orchestrated event.

Are the ideas good or bad? Are they logical conclusions or dreams? The business plan process allows a forum to analyze and put together a logical and understandable document of the ideas. Questions will have to be answered:

What is the impact on the staff of a proposed idea?

What are the financial ramifications of the implementation of a plan?

Will new employees who bring new skills to the firm, as in the case with CAD, have to be hired?

Will employees have to be let go?

Is the firm legally protected from letting employees go when there may be enough work in the firm to keep them on?

Do the issues facing the firm correspond to the ideas concerning the solution?

What is the overall direction of the firm?

What are the issues and risks facing the firm?

The questions go on. The writing and rewriting processes provide the opportunity to ask questions and to adjust ideas until a balanced plan is arrived at.

The actual process of developing a business plan for an office might be as follows. Start with the title page; insert the purpose of the plan. This step makes sure the plan is focused. Next, fill out the contents following another plan as a guide, such as the one in this book or the firm's format. Move to the executive overview, and write as much as possible about the purpose of the plan and perhaps a sketch of the conclusion. These are the preconceived ideas you carry in your head. Use these ideas as constructive starting points, then let them develop and flourish. Psychologists say you will not let go of these ideas until you try to use them, so let the plan revolve around them, let them be tested, and let them lead to new ideas.

Then, move on to the positioning section and develop as much detail as possible. Prepare the opportunities and issue analysis next. Follow that by the goals and objectives section, which tends to address the issues that have been developed. At some point market research needs to contribute information. As this information comes in, ideas will develop as to the potential marketing strategies. Likewise, one has to know what kind of budgets a firm has, what the profit and loss profile of the firm is, and what other financial information there is. Prepare this information.

As all of this information develops, it goes into separate files; thus, ideas on marketing strategies are in one file and goals and objectives are in another. Work through the plan to the end, using the best try attitude to get information down on paper. The result might be from 10 to 20 sheets of paper loosely organized in the form of a business plan with a considerable number of holes in it. You will also end up with several files of supporting material. Now you are in a position to sit back and take an honest look at what you have and do not have. Additional questions will have to be answered:

Where are the holes in the plan?

When do marketing researchers have to go out and substantiate ideas, or develop new ones?

Where is the financial weakness of the plan?

Are there employee ramifications?

Are the goals and objectives in line with the mission statement?

Are the goals and objectives real and obtainable?

Are the marketing strategies in line with the rest of the material?

Are there other solutions to the problem or to the goals and objectives?

What are they?

And the list goes on. What you have arrived at is a starting point for the analysis and discussions that will truly get into the heart of the business plan ideas. Now the process is one of refinement. There is a rough outline providing a sketch of where the plan wants to go and how to get there. It is now up to the person in charge of the marketing effort to develop the analysis necessary to fill the aforementioned gaps. There are several ways to tend to this task, but writing and developing ideas is essentially the task of rewriting and a lot of reflective thinking.

First, go back to the mission statement and make sure the statement reflects exactly what the firm wants to be. Then, go through the plan making sure the different sections reflect what the true interest of the firm is, the goals reflect the objectives, and so on. As these areas are refined, more ideas will develop as to how the firm can accomplish the objectives through new opportunities, and so on.

Next, make a list of all the marketing strategies you can think of that apply to the given situation as preparation. It is hoped that this will lead to a brainstorm session, where alternatives lead to other alternatives, and so on. At the end of these meetings it is important to summarize the results so the participants know exactly what information has been developed and the group consensus to the situations presented.

In the case where the business plan is addressing one specific problem or project, the same process can be used. In some respects this is an easier plan to write because you know exactly where you are going and how you are proposing to get there. The actual outcome may depend upon the financial analysis, and thus, like all plans, the summary should reflect the situation with realistic views of the intended project.

Business plans can be formal or informal, depending upon the purpose and the parameters of the plan. If the plan were for a financial institution for review of a loan, it would be formal in appearance and tone. If the plan were for internal use, it might be more informal in its presentation.

Sole proprietor and the small firm

The process of preparing a business plan for the sole proprietor is the same, except with less reliance upon staff members. The architect or engineer of a small-to-medium-size firm can get advice and business counseling from consultants who will address specific issues and prepare and present the outcome of the report. The firm, however, must have the necessary financial resources. Or the small firm can take a serious appraisal of one's situation, with a view of what one is trying to accomplish. A small architectural firm might look into developing a small advisory board of a minimum of three outsiders who advise the firm's principals. The charter of this group is to address certain issues presented to it by the principals. The group may meet as often as the principals feel necessary. Meetings might be during the development of the annual plan, then at one-third points throughout the year. The advisory group responds with their expertise and suggests a course of action, corrective measures, or whatever the situation merits. The meeting might be after work, then continued over dinner.

Who should the architect or engineer ask to be advisors? Some advisors are generally known to the principals as associate businesspeople and are asked to join for their expertise. The firm's accountant might be a member; an architect from another city whom the principals know might be another member. Other candidates are found by asking business acquaintances for recommendations. There may be a fee of $100 (plus) per meeting, plus dinner, and so on, depending on the circumstances. The price does not have to be overwhelming, since for many businesspeople meeting the challenge is the real reward.

The advisory group should start where the firm is and continue from that point. If there is no business plan, the first meeting can start by working toward one. A good advisory group will jump in and address whatever issues it needs to. Their reward is seeing the business change and grow as different issues are confronted and analyzed and courses of action are adopted. The firm may have a list of issues for the group to address developed from the O/T and S/W analysis. Each meeting should have a written agenda of the items to be covered with appropriate supporting material, usually sent out in advance. The advisory meetings may be chaired by an advisory member, as opposed to a principal who is preparing the material for review. The chairperson's role may change from year to year and rotate among the members. Basically, whatever the principals decide is in the best interest of the firm can be used as guidelines. The main goal is to develop the advisory group into a real business tool that becomes a valuable resource for the firm.

Another idea is to attend national conventions, such as the AIA, CSI, or AEC, on a regular basis and take part in seminars and programs dealing with this subject. This exposure will serve as a platform to meet those in other small offices interested in the same ideas. Associations may develop that can serve as a way to discuss business planning ideas. Also, professional organizations, such as the AIA, may have local programs to assist the architect or the engineer.

Existing business plan

Another situation is the case where a business plan already exists and it's time to do a new one. There is an advantage and a disadvantage to this situation. The advantage is that much of the material and format have been developed and will minimize the work in getting an annual plan together. The danger is that next year's plan can be rubber stamped. Just because a plan exists does not mean it's right. What opportunities have developed during the year that might suggest a change in strategy? When was the last time someone looked at the mission statements and the goals and objectives of the firm? Did the firm make its number? What about expenses? The firm will be at a true disadvantage if these questions and many others are not asked and therefore not addressed.

It is true that a marketing strategy might take several years to implement and show results. However, if it seems that the boat is going over the falls, someone should chart a new course. The business plan is the time to look seriously at the marketing programs and all other aspects of the annual plan and to weigh them carefully as the plan is prepared. Thus, in dealing with an existing plan, it's basically a massive rewrite task with more precise numbers and a better sense of which programs are working and not working. It's the time to fine-tune the plan in preparation for the next year's events.

All plans are not alike

Again, it is important to understand that plans develop for different reasons, and a plan may be put together simply to explore an idea further. As an example, consider a principal who decides to move the office to another town. One prepares a plan that outlines the costs and benefits and the pluses and minuses of such an undertaking. To continue the example, say there are two principals in the firm who are divided as to the move. The plan is going to help decide the issue. Here is a perfect example where the purpose of the plan is clearly outlined.

Whether the firm moves, however, depends heavily upon the ramifications of making such a move and the resulting financial effect. In addition, the obstacles and risks, or the threat analysis, become very important. Here the threat of losing customer identity can be analyzed along with the downtime of the move and all the other multitude of risks one might undertake in such an endeavor. In essence, here is the plan to accomplish this objective; however, here are also the risks one incurs in doing so. Another possible conclusion is alternative ways to reach a solution, such as a joint office in two locations. One could also reach the conclusion that the move is not feasible and specify the reasons why. The advantage of the business plan process is that all the information needed to make a good solid business decision is on the table in a logical sequence. The plan never makes the final decision—management does. Management is the engineer or architect wearing another hat.

Plans with biased opinions

It's possible to color a plan one way or another. The author of a plan may have an affinity for a particular outcome. One could take a position to always present his or her side a little bit more positively, with more supporting facts. Essentially, one has to know where to draw the line. A person asked to author a business plan will, after investigation, tend to favor one solution or group of ideas over another based upon his or her business experience. The result is a natural tendency to support that conclusion more effectively. The problem arises when one supports a conclusion by leaving out important details that support a contrary opinion. There are many ways to do this. This coloring of a plan to support one side falsely to gain acceptance will eventually be detrimental to the firm—and to the author of the plan. The fastest way to lose credibility is to be caught manipulating data through omission or inaccurate facts to make one side look better.

The solution to this problem is for management to take an active role in the plan's preparations. A sharp manager will not let obvious holes in a plan escape. The easiest way to manage this process is to review the plan and point out shortcomings and omissions. The plan is then returned for changes and completions. If the plan is done honestly and with diligence, obtaining the necessary information and input, this will be a minor occurrence. The best course for any business and marketing plan author is to do the best job possible under the constraints of the assignment. Sooner or later, a firm will find the proper business balance, and the business plan will become even more meaningful.

Plan outline

The outline of the business plan discussed in Chap. 2 is one of many combinations. Here is a business plan illustrating the fundamental parts. There are alternatives and other word choices and methods of organizing titles of sections, and so on. In addition, the same plan could be more complex, with detailed marketing strategies, and so forth. After enough practice, you can develop your own style and method of organization. The following business plan is presented for discussion.

Annual Operating Business Plan

In an effort to explore business planning of an architectural or engineering firm, without focusing on any one firm, a fictitious business will be used. This is the technique developed by the AMA and is well accepted. The important point is to go beyond the example and apply the business concepts to your environment.

The fictitious business, *Sample, Inc.,* is a growing firm feeling the pressure of outside competition and, at the same time, feeling a downturn in the market. These problems are everywhere, and the city architect or engineer, the suburban architect or engineer, or the small town architect or engineer will be able to identify with the dilemmas and proposed solutions. The important concept to remember is how a business plan is assembled into a logical cohesive presentation, not the specific conclusions or recommendations developed in the plan. The example illustrates the process of business plan writing for architects and engineers.

Sample, Inc., is located in Ukiah, California. It is in Mendocino County, part of the wine country. To the north are the redwoods, and about 30 miles to the west is the ocean. The region is feeling the pressures of growth as the freeways allow easy commute travel to Santa Rosa, about 50 miles south of Ukiah. The architecture is predominantly regional in nature, such as California ranch style, with some Maybeck influence on the older homes. Small strip-type shopping centers have sprung up in the last 10 years along a freeway east of town; there's also a sprinkling of homes in the oak-covered hills. The wine country is a mixture of grape and pear ranches, with small wineries dotting the landscape. The fall is a bustle of activity, as the grapes are picked and trucked off to the crushers. The ranchers vie for space with the developers and opportunists, who sometimes are disguised as ranchers.

Sample, Inc., has a total of 12 people on its staff. The two principal architects are owners and equal partners. The first principal is responsible for the design, construction, documentation, and observation of the work. Under the design architect are two project architects who have different numbers of years of experience. They are assisted by six drafters, also with different levels of experience, who generally work on several projects. Two of the drafters are assigned projects from beginning to end as a backup to the project architect; these drafters are further ahead with their licensing requirements. This process serves as a stepping stone and as an interoffice informal ranking system.

The second principal manages the business, attends to the clients, oversees the administration and all contract administration, and, as in any small firm, occasionally spends time on the boards when business necessitates it. His or her input in the design is one of a sounding board and as a critic. This partner usually assists in client meetings and is considered the firm's chief presenter. The office is supported by a full-time receptionist and part-time bookkeeper. The firm uses outside consultants for mechanical, electrical, and structural engineering.

Annual Operating Business Plan
for
Sample, Inc.
An Architectural Environmental Design Firm

The purpose of this plan is to outline next year's
operating guidelines and marketing strategies.

Prepared by

_____

_____

November 15, 199 __

Contents

I. Executive Summary

II. Positioning
- Mission Statement
- Market Characteristics
- Competition

III. Opportunities and Issue Analysis
- Strength and Weakness Analysis
- Opportunities and Threats Analysis
- Issues and Risks

IV. Goals and Objectives
- Financial Objectives
- Marketing Objectives
- Human Resource Objectives
- Goals and Objectives Summary

V. Marketing Strategies
- Marketing Strategy Statement
- Action Plan

VI. Financial Strategies
- General Financial Overview
- Projected Income Statement (P&L)
- Financial Resources
- Cash Flow Projections

VII. Conclusion

VIII. Appendix

I. Executive Summary

Sample, Inc., has matured into a stable architectural firm with a strong consciousness regarding environmental problems facing communities, owners, and developers today. The firm has positioned itself well within the community as a regional architect and thus receives its share of residential and commercial projects. In light of the present economy, however, the forecast is for a slowdown in construction starts in the residential sector, as well as a tightening of commercial funds resulting in a projection of lower commissions and fees over the next 5-year period.

Consequently, this business plan addresses next year's operating structure and suggests and recommends a growth policy that will position *Sample, Inc.,* as a strong player in the community, with additional exposure to new markets and services. Specifically, it is recommended that *Sample, Inc.,* considers two marketing strategies:

1. Position ourselves to take advantage of institutional work that is forecasted for Mendocino County within the next 5 years.
2. Position ourselves for a merger with another architectural firm to expand our market and our services.

The objective of *Sample, Inc.,* is to attack the forecasted downturn aggressively with no suggestion of financial instability to the public and our clients. With this posture, *Sample, Inc.,* will be prepared to take advantage of any opportunity we uncover, as well as the opportunities less-fortunate firms will provide by their departure. With a solid business plan in place, well fortified with an implementation strategy and combined with an aggressive attitude, *Sample, Inc.,* is in a position to prosper and to grow.

II. Positioning

Sample, Inc., has now completed its eleventh year of practicing architecture in Ukiah. It has grown to an office of 12 people and has occupied the same facility for the last 3 years. We designed the Bankers Office Park complex where we are located. The identity of *Sample, Inc.,* has been with the residential sector until several years ago, when our residential clients began to prosper in their own businesses and came to us for help with commercial-oriented construction. This strategy of growing with the customer has worked well during the last 7 years. However, the forecasted downturn in the residential and commercial sectors necessitates rethinking our marketing philosophy. In order to survive and grow and to enjoy the same quality commissions, *Sample, Inc.,* must itself grow in philosophy and look further into the market for opportunities.

Mission statement

In the past, the company's goal has been one of survival, basically a year-to-year, month-to-month, hand-to-mouth effort. Last year a business planning methodology was introduced to the firm, with the intent of providing a business planning structure, as well as informing our employees about our direction as a company. This planning methodology also communicates to our clients who we are and what we are about through the different programs we implement. That same concept continues this year, with a redefined mission statement designed to clarify our firm's direction and refine our goals and objectives.

Sample, Inc., Mission Statement

Sample, Inc., is a growth-oriented architectural firm that takes a special interest in the environment's preservation and use when creating exterior space relationships that serve to complement a building's function while maintaining the environment's integrity. Our design goal is to create usable and interesting space for users within the context of the owner's architectural program. We strive to take advantage of high technology and to pass that advantage on to our clients and users of our buildings. *Sample, Inc.,* provides quality design and service.

Our intent is clear as a firm. We are in a growth mode and seek profitability. We wish to be the leader in the use of high technology, both to create the building and to create a tool for users to manage the facility. We have special concerns with the environment as we try to create exterior spaces that are unusual and usable. We provide quality service and design. The direction and intent of *Sample, Inc.,* is a balanced mix of practical goals, design philosophies, and sensitivities to the changing aura of high-tech architectural practice.

Market characteristics

The architectural market *Sample, Inc.,* operates in is characterized as having peaked. The demonstrative effects of developers pushing the planning commissions for zone changes have slowed the bulk housing market, particularly with the forecasted economic trends of a slowing economy. The commercial market continues with projects set in motion more than 2 years ago. The planning department has indicated a strong interest in inner city beautification with all recent commercial projects. *Sample, Inc.,* has been fortunate to have catered to the early residential crowd that later followed with commercial projects; however, the forecast is for a definite fall off of commissions.

Our target market is within a 50-mile radius of Ukiah and is composed of several different building types as indicated in the following chart.

Sample, Inc., 3-Year History (in %)

	1987	1988	1989
Residential	28	19	4
Commercial	35	51	65
Planning	10	13	14
County	2	5	8
Farm related	25	12	9

In the past, the dominant trend has been the fall off of residential and growth of commercial work, which is the primary emphasis of the firm. Now, residential clients are usually a commercial client that wishes to use our services. This is usually done as a favor, since this type of work is essentially unprofitable unless high commissions are obtained; even then it can be a push. The primary clients are the mainstream businesspeople who have been successful and are building on that success with new business developments. The commercial work is much more profitable than the typical residential customer, as the commercial client understands an architect can be of great assistance and thus does not need the training and coaching a residential client requires. The commercial client generally provides repeat business, whereas the custom residential work is essentially a one-time project.

The regional forecasts indicate an overall slowdown. Local lumber mills have laid off workers, indicating there are fewer orders from building material suppliers and a slowdown in housing starts. Commercial clients indicate no aggressive construction plans, as they settle into managing their own businesses until the trend changes. The market characteristic suggests a definite slowdown which can only be interpreted as a potential economic problem for *Sample, Inc.* Nevertheless, because of our strong architectural presence in the area, it is felt we will generally outlast the competition.

Competition

The main competition comes from the outside. Santa Rosa has several architectural firms with projects in the Ukiah basin. There are reasons for this phenomenon: Pressures from the Bay Area and from Santa Rosa push development north. The developers who are local to Santa Rosa have worked with architects in that area and thus have established an architect-developer relationship. Santa Rosa architects who wish to expand their own market area understandably cater and encourage this activity. Also, new residents in the Ukiah Valley, not knowing any specific architect, opt for a larger, city architect. The psychological factor is difficult to deal with but does indicate a need for more aggressive marketing by us.

The local architects who compete with us are responsible members of the profession. Some are more experienced than others, and *Sam*

ple, Inc., generally only competes directly with two firms. Both these firms are established, have strong regional ties, and are somewhat smaller in size. There are some out-of-school architects who represent no real threat. Each architect seems to have his or her own client following and competes only on public and commercial projects. *Sample, Inc.,* has not had its share of public work, and even though we are larger in size, it appears to be where the competition has the predominant edge over us. This is the niche area that immediately suggests we must become more aggressive through marketing.

Hence, the lack of play in the public sector is our definite positioning weakness. With the market trend slowing and our emphasis in commercial work, there is a need to develop a more comprehensive program that focuses our attention on the public sector and to explore more ways to serve our existing commercial clients.

III.   Opportunities and Issue Analysis

It is said that behind every problem there is an opportunity, and behind every opportunity there is a threat. Beyond this are all the issues that must be faced rather than avoided. By evaluating the opportunities and issues, *Sample, Inc.,* has a chance to gain and grow more prosperous than any other firm in our market area. The opportunities analysis is addressed by a summary of the strength and weaknesses (S/W) and opportunities and threats (O/T) in the following situational analysis chart. This analysis was completed by several staff members and the principals.

Strength and weakness analysis

The situational analysis chart is the best reflection of the firm to date. It points out *Sample, Inc.'s,* lack of success with institutional buildings. *Sample, Inc.,* knows this market is forecasted to grow due to government decisions made several years ago. More specifically, judicial buildings and correctional facilities are forecasted to increase due to the growing state prison population. Added to this are the state laws requiring existing jail systems to update their facilities to comply with applicable building codes. Another weakness is our rather slow involvement with high technology—particularly the use of CAD and project management systems.

The strengths continue to be our commercial experience and our expertise dealing with environmental issues. Our commercial work may serve nicely as a platform for this upcoming

Situational Analysis
Sample, Inc.

	Current		Future	
Strengths	Weaknesses	Opportunities		Threats
Commercial	Institutional work	Institutional buildings • Correctional facilities • Judicial facilities • Code compliance work		*Sample, Inc.*, will not be prepared or competitive
Local and regional work	Exposure outside our geographic area	Expand via merger		Complex and managerial intensive; $s at risk
Strong operational planning methodologies	Lack of CAD expertise Lack of project management expertise	Become the expert in CAD		Outside architects or engineers will get the work Some government projects require CAD
Environmental design		Market this environmental image		
Residential	Have not pursued residential for a number of years	Seek out custom residential projects		Must be closely managed to be profitable

Developing issues
• Commercial vs. institutional architecture?
• Capital investment in CAD and project management?
• Geographic expansion?
• Custom residential?
• Merger?

institutional work. We also have not pursued the residential sector, where we were once strong, for a number of years.

Opportunities and threats analysis

The opportunities are also our weaknesses and are evidenced by the amount of correctional facility work forecasted both statewide and countywide. This is truly an opportunity, as no local architect has any jail experience of any kind. The threat is that outside architects from San Francisco or further away will be competing for our dollars and may win the commissions, since we may be unprepared or considered unqualified. An additional threat is the impact of losing a project because our present CAD system is not being operated to its fullest capability. This is further compounded by the fact that many government jobs may require the submission of electronic files at the completion of a project.

Issues and risks

The conclusions of the S/W and O/T analysis are the issues facing *Sample, Inc.* They are presented as alternative questions and based upon the answers will define the goals, objectives, strategy, and tactics of the plan. Associated with the issues are the risks, which are essentially a down payment for taking advantage of an opportunity. The issues are as follows:

Should *Sample, Inc.*, continue to stress its commercial services?

If we continue to market or attract commercial work, should price and promotion strategies change in any way?

Should *Sample, Inc.*, look at a long-term strategy of developing an expertise in institutional buildings?

What does it take to compete in this marketplace?

Should *Sample, Inc.*, reexplore the residential custom market?

Should *Sample, Inc.*, increase its capital investment in CAD technology and spend less money on promotions?

Should there be an infusion of additional capital monies by the partners to implement the long-range strategy?

What does it take besides money to implement CAD successfully into an office?

Will CAD help *Sample, Inc.*, become more competitive?

Should *Sample, Inc.*, look at expanding into another geographic location to take full advantage of our entrance into institutional buildings?

What is the easiest way to expand?

Should *Sample, Inc.,* simply put money into promotion, such as brochures, direct mail, and personal contact to expand our present services?

These identified issues are the basis for the development of goals and objectives, which in turn will be interpreted as marketing strategies and tactics for *Sample, Inc.,* to follow.

IV. Goals and Objectives

The issues facing *Sample, Inc.,* clearly indicate that certain decisions must be made to facilitate sustained growth. Discussion of the issues has resulted in the following goals and objectives. The financial, marketing, and human resource objectives of the firm and resulting goals serve further to add definition to the company's mission statement and provide direction to the marketing strategy and, hence, the eventual financial plan of *Sample, Inc.*

Financial objectives

Following are the financial goals and objectives that represent the direction of *Sample, Inc.,* and its mission statement. This is what the firm wants to be.

1. Become a million dollar firm in billable gross income within the next five years.

   Goals
   a. Minimize the loss in 199__ .
   b. Continue to generate a positive cash flow.
   c. Stabilize the income level at year 5.

2. Produce a net profit greater than 10 percent in year 5.

   Goals
   a. Increase billable services.
   b. Decrease cost of providing services.

3. Create a cash flow situation.

   Goals
   a. Generate, implement, and use a monthly financial plan based on the annual plan.
   b. Adjust the resulting budgets on a monthly basis to meet the plan at end of year (EOY).

Marketing objectives

The marketing goals and objectives are an interpretation of the financial objectives and lay the foundation for marketing strategy.

There is a projected loss at the EOY 1 of approximately 6 percent, which is largely due to the implementation of a marketing strategy that begins to realign the services offered so as to be in position to take advantage of future correctional institutional work.

1. Achieve a total sales volume (EOY 1) of $575,280.

   Goals

   a. Increase residential to 10 percent or $57,528 in sales.
   b. Maintain commercial at the 65 percent level or $373,932 in sales.
   c. Decrease planning to 5 percent or $28,764 in sales.
   d. Increase county work to 17 percent or $97,798 in sales.
   e. Decrease farm-related agriculture buildings to 3 percent or $17,258 in sales.

2. Increase the promotion plan to include correctional institutional exposure.

   Goals

   a. Develop an "institution" awareness.
   b. Develop in-house expertise.
   c. Develop a consultant relationship, and promote the association.
   d. Develop an awareness of the county's and state's processes for being selected.

3. Review the firm's use of all contracts and services.

   Goals

   a. Review our existing contractual relationships to verify we are properly compensated.
   b. Review the architectural and other services we offer to determine what other service we should be actively marketing.
   c. Review our legal posture regarding contracts to eliminate any downside risks.

4. Position ourselves for expansion into outside markets.

   Goals

   a. Develop expansion alternatives.
   b. Develop relationships with outside architects and consultants.

5. Develop a full CAD and computer system, with the aim of being the most sophisticated high-tech architectural firm in the valley.

   Goals

   a. Work toward a 90 percent CAD solution within 5 years.
   b. Develop a database for our use and for the use of potential clients.
   c. Hire a CAD manager who can implement and manage such a program.
   d. Develop CAD into a marketing program.

Human resource objectives

The employee relationship objectives provide the personnel for accomplishing the above goals and objectives, while at the same time the necessary working environment required for the firm to grow and attract new help. Staff turnover, particularly to the competition, is recognized as being costly in downtime, resulting in lost contribution and office knowledge. Particular care should be taken to ensure a good employee life, where one looks forward to coming to work and contributing to the firm's success and his or her future.

1. Improve the quality of work life.

   Goals

   a. Establish an employee and employer review system.
   b. Establish a bonus program based upon profits, contribution, and performance.
   c. Establish a sense of office identity.

2. Improve the employee.

   Goals

   a. Establish an employee training program.
   b. Develop an architectural intern program.

Goals and objectives summary

The objective of *Sample, Inc.,* is clear in that we are to be a $1 million company in 5 years. The financial goals and objectives set the stage for creating the momentum to get there, even with a forecasted down economy and a projected loss for next year. The thrust of the marketing objectives is to develop a different mix of work to accomplish the financial objectives. To prepare for the future, a decrease of planning work, which has been developer oriented, a decrease in farm agriculture buildings, which are low profit jobs, and an impressive increase in county work are recommended. The increase in county work is important since we need to build our relationship with these agencies if we are to position ourselves to accept future local, state, and government commissions. An increase in residential work is in order in that we now turn away this work. This new interest in the custom home market will broaden our exposure if a downturn is greater than predicted. Although these jobs tend to be as sophisticated as commercial work, we can charge larger fees and take more of an active role in construction management than we have in the past. We thereby can gain additional experience in construction management, which we can develop into a marketing feature that may be very desirable for future work.

Marketing issues are very important in this year's plan and achieving the next 5-year bottom line goals.

V.   Marketing Strategies

The marketing approach that will be used to achieve the objective of becoming a $1 million billable firm within 5 years is a combination of strategies that sets the course of our business in a direction that takes advantage of the federal, state, and local construction dollars forecasted due to judicial and correctional facilities being built or remodeled. Marketing strategy is essentially the desire to gain a competitive advantage over the competition, leading to strength, profitability, and ensured stability. The emphasis of all programs is focused on this effort. Product, place, price, promotion, and people issues will all be tailored to accommodate the growth and the change in the firm's direction, as well as the acceptance of CAD as part of the basic strategy. The strategy is summarized below.

Marketing strategy statement

Target market. *Sample, Inc.,* will continue to develop its role in the commercial market, with a long-term objective of developing a presence in the correctional facilities marketplace and other judicial and government-oriented buildings. Increased emphasis in county and state work will be the staging ground for future correctional facility work.

Positioning. *Sample, Inc.,* will initiate a four-step marketing strategy to enter the correctional market:

1. Establish a relationship with a consultant in the correctional and judicial field.
2. Establish alliances with other firms doing institutional work to expand our knowledge and become more competitive within this market area.
3. Develop a program for identifying other architecture or engineering firms that will become targets of acquisition to expand our market area outside of the Ukiah Valley and to expand our expertise.
4. Develop a program to expand CAD and the use of computers to take advantage of the computer's leverage and attractive marketing alternatives.

Services offered.   The basic service will be represented to all clients as the minimum service they will need. Additional work as might be generated due to the nature of the design will be stressed by presentations that unequivocally show that it is to the client's advantage to have us provide a broader scope of service rather than have the client go elsewhere. The use of the computer will be emphasized for its efficiency of the database of information created using the CAD system. We must distinguish ourselves from our competitors in every possible way, and our unique marketing message must be promoted.

Price structure. The philosophy of this firm regarding price is to charge a fair and competitive amount that is not changed because other architects charge a lower amount. When clients tell us the price is too high, they are really telling us that they do not understand the depth and breadth of the services we are offering in relationship to their particular project and do not understand how the scope of our services combined with our professional experience will, in the long run, save them money. This situation also means that we are not properly communicating this information to our prospective clients, which indicates we need training and to look at our presentation skills. *Sample, Inc.*, strives to achieve an awareness of the selling environment; we are highly profit motivated, which we believe is the key to being able to offer quality architectural designs in the future. The principals' time will not be free, and they will actively participate in all projects as required. However, a larger portion of the principals' time will be allocated to marketing and sales.

Marketing research. A budget for market research shall be established with the emphasis on long-term future markets and targeted prospects. This program will feed into the different promotional campaigns. The intent is for marketing research to get a handle on what is happening in our market area so as to put us in a position to be more competitive.

Contractual. An emphasis on legal ramifications of all contracts shall be reviewed by legal counsel on a regular basis, especially before any contract execution. Particularly important are legal problems arising during practice, such as fee collections, construction-related problems dealing with interpretations of the contract, arbitration, and limitation of risk clauses. In addition, at the appropriate time, guidelines for acquisition of another firm and transition philosophies will be addressed by legal counsel. In short, a full protective legal blanket is viewed as an essential ingredient for *Sample, Inc.'s,* success.

Promotion. There will be six on-going promotional campaigns that will serve to generate leads and establish a county or state and local presence. The use of an advertising agency to assist the principal architects in implementing the basic promotional campaigns to achieve our goals shall be a basic marketing strategy. *Harvest and Partners, Inc.*, assisted us in the following promotional program and will assist us in its implementation:

1. Develop an appealing brochure that demonstrates the design capabilities of our firm, as well as the successful completion of several different types of work. The brochure will be of the type that projects and/or promotional material can be taken out or inserted, allowing us to customize each presentation. This will also allow us to make changes as *Sample, Inc.,* grows.

2. Develop a computer model of the downtown corridor that can be used by city officials and make the use of our firm attractive for city and county work. This is an on-going, long-term project.

3. Develop a direct-mail campaign for prospects identified by market research.

4. Develop a telemarketing program to survey existing customers and conduct market research and other programs that are in line with *Sample, Inc.'s,* goals and objectives. Outside professional telemarketing consultants should be used to assist in the design and implementation of the campaign.

5. Develop an after-action follow-up campaign to ensure that clients are satisfied with our work. Identify areas upon which we can improve.

6. Develop a networked computer system that is used in all areas of the office. Particularly important is the CAD system that must be used to generate excitement with the client.

Plan implementation.   The implementation of the components of the marketing strategy, which interprets the goals and objectives and basic mission statement, is accomplished through assignment of responsibilities, or management by objectives. This delegation will divide the tasks and make each part known to the individual responsible; the procedure will be used as a guideline for assessing each one's performance. The principals will author an action plan under a separate cover that further breaks down each goal and objective into areas of responsibility with appropriate references to completion times. The action plan for *Sample, Inc.,* follows.

Action plan

Managing partner.   The managing partner will primarily be responsible for the marketing and promotional aspects of the firm, along with the financial plan.

Design partner.   The design partner will be responsible for the cost of the service provided by the firm on each and every project.

VI. Financial Strategies

The marketing strategies are implemented through a sound financial plan that is a basis for measuring the performance of the firm in relationship to our goals and objectives. Costs, along with forecasted profits, are projected for our new marketing strategies. As managing principals, our responsibility is for the firm's economic survival and profitability. We therefore have taken an aggressive role in managing the firm, rather than a sit back and wait and see attitude.

General financial overview

Briefly, the financial overview of *Sample, Inc.,* is as follows:

Sample, Inc., generated fees at the $612,000 income level this year but is projecting a sharp decline in profitability next year. Current gross margin is 45 percent of total revenue with general and administrative (G&A) at 30 percent, producing a 14 percent net income. The cash flow is stable but declining. Costs are at the required level but must be watched carefully in light of current jobs that are now in schematic design phase.

Projected income statement (P&L)

Based upon the marketing strategies, the following is a projection of income and expenses for the next fiscal year.

Projected Income Statement

	199 __		EOY 1	
	($)	(%)	($)	(%)
Total revenue	612,000	100.00	575,280	100.00
Total direct cost	333,849	54.55	392,363	68.20
Gross margin	278,151	45.45	182,917	31.80
Total G&A expense	187,788	30.68	220,996	38.42
Total expense	521,637	85.23	613,359	106.62
Net income (loss)	90,363	14.77	<38,079>	<6.62>

$38,079 is the projected loss for next year; however, *this is due to the increase in expenditures to change the marketing direction of the firm.* This increase in expenditures is considered both risky and critical to *Sample, Inc.'s,* success. It is apparent that the mix of future jobs is going to change, and it is our job to adapt and exploit the opportunity.

Financial resources

Each year *Sample, Inc.,* increases its budget by increasing expenses due to inflation and other normal operating parameters. This year, there is an increase in the amounts expended due to the results of the long-range planning and marketing strategies. Hence, an additional $66,371 is allocated to implement the plan. The money is generated from three sources:

Bank loan

Savings

Cash flow

The decision to borrow money is based upon not wanting to deplete the firm's cash reserves totally, as well as the desire to continue to develop a good solid banking relationship. The remainder is from cash flow and will fluctuate each month depending upon the monthly forecasted demand. The principals will take less of a draw this year to facilitate the firm having financial flexibility and cash reserves.

Following are the increased figures for the coming year that are required to implement the above marketing program.

$66,371 Cash Requirement above Normal Budget

	Additional $s
Marketing	
Advertising	750
Promotion	1,100
Brochures	2,400
Direct mail	115
Telemarketing	485
CAD	
Equipment	11,700
Training	3,450
CAD manager	38,955
Consultant fees	3,570
Supplies	1,191
Repairs and maintenance	2,654
Total	$66,371

This investment of $66,371 puts *Sample, Inc.,* on track for meeting its goal of growing the company. All other normal operations and marketing can be accomplished within the normal budget framework.

Cash flow projections

The cash flow projections allow the firm to operate normally with no major financial difficulties during the year. In December, a $35,000 bank loan is suggested so the firm has operating capital for the following months. At this time, the income should be stabilized. Future annual plans will continue to address the financial resources of the firm and the return on investments.

In the plan appendix are *Sample, Inc.'s,* financial statements for the year just ended, 5-year financial plans, and cash flow projections. These projections are meant to be used as a guideline for developing and approving various projects that support the firm's financial objective of being a million dollar billable company in 5 years.

VII. Conclusion

Sample, Inc., can aggressively use its marketing expertise to seek out new opportunities with the services we have to offer. By discovering prosperous courses of action through seeking new opportunities, such as the correctional marketplace, we are actively participating in the firm's future. We are making business decisions based upon planning. *Sample, Inc.,* will only become a better firm for the effort it expends to develop the necessary expertise. Given the knowledge that there will always be work available and *Sample, Inc.,* is one of the most sought after firms, enlarging our target area and becoming known more on a statewide basis will enhance *Sample, Inc.'s,* market position.

It is our underlying philosophy that being aggressive gives us the chance to prosper. More important, the prosperity allows us the opportunity to produce quality design and create the spaces we envision. Hence, the plan as submitted is recommended to be implemented. The financial resources of *Sample, Inc.,* are strong, and the investment is necessary to achieve our goals.

VIII.   Appendix

I. Balance Sheet

II. Income Statement (P&L)

III. Next Year's Budget

IV. Five-Year Plan

V. Pro Forma Cash Budget for Next Year

Sample, Inc., Balance Sheet as of December 31, 199 __

Assets ($)

Current assets	
Cash: checking	8,901
Petty cash	50
Accounts receivable	16,427
Bank savings	31,411
Total current assets	$ 56,789
Fixed assets	
Office equipment	6,946
Technical equipment	17,500
Transportation	19,765
Furniture	21,986
Less: Accumulated depreciation	<6,700>
Total fixed assets	$ 59,497
Total assets	$116,286

Liabilities and equity ($)

Current liabilities	
Accounts payable	26,495
FIT and FICA payable	4,500
Total current liabilities	$ 30,995
Long-term notes	
Long-term notes payable	8,500
Total liabilities	$ 39,495
Owner's equity	
Common stock	36,500
Retained earnings	12,805
Profit (loss)	90,363
Less: Owner's salary	<62,877>
Total equity	$ 76,791
Total liabilities and equity	$116,286

Sample, Inc., Income Statement January 1, 199 __ to December 31, 199 __

	199 __	
	($)	(%)
Revenue		
Professional fees	434,337	71.07
Additional service fees	113,209	18.50
Reimbursable expense	63,854	10.43
Total revenue	$612,000	100.00
Direct cost		
Salaries	201,484	32.92
Consultant fees	78,000	12.75
Contract labor	12,607	2.06
Blueprint & eng. services	17,890	2.92
Travel	6,854	1.12
Drafting & CAD supplies	17,014	2.78
Total direct cost	$333,849	54.55
Gross margin	$278,151	45.45
General & administrative (G&A)		
Administrative salaries	28,388	4.74
Accounting	5,203	0.85
Advertising & promotion	13,220	2.16
Office lease	34,568	5.65
Payroll taxes	12,853	2.10
Transportation	6,733	1.10
Depreciation: Trans.	5,264	0.86
Depreciation: Other	16,893	2.76
Capital equipment	5,201	0.85
Repairs & maintenance	8,630	1.41
Telephone	3,428	0.56
Utilities	3,618	0.59
Legal	8,752	1.43
Licenses	1,592	0.26
Insurance	25,093	4.10
Contributions & subsc.	1,225	0.20
Postage & freight	2,858	0.47
Misc. expense	3,672	0.60
Total G&A expense	$187,791	30.69
Total expense	$521,640	85.24
Net income (loss)	$ 90,360	14.76

Sample, Inc., EOY 1 Analysis

	199 __ ($)	(%)	Normal operating budget ($)	(%)	Increase	New EOY 1 budget ($)	(%)
Revenue							
Professional fees	434,937	71.07	408,841	71.07		408,841	71.07
Additional service fees	153,209	25.03	144,017	25.03		144,017	25.03
Reimbursable expense	23,854	3.90	22,423	3.90		22,423	3.90
Total revenue	$612,000	100.00	$575,281	100.00		$575,281	100.00
Direct cost							
Salaries	201,484	32.92	207,528	36.07	38,955	246,484	42.85
Consultant fees	78,000	12.75	80,340	13.97	7,020	87,360	15.19
Contract labor	12,607	2.06	13,742	2.39	0	13,742	2.39
Blueprint & eng. services	17,890	2.92	18,248	3.17	0	18,248	
Travel	6,854	1.12	7,814	1.36	0	7,814	1.36
Drafting & CAD supplies	17,014	2.78	17,524	3.05	1,191	18,715	3.25
Total direct cost	$333,849	54.55	$345,196	60.01	$47,166	$392,363	68.20
Gross margin	$278,151	45.45	$230,085	40.00		$182,917	31.80
G&A							
Administrative salaries	28,988	4.74	30,727	5.34	0	30,727	5.34
Accounting	5,203	0.85	5,307	0.32	0	5,307	0.92
Advertising & promotion	13,220	2.16	13,370	2.32	4,850	18,220	3.17
Office lease	34,568	5.65	36,297	6.31	0	36,297	6.31
Payroll taxes	12,853	2.10	14,267	2.48	0	14,267	2.48
Transportation	6,733	1.10	7,271	1.26	0	7,271	1.26
Depreciation: Trans.	5,264	0.86	5,843	1.02	0	5,843	1.02
Depreciation: Other	16,893	2.76	18,751	8.26	0	18,751	3.26
Capital equipment	5,201	0.85	6,501	1.13	11,700	18,201	3.16
Repairs & maintenance	8,630	1.41	8,325	1.55	2,654	11,579	2.01
Telephone	3,428	0.56	3,805	0.66	0	3,805	0.66
Utilities	3,618	0.59	4,016	0.70	0	4,016	0.70
Legal	8,752	1.43	8,927	1.55	0	8,927	1.55
Licenses	1,592	0.26	1,607	0.28	0	1,607	0.28
Insurance	25,093	4.10	27,853	4.84	0	27,853	4.84
Contributions & subsc.	1,225	0.20	1,249	0.22	0	1,249	0.22
Postage & freight	2,858	0.47	3,001	0.52	0	3,001	0.52
Misc. expense	3,672	0.60	4,076	0.71	0	4,076	0.71
Total G&A expense	$187,791	30.69	$201,793	85.07	$19,204	$220,997	88.41
Total expense	$521,640	85.24	$546,988	95.08	$66,371	$613,360	106.61
Net income (loss)	$ 90,360	14.76	$ 28,292	4.92		<$38,080>	<6.61>

Sample, Inc., Five-year Income Statement Projection

	199 __ ($)	(%)	EOY 1	EOY 2	EOY 3	EOY 4	EOY 5	(%)
Revenue								
Professional fees	434,937	71.07	408,841	461,990	526,669	605,669	714,689	71.07
Additional service fees	153,209	25.03	144,017	162,739	185,522	213,351	251,754	25.03
Reimbursable expense	23,854	3.90	22,423	25,338	28,885	33,218	39,197	3.90
Total revenue	$612,000	100.00	$575,281	$650,067	$741,076	$852,238	$1,005,640	100.00
			< 0.06 >	0.13	0.14	0.15	0.18	
Direct cost								
Salaries	201,484	32.92	246,484	261,273	306,273	324,649	369,649	36.76
Consultant fees	78,000	12.75	87,360	98,717	112,537	129,418	150,125	14.93
Contract labor	12,607	2.06	13,742	14,704	15,439	15,902	16,379	1.63
Blueprint & eng. services	17,890	2.92	18,248	18,613	18,985	19,365	19,752	1.96
Travel	6,854	1.12	7,814	8,986	10,424	12,196	14,391	1.43
Drafting & CAD supplies	17,014	2.78	18,715	20,586	22,645	24,910	27,401	2.72
Total direct cost	$333,849	54.55	$392,363	$422,879	$486,303	$526,440	$ 597,697	59.43
Gross margin	$278,151	45.45	$182,918	$227,188	$254,773	$325,798	$ 407,943	40.57
G&A								
Administrative salaries	28,988	4.74	30,727	32,571	34,525	36,597	38,792	3.86
Accounting	5,203	0.85	5,307	5,466	5,684	5,969	6,327	0.63
Advertising & promotion	13,220	2.16	18,220	20,042	22,046	24,250	26,675	2.65
Office lease	34,568	5.65	36,297	38,111	40,017	42,018	44,119	4.39
Payroll taxes	12,853	2.10	14,267	15,837	17,579	19,512	21,659	2.15
Transportation	6,733	1.10	7,271	7,853	8,481	9,160	9,893	0.98
Depreciation: Trans.	5,264	0.86	5,843	6,485	7,199	7,991	8,869	0.88
Depreciation: Other	16,893	2.76	18,751	20,813	23,103	25,644	28,465	2.83
Capital equipment	5,201	0.85	18,201	28,201	20,201	12,201	5,200	0.52
Repairs & maintenance	8,630	1.41	11,579	9,579	10,633	11,802	13,101	1.30
Telephone	3,428	0.56	3,805	4,224	4,688	5,204	5,776	0.57
Utilities	3,618	0.59	4,016	4,457	4,948	5,492	6,096	0.61
Legal	8,752	1.43	8,927	9,105	9,288	9,473	9,663	0.96
Licenses	1,592	0.26	1,607	1,624	1,640	1,656	1,673	0.17
Insurance	25,093	4.10	27,853	30,917	34,318	38,093	42,283	4.20
Contributions & subsc.	1,225	0.20	1,249	1,274	1,300	1,326	1,352	0.13
Postage & freight	2,858	0.47	3,001	3,151	3,308	3,474	3,648	0.36
Misc. expense	3,672	0.60	4,076	4,524	5,022	5,575	6,188	0.62
Total G&A expense	$187,791	30.69	$220,997	$244,234	$253,980	$265,437	$ 279,779	27.81
Total expense	$521,640	85.24	$613,360	$667,113	$740,283	$791,877	$ 877,476	87.26
Net income (loss)	$ 90,360	14.76	<$38,080>	<$17,046>	$ 794	$ 60,361	$ 128,164	12.76

Sample, Inc., Pro Forma Cash Budget—Year One

	Jan.	Feb.	Mar.	Apr.	May	June	July	Aug.	Sept.	Oct.	Nov.	Dec.	EOY 1 Total
Financial resources													
Professional fees	32,707	36,796	40,884	57,238	28,619	24,530	20,442	28,619	32,707	32,707	36,796	36,796	408,841
Additional service fees	11,521	12,962	14,402	20,162	10,081	8,641	7,201	10,081	11,521	11,521	12,962	12,962	144,017
Reimbursable expense	1,794	2,018	2,242	3,139	1,570	1,345	1,121	1,570	1,794	1,794	2,018	2,018	22,423
Total cash	$46,022	$51,776	$57,528	$80,539	$40,270	$34,516	$28,764	$40,270	$46,022	$46,022	$51,776	$51,776	575,281
Use of cash													
Salaries	20,540	22,184	18,897	22,594	21,362	20,540	18,486	19,719	20,540	13,146	21,567	26,908	246,484
Consultant fees	7,280	7,862	6,698	8,008	7,571	7,280	6,552	6,989	7,280	4,659	7,644	9,537	87,360
Contract labor	1,145	1,237	1,054	1,260	1,191	1,145	1,031	1,099	1,145	733	1,202	1,500	13,742
Blueprint & eng. services	1,521	1,642	1,399	1,673	1,582	1,521	1,369	1,460	1,521	973	1,597	1,992	18,248
Travel	651	703	599	716	677	651	586	625	651	417	684	853	7,814
Drafting & CAD supplies	1,560	1,684	1,435	1,716	1,622	1,560	1,404	1,497	1,560	998	1,638	2,043	18,715
Administrative salaries	2,561	2,765	2,356	2,817	2,663	2,561	2,305	2,458	2,561	1,639	2,689	3,354	30,727
Accounting	442	478	407	486	460	442	398	425	442	283	464	579	5,307
Advertising & promotion	1,518	1,640	1,397	1,670	1,579	1,518	1,366	1,458	1,518	972	1,594	1,989	18,220
Office lease	3,025	3,267	2,783	3,327	3,146	3,025	2,722	2,904	3,025	1,936	3,176	3,962	36,297
Payroll taxes	1,189	1,284	1,094	1,308	1,237	1,189	1,070	1,141	1,189	761	1,248	1,558	14,267
Transportation	606	654	557	667	630	606	545	582	606	388	636	794	7,271
Capital equipment	1,517	1,638	1,395	1,668	1,577	1,517	1,365	1,456	1,517	971	1,593	1,987	18,201
Repairs & maintenance	965	1,042	888	1,061	1,004	965	868	926	965	618	1,013	1,264	11,579
Telephone	317	342	292	349	330	317	285	304	317	203	333	415	3,805
Utilities	335	361	308	368	348	335	301	321	335	214	351	438	4,016
Legal	744	803	684	818	774	744	670	714	744	476	781	975	8,927
Licenses	134	145	123	147	139	134	121	129	134	86	141	175	1,607
Insurance	2,321	2,507	2,135	2,553	2,414	2,321	2,089	2,228	2,321	1,485	2,437	3,041	27,853
Contributions & subsc.	104	112	96	115	108	104	94	100	104	67	109	136	1,249
Postage & freight	250	270	230	275	260	250	225	240	250	160	263	328	3,001
Misc. expense	340	367	312	374	353	340	306	326	340	217	357	445	4,076
Total cash disbursement	$49,065	$52,987	$45,139	$53,970	$51,027	$49,065	$44,158	$47,101	$49,065	$31,402	$51,517	$64,273	$588,766
Opening cash balance	$40,363	$37,321	$36,107	$48,497	$75,066	$64,309	$49,762	$34,369	$27,537	$24,496	$39,117	$39,375	
Net monthly cash flow	<$3,041>	<$1,214>	$12,389	$26,569	<$10,757>	<$14,547>	<$15,393>	<$6,832>	<$3,041>	$14,622	$ 258	<$12,498>	
Closing cash balance	$37,322	$36,107	$48,496	$75,066	$64,309	$49,762	$34,369	$27,537	$24,496	$39,118	$39,375	$26,877	
Loans	0	0	0	0	0	0	0	0	0	0	0	$35,000	Loan
Closing cash balance after loans	$37,322	$36,107	$48,496	$75,066	$64,309	$49,762	$34,369	$27,537	$24,496	$39,118	$39,375	$61,877	Cash on hand

85

Business Planning—The Reasons Why

This plan was written to introduce the business plan process and show how architects or engineers might construct a plan. It makes a rather bold move of investing money and thereby creating a loss in an effort to curb a projected downturn in business. The plan was submitted as an example of what could happen; each individual plan decision must be made on its own merit. A plan can be much more complicated, with many more detailed financials and ratio analysis, or it can be simpler, with just a sketch of the essential points. For the business plan which looks at a specific project, the planning process provides a framework for making sure a careful and complete evaluation is done. In the case of an annual operating plan, the importance is in having a review process that allows one to compare and benchmark the progress of a firm against its goals. If there are no objectives, one may never have the chance to change and adapt to conditions that threaten a practice. Architectural and engineering practices do not fail because of poor architecture or engineering; they fail because of how the practice was managed. Business planning is a tool to help one manage.

Who will benefit?

This business plan was written with small- and medium-size firms in mind that do not have the necessary expertise on staff and thus need a starting point. A sole proprietor can have an operational plan just as a large firm can. The more hands-on control one has, the more one can control the outcome. The more business plans one can read, the better one is prepared to write his or her own. Architects and engineers who work for large firms will also find this plan valuable in that it explains what is happening at the management level above them. Also, architects and engineers will find the planning guidelines useful as they prepare to go out on their own.

Writing a plan

This example of a business plan can be used as a guide for the annual business plan or with adjustments for a business plan that deals with a specific subject. As you gain experience you can add material or present it in different formats. It is suggested that you put your own business personality into a business plan. This plan is a starting point. See the appendix for additional business plan outlines that illustrate the flexibility you have in putting a plan together. The words may change, but for the most part the content doesn't. As a starting point, use the index as a guide to ensure that all major parts of the business plan are included.

The first plan is always the hardest one to write, since you are also learning the process. Once the plan has been completed, the second year's effort will be quite different. Now everyone understands the format and what it takes to complete the plan on time. The difference is going to be the vastly improved communication process as meetings are held to review the year's events and discuss changes. Now there will be sophisticated conversations about what was good, what was bad, what didn't work, and so on. In the second year, the plan is operating as a benchmark and leading the firm in its discussions. The office staff is now thinking in terms of planning throughout the year. They may very well offer their own stratagems for consideration in future meetings.

Who should participate?

One last question is in order: Who should participate in writing the plan? First, and foremost, there must be a leader who drives the plan, who is responsible for approving the content, who is essentially responsible for the firm's bottom line, and who is not afraid to make decisions. This is most likely the owner. In any case, there must be a hierarchy of decision makers who work toward a course of action that is resolute in their commitment to make the firm successful and profitable. Other participants should include as many people who can be accommodated in the planning process comfortably.

Sole proprietors may find themselves in a position where they are responsible for all of the planning and marketing. If they don't want this degree of control, they can begin to share the responsibility with other members of the firm. As mentioned before, small offices can also be set up with an informal advisory board to assist in planning efforts.

The managers responsible for the delegation of objectives and carrying out the plan's intent should be included. This does not mean that everybody goes to every meeting; quite the contrary. Upper-level management should meet to evaluate the financials and discuss the general condition of the firm. These should be preparatory meetings before the general staff meetings. The staff may not have an intimate financial knowledge of the firm but does have a solid grasp of operations and thus opinions of what will work and what will not work. Likewise, the staff can have lower level meetings to review ideas and discuss the nuances of different planning ideas. As the aspiration of the firm becomes known and more people are included in the process, the firm's energy and drive will increase. This will do more for a firm's harmony than perhaps any other process as the staff is being included in the firm's future.

The mere fact that a firm comes to anticipate the year-end planning meeting puts it on a conscious course of planning. Now it will understand that what it is asked to do is for a reason, even though it may not have participated in that decision. If an individual has the desire to seek management responsibility, he or she will now have something to work for—participation in the firm's planning process.

Strategy and Marketing

Strategic planning and marketing are often confused. But they are different and equally important to the business plan. It is therefore important to understand what each means and how architects and engineers can use these concepts to further their business interest. The purpose of discussing these concepts together is to emphasize that marketing can be thought of as "the doing" of the strategic positioning process.

All the nuances of strategic planning and marketing cannot be covered in one chapter; however, this chapter will provide a starting point for developing a business plan. It will provide structure in these areas that will suggest new ways of thinking about an architectural or engineering practice and provide a framework for future reading and investigation. First, strategy will be discussed, then marketing. Together, they provide a vehicle for creating ideas and implementing them into an action plan.

Strategy

Setting a strategy for a firm is generally approached with much trepidation. It is often easier to continue doing what one has always been doing and hope for the best. The odds seem insurmountable in setting the right strategy in place, whereas the repercussions seem endless. Ideas always seem to appear as tangled thoughts without organization. The process of setting a strategy is always fraught with fears and hesitation. These feelings can best be offset with a better understanding of what strategy means and how the strategic planning process can fit into the business planning process.

One could say that strategy is marketing or marketing is strategy; both are right. In order to understand these ideas, strategy will be defined first so you will have an understanding of its definition. Then, three examples of strategic planning tools will be introduced:

Planning pyramid	To organize and to relate strategies
Three C's	How to view one's self in the marketplace
Competitive advantage	Seeking a way to be more competitive

As a result, you will have several tools for evaluating an idea from a strategic vantage point. This discussion is a starting point to get a handle on strategic planning as applied to marketing. It is not an exhaustive dissertation; it is an outline and definition so you can later address the issues in more depth.

A company without a strategy is like a building without a foundation. Sooner or later it's going to sink. Sooner or later a practice is going to be a worst case scenario. Marketing strategy is of prime interest to architects and engineers because of the service orientation of the businesses. There are many misunderstandings about strategic planning, and most of it is due to a misunderstanding of what strategy is all about.

The term *strategy* is closely associated with military terminology, meaning what an adversary might or might not do. In fact, the dictionary[8] defines strategy as follows:

1. The overall planning and conduct of large-scale military operations

2. The art or skill of using stratagems as in politics and business

3. A plan of action

Likewise, stratagem is defined as a maneuver designed to deceive or surprise an enemy.[8] Some of the first discussions about strategy were by Sun Tzu. He wrote *The Art of War* in which the first military principles of strategy were outlined.[3] For our purposes it is best to say that strategy is a plan of action used to achieve an objective with a given resource. In other words, strategy is related to the goals and objectives and, hence, to the mission statement. It is easy to see why strategy is an important business planning issue.

It is important to understand that there are many strategies and many plans of action within a given company. Strategy is the name given to a process when addressing a plan of action to accomplish an objective or a goal.

To complicate matters, the words *strategic* and *strategy* are used in different parts of a plan. For example, you might have a brilliant strategic plan for turning a company around, and the plan's advertising section is labeled "strategic advertising plan." The point is that the labels "strategy" and "strategic" are used at many different levels and the terms are essentially interchangeable. In many business plans, they are used in all sections. In fact, the terms tend to be overused. However, if you think of strategy (or strategic) as a process, as opposed to a magical answer, it begins to help you understand the planning and the marketing process.

Many companies contend strategic planning is a waste of time and that it should be avoided. It's not. Strategic planning is an integral part of the planning process and the name given to the direction a firm takes with regard to an objective. Not using strategic planning in a firm that is creating a business plan would be like going on a vacation with no destination. You don't know where you're going, and when you get there you wouldn't know to stop. You wouldn't even know what to pack or when to leave. Therefore, consider strategy as a plan of action used to achieve an objective with a given resource.

To explore how marketing strategy can be of help to the architectural or engineering firm, three ideas will be presented: planning pyramids and a way to visualize strategy as a concept, the three C's, a strategy that develops a methodology for looking at the architect's or engineer's marketplace and relationship to the competition and the client, and competitive advantage on how one seeks a way to be more competitive. Knowledge of these three ideas, coupled with an understanding of how strategy fits into the planning process, will provide a handle for developing a business plan.

Planning pyramid

In any business, there are levels of policy making. Not all of these levels deal with all of the strategic planning issues a firm may be exploring. It's a matter of degree and a matter of delegation. Upper management deals with broad issues of planning and direction; middle management deals with issues that relate to implementation. Both of these levels require strategic planning, or strategy. Usually in the architectural or engineering world there are one or more principals who are usually owners. Below them are associates who may or may not have a vested interest. Below them are the project architects or engineers, then the draftspeople. These professionals are assisted by administrative people. In the case of the small office, or the sole proprietor, the principals deal with all the issues. Strategic planning principles apply equally to the large office and the small office. Implementation is the only thing that is different.

Most of these levels could have some sort of strategy, or a plan of action to accomplish their respective goals. That is the confusing part when trying to understand how strategy is used. Because of this confusion, it's recommended that strategy or strategic planning be used in conjunction with goals and objectives and tactics of a specific program. In this light, at one level you can have a strategy to increase market share, and at another level you can have a strategy for promotions without getting them confused. They are part of the same plan but are not on the same level in terms of allocation of resources.

One is a broad statement about the direction of the business; the other is a specific marketing campaign. But they both use the word strategic or strategy; it's a word that suggests completeness. See Fig. 4.1, which provides a method for viewing strategy within the context of a particular level.

The pyramid in Fig. 4.1 illustrates that the focus is the mission statement. In order to interpret and implement the mission statement, it is broken into objectives. The mission statement and objectives are supported by the strategy, goals, and tactics, or the action plans. With this concept, you have a tool for providing a visual perspective of relating strategy back to the objectives and the mission statement.

Such planning pyramids can be used as vehicles for presenting ideas in the body of a plan or for organizing a discussion on a particular idea. For example, see Fig. 4.2, the planning pyramid for *Sample, Inc.,* and Fig. 4.3, the pyramid for the promotion portion of the business plan. These pyramids represent the intent of the business plan; however, they are at different levels, use different strategies, and are implemented by different people. The point is that strategic planning can appear at all levels of an organization—it is a planning concept that is an organizational tool.

The strategic pyramids in Figs. 4.2 and 4.3 show the mission statements, the objectives, the strategies, the goals, and the action programs, or tactics, of their respective programs. These plans appear at different parts of the management structure. The first one shows an upper management commitment to growing the business, requiring allocation of funds, a specific time frame, and so on. It's a 5-year plan. The second pyramid is a diagram of the promotion plan for the first year. It also shows the related strategies, the goals and objectives, and the action items. These diagrams force one to relate a strategy to an objective and to the subsequent goals. It's this organizational tool that allows one to develop strategies at all levels of a firm, without getting confused as to what strategy belongs where.

These diagrams are very useful in a business plan in that they clearly illustrate the direction of a firm and its different programs.

Figure 4.1 Planning pyramid.[9]

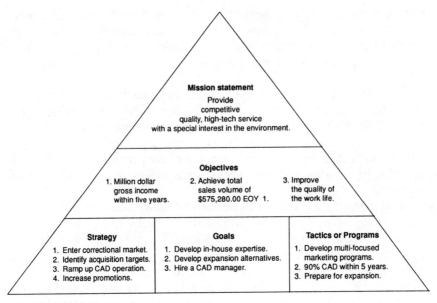

Figure 4.2 *Sample, Inc.,* planning pyramid.

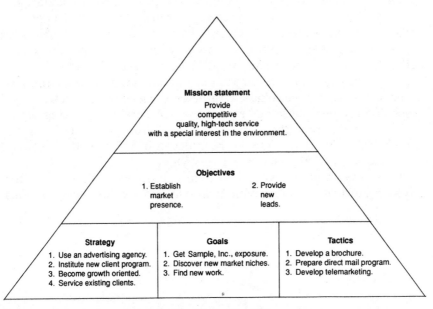

Figure 4.3 *Sample, Inc.,* planning pyramid for promotions.

They could be included within the text or in an appendix. They ensure that different strategies will not be confused. They also make excellent tools for presenting ideas and can be the focus point for meetings in which people discuss the business plan under development. Because programs can become quite involved, all of the components of a particular program may not fit within a planning pyramid. Thus, the pyramid represents the thesis of the structure and aids one in sorting out ideas and how they relate to one another.

This planning tool relates an organizational method for different strategies; there are also tools for looking at the market in relation to the client and the competition.

Three C's: client, corporation, and the competition

When developing a strategic plan, or any plan, it is important to look at the competition from the client's perspective, as well as to look at your firm's position relative to the marketplace. One tool for doing this is mentioned in Dr. Kenichi Ohmae's book *The Mind of the Strategist.*[10] He refers to a *strategic triangle* as the relationship between the corporation (the architectural firm), the customer (or in our case, the client), and the competition (the architect or engineer down the street). Figure 4.4 illustrates the relationships Ohmae discusses.

Each of the three market segments in Fig. 4.4 has its own interests and objectives and thus views the same marketplace differently. According to the figure, strategy can be defined as the way in which a corporation endeavors to differentiate itself positively from its competitors, using its relative corporate strengths to better satisfy customer needs.[10] This interpretation of strategy is a restatement of the earlier

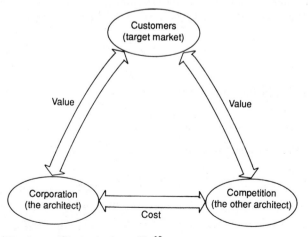

Figure 4.4   Strategic three C's.[10]

definition; that is, strategy is a plan of action used to achieve an objective with a given resource.

As mentioned earlier, preparing an annual plan is mostly unrelated efforts that come together in a cohesive presentation. It's impossible to write a plan from beginning to end in one sitting. One has to go back and fill in the blanks and adjust the plan as information is processed. During this evaluation and research period, a useful tool is the three C's diagram, or the strategic triangle. It provides a vehicle for examining the forces in the marketplace by looking at them from different positions.

For example, as Ohmae mentions, the "job of the strategist is to achieve superior performance, relative to the competition."[10] In addition, the strength of the strategy must match the strength of the corporation with the needs of the market. To be more specific, let's look at *Sample, Inc.'s,* strategy and relate it to Fig. 4.4.

Reviewing the planning pyramid in Fig. 4.2, you can see that the strategy to become a million dollar gross billable firm within 5 years is to do the following:

1. Enter the correctional market

2. Identify acquisition targets to facilitate growth

3. Ramp up the CAD operation

4. Increase promotions

Looking at the three C's strategic triangle, you can ask several questions. You must assume that sooner or later everyone knows everyone's strategy; thus, all questions that might shed some light on the ideas should be asked. Take the position that the competitor is in the room and asking questions, or that the evaluation team of a client is asking the questions, or that a competing architect or engineer is asking the questions. Put yourself in their shoes, and look at the problem from different perspectives.

From the corporation's view (i.e., from your point of view):

Does the correctional marketplace really exist?

What marketing research report supports its growth?

Are acquisitional targets available that will genuinely increase our growth?

Can they be acquired reasonably?

Is the competition going to do the same thing once they learn of our strategy?

How can we implement a better plan?

Will increasing promotions have to be addressed to a specific market, or are we looking at more of an image public relations campaign?

Does the competition really know the intensity of our commitment to win?

From the competition's view (from the office down the street):

Can we match *Sample, Inc.'s,* efforts in preparing for the future correction market in some other way?

Would being acquired by this firm hurt or help us?

Is the client really going to be there?

Is a full CAD department really going to make *Sample, Inc.,* more competitive?

What should we do?

Should we try and hire away their strength?

From the customer's view (your client or future client):

Do we want to deal with a firm that is totally CAD oriented?

One that is not CAD oriented?

What happened to creativity and the person at the drawing board?

Is CAD going to cost us more in fees?

Do we want to work with an architect or engineer who may eventually become a large institutional planner?

Do we want them to do my residence?

Is institutional architecture rigid and inflexible?

Do we want to deal with an architect or engineer who promotes him or herself?

As you can see, by using the three C's planning pyramid, questions can be asked from every angle about a specific strategy. Viewing a situation from different vantage points allows you to question whether the strategies are sound, thoughtful, and manageable. Also, the questions can be quite pointed and direct. But by asking these questions now, you can be better prepared to meet the competition in the future. Taking a different path may produce avenues of opportunity that others would not see. But the secret is in the doing, in setting goals, working the plan, charting the progress, and evaluating the outcome. If the competition does the same thing in a different way, say in a less expensive way, will they win? Will this strategy be for naught? Continually evaluating relative positions in a strategic war is important. Perhaps the competition only thinks it knows your agenda—perhaps there's a deeper strategy which only upper management knows. The possibilities are endless.

Competitive advantage

A popular phrase in the marketing arena today is "competitive advantage." It's probably one of the greatest strategic concepts to have developed—although its origins have been around for years. Marketing theory has always been based upon a process whereby the needs of the customer are satisfied through the production and promotion of a product or service. Hence, a customer-oriented philosophy is developed. It is easy to say that architects or engineers are basically customer oriented, that they satisfy the customer's needs and in the process produce individualistic pieces of architecture. Architects and engineers like being individualistic, which is why one hires one architect or engineer over another. Each architect or engineer satisfies the needs of the public in a different way, and that is the basis of modern marketing theory.

Fortunately, strategic thinking does not have the burden of accepting the commonplace, and out of this position have grown many new ways of looking at the market. Strategic planning, having its origins in military thought, has led many modern-day marketing strategists to think in terms of attacking the competition, defending positions, flanking competitors, and mixing it up with guerrilla tactics. Al Ries and Jack Trout sum it up nicely in their book *Marketing Warfare*. In it they state that "The true nature of marketing today involves the conflict between corporations, not the satisfying of human needs and wants."[11] From this perspective, the focus is on the competition, and everything takes care of itself (i.e., the client's needs and wants are satisfied). In other words, focusing on the competition and working toward gaining a competitive advantage places the emphasis on being competitive in order to survive and to profit. Human needs and wants serve as traffic lights and invariably get satisfied in the process of the competition, but the competition itself is the cutting edge of the creative process. This is the same competition felt in architectural and engineering schools as classmates struggle for the acclaims of their instructors. It is the same competition that occurs in all levels of design, where striving for the award, the nod to go ahead, is the true source of inspiration and thought. It is this competitive process that is the heart and soul of architecture and engineering; it is what dreams are made of; it is what holds the profession together. Therefore, this process should be magnified and used to an architect's or engineer's positional advantage. Then, in the end, basic marketing theory, the human needs and wants of the client, will be fulfilled.

Another way to look at marketing is as a strategy involving a competitive advantage. Kenichi Ohmae states, "Without competition there would be no need for strategy, for the sole purpose of strategic planning is to enable the company to gain, as efficiently as possible, a sustainable edge over its competitors."[12] Hence, the focus is on the competitors. When significant advantage over the competitors has been achieved, at an acceptable cost to itself, it has developed a good business strategy.[13] Ohmae goes on to discuss four separate strategies, all based upon gaining a competitive advantage:[10]

- Key factors for success (KFS)
- Relative superiority
- Aggressive initiatives
- Strategic degrees of freedom (SDF)

The *KFS strategy* is a business strategy based upon the key factors for success. All architectural and engineering firms have resources, such as people with specific talents and different degrees of experience, as well as financial strengths. If all firms allocated their resources in the same way, no one would have a competitive edge. Thus, progressive firms must identify the key factors for success and apply resources in these areas to amplify the possibility of developing a competitive advantage.

Ohmae discusses two approaches to identifying the key factors for success. The first one is to dissect the market in an imaginative way so as to identify the key segments. In the business planning process, the architect or engineer is given the opportunity to look at the market relative to his or her position and to take it apart. Therefore, one has the opportunity to take a fresh look at what makes up the marketplace—what makes up the segments.

For example, in the case of *Sample, Inc.*, the analysis pointed toward a clear segmentation of the building types and the relative ability to serve that market. By allocating its resources over the next 5 years to take advantage of the particular market segment, *Sample, Inc.*, is applying a key factor for success to gain an advantage over the competitors. Other views might show that the market is made up of a lot of office lease spaces and that by developing and offering services that help a developer manage these areas, the architect will most likely enhance his or her ability to get interior design jobs to finish the roughed out spaces for the new tenants. Market segmentation is another way to look at the architectural or engineering practice within the context of the working environment and make a determination that may give one a superior advantage.

The second approach to identify KFS is to discover what distinguishes winning companies from losing companies. Looking at *Sample, Inc.*, again, one of its decisions was to expand the target market area to gain an advantage. This is based upon the analysis that *Sam-*

ple, Inc., believes that having a broader exposure in its market area will serve to identify it as a leader. Another analysis showed that successful offices have sophisticated CAD operations that distinguish them from the competition. This is another factor that distinguishes winners from losers.

Thus, by dissecting the industry as seen by architects or engineers in their immediate working environment and by looking at what makes up winners and losers, an engineer or architect is able to determine and apply resources to the key factors for success and thus able to gain that sought-after advantage. There are risks involved, and the strategic decision to take a different path may be the only thing that separates you from competitors. The key is the application of resources to KFS in such a manner that your view of the market segmentation, and what makes a winner and a loser, enables a firm to gain that competitive advantage at an acceptable risk.

The second strategy is to build a *relative superiority* by identifying unique services that one offers that the competitor doesn't, then build upon that advantage to develop market share. The predominant vehicle for doing this is a side-by-side comparison of one firm to another showing how service, operational strategies, marketing, and so on, differ. This is not a segmentation of what is the difference between winners and losers, but a one-on-one, blow-by-blow analysis that will often reveal strengths that can be capitalized upon and weaknesses that should be fortified. This should not be construed as a comparison of architectural styles.

Architects or engineers seldom put themselves in a position where they look closely at services they offer compared to a competitor. It's the nature of the profession to go it alone and not acknowledge the other person. *It is important to know what the other person is doing— the other person represents what you are not doing.* For architects or engineers who wish to learn about themselves and gain strategic insight that might make the difference in the future, developing a relatively superior advantage is a good starting place.

The task here is to make a business analysis of competitors looking at the following:

What service do you present to the market?

What services do your competitors bring to the market?

How are these services offered?

Why have clients chosen your firm over another?

Why did you lose a commission to the architect or engineer around the corner?

It is hoped that from this analysis differences will emerge that will be significant and, with the proper promotion and emphasis, will be key building blocks in gaining a strategic advantage.

An example using *Sample, Inc.,* is deciding to increase the use of CAD. Questioning an existing client over a business lunch might disclose that the reason *Sample, Inc.,* was selected was because of its CAD exposure. The client felt that the use of CAD was an indication the firm was current and was making the investment to be at the forefront of its profession. This bit of market intelligence indicates a client's perception that can be developed into a competitive advantage. When this CAD image is confirmed by other clients, one has good reason to think of CAD as a competitive advantage. Using the strategy of relative superiority, *Sample, Inc.,* has chosen to make a financial commitment to be 90 percent CAD within 5 years. There is no doubt it will have that competitive advantage due to its relative superiority in CAD.

A third strategy is pursuing *aggressive initiatives,* which simply means "to challenge the prevailing assumptions with a single question: Why?"[14] This method is to relentlessly question why something is done in a particular way. This technique is often used by efficiency experts in developing cost savings for customers. But the strategist is not necessarily after cost savings, although ways of reducing costs are invariably found. They are looking at ideas that lead to improvements that give the architect or engineer an advantage—a competitive advantage.

Here are some questions that might be asked:

Why do you only present basic services at client introductory meetings?

Why do you take a client on a tour of completed work on the second visit?

Why not build a computer model of the city to generate excitement and exposure when making planning presentations?

Why do you get nervous during your presentations?

Why do you design only one building for a client?

Why have you turned down jobs?

Why do you always lose money during the design phase?

Why don't you become the driving force behind historical buildings and their renovation?

Why don't you have additional services to offer after a building is completed?

Why do you use ink for check prints, then throw the drawing away? Is there an alternative?

Why don't you use CAD more? How?

As you can see, these are standard questions for an architect or engineer. Asking why and applying the answers wisely will generate ideas that will give that advantage. This is a technique used by all strategists; asking why is akin to brainstorming, where wild ideas find a home in relative practicality. As mentioned before, for a long time the Japanese have spent more time on defining the question to ask than on the answer. They view the real problem as asking the right question. Likewise, for a long time inventors have shown that questioning the commonplace suggests new ideas that eventually can turn into realities. Architects, engineers, inventors, scientists, and businesspeople are no different when it comes to creative methods of investigations.

The fourth strategy is exploiting *strategic degrees of freedom.* Specifically, this refers to the options one has once the KFS has been determined. For example, *Sample, Inc.,* determined that one key factor to gain a competitive edge was the ability to do large institutional type of work because the forecast for this type of work was increasing while at the same time a downturn in traditional developer-oriented projects was occurring. The strategic degrees of freedom as applied to this KFS *are the ways this idea could be developed.* In other words, the analysis doesn't stop when the particular KFS is determined. One must look at the way the idea can be exploited in relationship to the objective function of the mission statement—to increase stability, revenue, and profitability. This means an analysis of the ways this KFS can be developed, such as the following:

Hire an architect or engineer with institutional experience, particularly in the correctional area.

Hire a consultant with these specialties so they are associated with the firm.

Acquire a firm with these capabilities.

Start immediately to gain experience by bidding on small jail remodeling that becomes available in the county.

Plan to take seminars on correctional facilities.

Associate with a firm to do site observations and gain exposure.

Tour major prison complexes at every available opportunity.

The key factor for success has been determined; the above choices represent the methods that can be used to gain a competitive advantage. Some of the choices are economical and powerful. For example, imagine the effect when interviewing in front of a city council, if you have personally toured and inspected every major correctional facility in the state and several noted ones out of state. This fact would certainly impress a city council and put you in a favorable position. But the overall decision is to determine where to apply the financial resources of the firm and in what amounts to achieve the desired results.

Hence, the strategic degrees of freedom allow one to look at a key factor for success from several different viewpoints, then determine the course of action.

Summary of strategy alternatives

All architectural and engineering services are offered based upon a company backing what it believes to be the key factors for success and services that affords them an advantage in the marketplace. It hopes the strategy will be difficult for the competitor to imitate. All this is done as a matter of choice, for the strategies described are a sophisticated way of approaching the marketplace. No longer is the profession curtailed by suggestions that engineers or architects should take a let's see what happens attitude. They must manage their own business affairs. The four strategies discussed help the strategic planner when developing new ideas and directions for a business by looking at the same problem from different perspectives. It's no longer a simple brainstorming exercise but a planned look at the architect's or engineer's business, the role, and how the business is done.

Likewise, the three tools described above provide a framework for strategic planning. They can assist the architect or engineer in the following ways:

Planning Pyramid: Develop a planning pyramid that helps organize and relate strategies at different levels of a plan or a corporation without getting them confused.

Three C's: Help a firm access its position with the target market by looking at itself from different points of view and determining where it wants to be and suggest alternatives for getting there.

Competitive Advantage: Help a firm establish a competitive advantage via one of four strategies:

1. KFS—looking at the parts
2. Relative superiority—looking at the competition
3. Aggressive initiatives—asking why one more time
4. Degrees of freedom—the choice of choices

These strategic planning tools provide a framework for developing positions and strategies for managing an architect's or engineer's business. It allows you to look at your business from a number of different perspectives and suggests questions you should ask. The result is a position that is not easily copied by competitors and that moves you one step closer to a plan that satisfies the mission statement and the goals and objectives. This strategic thinking process is the essence of annual and long-range planning and is very important to the marketing functions that logically follow. It's these activities that will help a firm find a productive, profitable market niche and weather probable economic storms.

Marketing

Marketing is one of the most important parts of an architect's and engineer's business. There are certainly other important parts, such as the ability to prepare clear and precise sets of construction documents and the ability to design quality work. But these abilities are givens, in that they are functions inherent in the nature of the profession. One reason why marketing is so important is because it's the last area to receive any real attention. The profession is going to have to take a close look at marketing in general and help architects and engineers understand that it's a necessity and skill needed to succeed. Marketing is important because it's how one communicates with the public. Marketing creates a climate of acceptance; it doesn't sell anything, it creates situations in which engineers and architects become attractive to specific groups and, as a result, form business relationships.

A business plan addresses many issues, and the marketing part is the focus of most planning efforts. Marketing concerns the infrastructure within the architect's and engineer's market area. The infrastructure is the network of all those who have an opinion that can influence a prospect choosing one architect or engineer over another. The financials are a scorecard of the marketing and cost control efforts. Sales brings the services before the prospect. Marketing is what holds everything together. As stated before, marketing is essentially the strategic positioning process. In a good economy, with strong marketing, a firm will prosper. In a good economy, with bad marketing, the firm's performance will vary; some marginally, some average. In some cases, a firm will make a good profit when the economy is strong and there is a demand for services. In a bad economy, marketing efforts will allow the firm to stabilize and hold its own. In a bad economy with bad marketing, the firm will be a poor performer, and its existence may be threatened. This concept is summarized in Fig. 4.5.

Marketing is the one controllable factor. One cannot control the economy, but one can control what services are brought to which markets in what time frame. This marketing effort satisfies the need of

		Marketing	
		Good	Bad
Economy	Good	Record sales (prosperity)	Good, average or bad sales (risk prosperity)
	Bad	Average sales (stabilized prosperity)	Poor sales (no prosperity)

Figure 4.5 Marketing and economic matrix.

the client. When this concept is furthered to impact the weaknesses of the competition, the marketing position is strengthened even more.

It is often perceived that marketing is simply doing quality architecture or engineering, then letting the building speak for itself. Granted, some people may take notice of a new building that is attractive and noteworthy, but how are they going to know the true value of the service offered by the architect or engineer without communication? The building can be promoted and used as a marketing tool, but there has to be a way to make a connection with future clients—that is what marketing is all about. Architects and engineers need to understand how marketing works and how using it can help address architecture and engineering business problems.

Marketing is rarely used to its fullest extent in the architectural or engineering profession, and, as a result, it is one of the least understood parts of the practice. For a long time marketing was considered taboo—if one marketed skills you were considered going against the grain of the architectural or engineering community. This, of course, is wrong, for marketing is part of managing a business. Architects and engineers were always proud that they didn't market their services or advertise and thus took on a haughty posture with regard to other professions. It's one of the reasons architects have seemingly separated themselves from other mainstream professions; for that behavior they have paid a price.

It would seem that architects and engineers would have advanced further in developing sophisticated marketing programs, for marketing seems right for architecture. But 1-hour seminars at national conventions are not enough. Marketing is not taught in architectural or engineering schools and is usually not at the top of the list as an elective. Four and 5-year schedules are crowded enough, and until there is a realignment of the architectural and engineering education to include some form of business management, marketing will be another subject that one is to learn in the field.

Marketing requires hands-on experience to be effective. Often, the only way to learn marketing is from the experience of being on your own. One reason for this is that seldom are architects or engineers called into the head office and told, "Today, I'm going to teach you marketing."

Marketing is the activity whereby a firm presents the services they offer to a specific group in order to create a climate of acceptance for the firm. Marketing's intent is to contribute to the firm's effort and commitment to accomplish its goals and objectives. Marketing is part of the action plan. As has been indicated, marketing involves the conflict (competition) between corporations, which in the process, satisfies the needs and wants of the target market. The focus on the competition stresses seeking out market niches and opportunities to provide a better service than the competition and in the process satisfy the needs and wants of the target market. Marketing is part of the process that sets goals and objectives and initiates plans of action to implement marketing tactics. Marketing is also the focus for gathering information on the market and presenting information that is helpful for all levels of the planning process. This is called *market research.* Strategic planning sets the strategy for what marketing does. Marketing then takes this information and puts it into action items that present these programs to the marketplace. For the purpose of discussing marketing within the context of business planning, several concepts will be examined that provide a starting point for marketing development. They are as follows:

- Marketing direction
- Marketing communication
- Market research
- The value of the architect or engineer

These marketing concepts form a core of marketing knowledge that can be used as a basis for furthering one's own marketing philosophies and integrating them in a business plan. They are a starting point.

Marketing direction

It must be clarified that architecture and engineering provide a service and thus are different from standard product marketing. A service business suggests to the public an intangibility and a variability in quality.[15] In addition, the engineer's or architect's product is often a pile of loose sketches, and if the project ends prematurely, the client often looks at the sketches and the bill for professional services rendered with apprehension and little imagination. This is complicated by the fact that some services are exploratory, which often leads to the conclusion that the project should not be undertaken. Also, a lot of projects are planning oriented, and if planning approval is not forthcoming, there is no project. In these cases attitudes change: "Why should I pay for something I'm not going to use?" This unsure intangibility regarding the architect's or engineer's product is difficult enough to overcome with paying clients, let alone nonpaying clients. This is all the more reason for architects and engineers to start *stressing the value* they provide to their clients.

Therefore, architectural and engineering services should be treated as intangible since there is little connection to the end product until the construction of the building starts. On the other hand, one may work with a truly professional client who recognizes and understands the value he or she is receiving in all phases of the architect's or engineer's efforts. Unfortunately, even the most experienced client often conveniently "forgets" the value of the work when a problem develops.

What follows is often a legal argument built around defending your position. It's likely that a jury of average people will have a more difficult time identifying with the architect's or engineer's product than the client, who now isn't on your side.

This example is, of course, a problem taken to the extreme. But what about the client who calls for a meeting and simply states he or she doesn't see the value of your work and doesn't want to pay the whole fee as outlined by the contract? This, and the previous example, are basically marketing failures—a failure to communicate what an architect or engineer does and the value of the services. As all successful salespeople know, when someone says no, one assumes the prospect does not have all the information to make a decision. So the sales process starts over, and in the process the objections are overcome and the sale is made. Marketing is no different. At this point, one must reeducate the client and bring him or her back to a comfort level where the person again understands the value of the service. That is why marketing is so important.

Hence, the main and most important marketing problem facing the architect or engineer is to link the marketing message to words or ideas that are tangible so an image is conjured up in the prospect's mind of the *value he or she is receiving for the architect's or engineer's efforts.* There are two ways to approach this problem. The first approach deals with making the services more tangible by providing something for the client to focus upon. The second involves focusing on the service provider rather than the service.[15]

The first approach uses slogans to identify and distinguish companies from each other as was discussed under goals and objectives for human resources activities. This is also a good opportunity to convey a substance and tangibility to the architect's and engineer's message. Examples are

The planning firm	Suggests careful thoughtfulness
The environmental firm	Suggests concern with environmental systems
Architectural excellence or engineering excellence	Suggests the best
Construction managers and planners	Suggests cost savings

The architect or engineer is not selling drawings on a piece of paper; he or she is selling planning and thoughtfulness, environmental awareness, cost savings, and quality. By centering the focus of what the architect or engineer does on something tangible with which the client can connect, it is much easier for the client to identify with what the architect or engineer does. The tag line should be used whenever the firm name is used, from brochures to title blocks. There are many ways to use the concept. For example,

Sample, Inc.: The Environmental Firm

Example Imaging Architects, Inc.
Construction Managers and Planners

As *Example Imaging Architects, Inc.*, develops other marketing messages and brochures, its tag line can be used to convey that it is a planning firm. Likewise, planning can be connected to saving money, which has a direct benefit to the prospect. The architect or engineer now has something to sell that is positive and with which the prospect can identify—saving money.

A comment is in order here. Never let it be said that an architect or engineer doesn't sell. The profession has long shied away from the image of actively selling, but the reverse has to be true. Architects and engineers continually must sell themselves, the work they do, the service they offer, and their style, personality, and vitality. Not to acknowledge these areas is unfortunate for the individual and for the profession. Nothing happens until something is sold. When the architect or engineer makes the sale and the commission is integrated into the office, it is the staging ground for an enormous amount of activity leading to construction and the employment of hundreds of people. Every person involved, from the owner who has to sell the project, to the financial lending institution, to the contractor who builds it, to the janitor who finally sweeps the empty halls of the completed building at night, has to sell him or herself in order to participate, in order to be paid, in order to exist. That's the way it is, and that's the way it will always be. The architect or engineer is only part of the process.

The architect and engineer should make every effort to connect the client to the end product during the phases where there is no visible evidence with which one can identify. Most clients do not relate to drawings the way architects and engineers do. They have no way of knowing that the sketch you just showed them took years of experience and knowledge of the local conditions to create accurately and efficiently. Thus, touring existing architectural or engineering work and letting clients experience the spaces is always effective. Having your office in a building that you designed or a space that was remodeled by you is very important in conveying your art and the real product of your work to clients. Having a luncheon meeting in a restaurant you designed that has a particular ambiance also works. Having clients meet and develop relationships with other satisfied customers can also be useful. These marketing and sales functions have a real purpose in conveying to clients an aura of substance and tangibility.

The second way of setting a marketing direction is by the image of the engineer or architect. The service provider—the architect or engineer in this case—is more tangible than the service itself. "The service provider usually has a level of skill and expertise that represents the service. As a result, advertising often focuses on the skill and technical competence of the service provider."[15] Architects must convey technical competence along with a degree of artistic sense in order to be readily accepted by a client. Since architects and engineers don't openly advertise, they must rely on other marketing communication techniques to convey this message.

Marketing communications

Marketing communications is an area that exists in all businesses— formally or informally. If you put up a sign outside your office, you have just entered the world of marketing communications. The size and shape, the choice of letters and color all leave a message about your practice to your customer. The choice of logos, letterheads, and business cards and how you communicate with a client are all marketing communication decisions. How you get the word out also falls under this category. In that architects and engineers don't overtly advertise, marketing communication becomes very important. It is rare to find a person dedicated to this in a small- or medium-sized firm— usually this is the task of the owner or architect. But firms large enough to employ a marketing director will find that person spending much time with marketing communication decisions.

Brochures. The first choice in marketing communications beyond business cards and letterheads is a brochure which illustrates the type of work the architect or engineer has completed. A brochure ranges from bound brochures, providing a complete presentation of the firm, to single sheets collated together to form a presentation package. One can also design special brochures of different sizes with different packaging. The collated brochure lets you add new work representing your graphic presentation at a reasonable cost. Also, when a firm has many building types, it can select the projects that most closely resemble the building type the prospect is seeking. For example, if *Sample, Inc.,* were to go after a new financial institution, it could include several sheets from bank projects so the presentation is targeted. This approach provides a great deal of flexibility.

Likewise, statements about the philosophy of the architect or engineer in terms of design, structural integrity of the building, the environment, and so on, can be included. Again, this is a chance to tell the client the value of the architect or engineer and the services he or she can offer. These statements can be intermingled with descriptions of completed projects. For example, here is a statement that might appear in a brochure:

> *Sample, Inc.,* recently completed a new bank commercial center for Sierra Banking of California. The design problem was to provide the max-

imum amount of leasable floor space while maintaining the integrity of the hillside site, which is populated with massive oak trees. The result was *Oak Tree Banking Center,* a project that allows the natural beauty of the site to integrate with the building's open circulation areas. Much of the interior views are natural, as the building essentially turns its back to the noise and traffic, and develop an interesting and pleasant work space environment. The building's exterior is predominantly wood of natural tones that suggest a further harmony with the site and landscape. "The building looks like it always belonged there," said the owner, Mr. Jones of Sierra Bank.

This description would be accompanied with different views of the finished complex and perhaps even sketches of when it was under development. Diagrammatic floor plans can also be included. The description imparts a sensitivity to the environment, while fulfilling the owner's needs for a commercial center.

Brochures can be used any number of ways and are often the primary method of presenting what the architect or engineer can do. As marketing should be an on-going activity, brochures should continually be updated. The brochure is the entry into a new account.

Direct mail.   Another excellent way a small firm can begin to develop a relationship with potential prospects is to use a direct mail program on a regular basis. A direct mail program is a marketing project designed to accomplish a particular goal. Its primary purpose is to educate prospective clients about who you are, what you do, and how the architect or engineer can help the prospect. Generally, each direct mail project should have a specific message with a specific task to be accomplished. For example, it may be to introduce the firm, to introduce a new partner, or to tell people about the completion of a project. Some leads may occur from this type of activity; however, it is generally difficult to acquire business in a service-oriented professional relationship business. Sales, of course, is the bottom line; but educating the public by creating a climate of acceptance is a specific marketing goal that can be addressed via a direct mail program.

In order to be effective, direct mail programs should be repeated often and convey essentially the same message to the prospect list over a regular time frame. They should be looked at as projects. For example, *Sample, Inc.'s,* strategic plan is to continue to seek commercial projects while preparing to enter the correctional institutional market that is developing locally and statewide in its target area. The first order of business is assembling a direct mail list from various sources. There might be two lists: One list could be of all people and companies associated with potential commercial projects, either as the owner, the contractor, or as major influencers such as banks or venture capital groups. A second list might include all people at local, state, and federal levels associated with correctional facilities. Both of these lists are developed over a period of time and are managed as they become a valuable resource for the firm. Some names might be purchased through list brokers or trade publications; others are acquired through personal contact and by reading trade journals.

Two direct mail pieces might develop. The first is a mailing done once a month for four months with a message concerning *Sample, Inc.'s,* relationship, contribution, and success in the commercial development field. Like all marketing campaigns, it's a designed campaign to convey a certain message. The intent of all the mailings is to build a relationship in the prospect's mind that associates *Sample, Inc.,* with commercial projects.

The second piece might be focused on *Sample, Inc.'s,* recent association with a correctional consultant. Or if a small correctional remodel is completed, it can announce this achievement. Again, the intent is the same: to develop a relationship in the prospect's mind with a particular message, in this case, *Sample, Inc.'s,* correctional experience and relationships.

Direct mail offers an opportunity to develop an indirect association through repetition. Generally, the first piece is thrown away. The second piece is glanced at. The third piece the reader reacts to by saying, "I remember seeing that before." And, finally, the fourth piece is recognized by the reader, who reads it and may make a mental note about the architect or engineer or file the business card. *Repetition and frequency* are of primary importance in direct mail, along with a sense of uniform presentation, logo, and overall style of the artwork. Also important are the day it arrives, the graphics, simplicity, and the tag line. Many references are available that will help you put together a direct mail piece. It can become a reasonably priced marketing communications tool.

Newsletters. A form of direct mail campaign that works well with architectural or engineering firms is a newsletter approach. This approach has recently become popular because of advances in desktop publishing that allow one to publish an attractive, eye-appealing newsletter without using outside design services. Through this marketing communications tool, a targeted list of clients, prospects, and businesses such as banks receives a newsletter about your firm, its activities, and other related information, usually monthly, bimonthly, or quarterly, depending upon the size of the firm and staffing. Quarterly is acceptable and relieves one of coming up with new material on a monthly basis.

The person with marketing responsibilities can generate material through various means such as guest columns each month or testimonials. Any and all information relative to the marketing message one wishes to impart can be used. Generally, the newsletter can convey credibility, provide marketing exposure, and illustrate expertise. Political issues should be avoided.

Just as in direct mail, there are some rules that should be followed. The newsletter should look like a newsletter. It should have a banner (or masthead) that ties into the firm's marketing message, such as the tag lines previously discussed. The newsletter should provide information important to the reader. Current projects, completed projects, new staff members, photos, guest editorials, and so on, can be included. Above all, the newsletter should be well written, using correct grammar and punctuation. Nothing distracts more than improper presentations. The goal should be the production of a newsletter readers look forward to getting. There should be ample opportunity to present the marketing message about your firm and the value you offer to your clients. This is a public relations piece with the intention of selling yourself.

Publicity.   Publicity offers another avenue for the marketing communication process. Public relations (PR) is essentially getting the name of your firm out in front of those who might use your services or are in a position to recommend your services. Publicity has several advantages for the architect and engineer. The major one is that it has a different image than outright advertising. Publicity may or may not be more costly than advertising, although it may require more constant attention. Publicity can come in many forms, shapes, and sizes.

A good starting place is local newspapers. Anytime an architect's or engineer's name is mentioned in a positive light, connecting him or her to an event, the completion of a building, or the success of a design, the benefits will be highly rewarding. Sunday newspaper supplements that address an audience interested in architecture, planning, and engineering are excellent locations for material about your firm. Lecturing at local schools, museums, and other civic organizations can also be beneficial. Participation in competitions and winning awards are also important. Anything that can get the name of the firm in a positive light in front of potential prospects is worth considering.

One important idea to remember is that newspapers, magazines, and so on, are always looking for new material. They have a requirement to provide information to their audience. Understanding how to be at the right place at the right time can be the deciding factor in constantly being in the paper. Having a press kit ready and having the necessary resources to announce new offices, an expansion of the staff, and so on, will make the difference in a publicity campaign. Often, an architect or engineer might be able to ride the coattails of a client who is setting up a campaign for a specific building project. The possibilities are endless and up to the architect or engineer to manage effectively.

Help in promoting and managing publicity can come from several sources. If an architectural or engineering firm has a marketing director, or a person in a similar position, this task will become his or her responsibility. If a firm has one of the managing partners take on the task, education in several different areas will be required to understand how to develop the publicity contacts and what material to prepare. Another avenue is to hire an advertising agency or a PR firm. These agencies are specialists in working on projects that get your name in front of the right people. Hiring an advertising agency may be one of the best investments a firm can make, particularly if the firm is well organized, knows where it's going, and knows how it's going to get there.

Advertising. For a long time architects and engineers were not allowed to advertise. Now, however, many of the constraints have been removed, and architects and engineers are free to consider these alternatives for promotion. There are still mixed feelings about the profession using advertising; however, ideas are changing as the advertising topic receives attention by all professions. Generally, the courts have indicated that forbidding one to advertise is a restraint of trade. Thus, professional affiliations cannot restrict you from promoting yourself in this manner. Local and state registration and practice laws should always be checked, however.

Advertising is not taught in architectural or engineering schools. One reason is the crowded schedules. Another has been the feeling that those who advertised were unethical. But if one looks at architecture or engineering as a business, then some advertising done properly can help those willing to spend the time and energy to do it right. Advertising for the architect or engineer tends to be promotional, since the overt ad is avoided.

Advertising can be done subtly and done well; it can help educate potential prospects about your services and the value you contribute. The best place to start is an advertising agency. The agency consists of professionals who can assess a marketing goal and prepare suggestions for a plan of attack. In fact, using an advertising agency to help with a combined PR campaign, selective advertising, and mailing lists for potential prospects can be one of the most important strategies an architect or engineer can use when putting together a marketing program.

The first step in this process is to interview several advertising firms that are recommended or that you select based upon some criteria. The next step is to have the firm make a presentation based upon specific guidelines. For example,

> *Sample, Inc.,* would be interested in looking at suggestions an agency can provide in promoting our impending move into correctional architecture and a program to enhance our image as one of the more successful commercial building architects in the Ukiah Valley.

The final selection should be based upon who you feel comfortable working with and who you feel will provide the best service. The selection is similar to what others go through in selecting an architect or engineer.

The key to working with an advertising agency is to be specific as to what you want to accomplish, then to work with the agency to develop a plan that is in concert with your own marketing plan. The plan must then be followed as designed, providing monetary restraints don't weaken it. Setting up and following a plan provides many benefits during and after the campaign. The success of many programs depends upon regular mailings at specific times to specific groups. After all has been done, a consistent record following the plan leads to a better evaluation of the efforts and of what works and what doesn't work. There are no guarantees in advertising, just experience and the ability to test, monitor, and adjust. A good advertising agency can offer a wealth of ideas and insight to help a firm take steps to accomplish its goals. Working with an agency should not be overlooked.

A small office can advertise without professional help. The best starting point is to observe what others are doing in your community as well as other communities. After a period of time, certain advertising vehicles will seem attractive and appropriate to your campaign and message. From there, you can start to build a program. It might be as simple as having your name in the *Yellow Pages* in a different way or perhaps putting up a different type of job sign at your construction sites. Advertising plays an important role in getting your name in front of the public, both for large and small firms.

Social contacts.   Another important area of marketing is social contacts and the business relationships that develop from these contacts. This is actually a form of publicity. Some architects and engineers are good at this; others shy away from it. It's largely a matter of personality that determines how well this approach is used as a marketing communications tool. Some firms are built upon its principal's ability to get around the community and make the proper contacts. Although this is changing somewhat as more and more architects and engineers look at the traditional business ways of marketing their services, it still plays an important role in the architectural and engineering world.

How much one contributes to community projects is a personal choice, but engineers and architects have much to contribute because of their vast educational experience and interest in social issues, such as the environment and low income housing. From a marketing and practical point of view, every engineer and architect should be able to find a comfortable niche that affords the opportunity of exposure, while making at the same time meaningful contributions. Building code boards of appeals, planning commissions, as well as social involvement all offer exposure for the architect and engineer.

Market research

Active market research for the architect and engineer is relatively new. The aspect of market research that's important is the information that helps target and get new commissions. The service nature of the architectural and engineering business essentially divides the marketing research role of new work into the area of who, what, when, and where. The marketing question is who is going to get the work, and why?

When you think about market research, think about the fact that marketing involves the conflict among corporations and that the needs and wants are satisfied as a result of those conflicts. Therefore, one way marketing research should be contributing to the effort is by having information on the competition. Knowing what kind of projects the competition is working on and how their services are being offered will shed some light on why they may be getting commissions instead of you. For example, if after monitoring your major competitors for a year, it turns out that all major projects include construction management services, you might conclude that customers need and want construction management services. Or you could conclude that the competition is selling this service and new customers *feel* a need for construction management. This may mean redefining your marketing strategy. Market research can be as sophisticated as you want or as simple as keeping files of clippings that track the strength and weakness of various competitors.

To be more explicit, market research is defined as follows: "Market research is the systematic design, collection, analysis and reporting of data and findings relevant to a specific marketing situation facing the company."[16] For the engineer or architect, this can be developed into an invaluable tool where categories of information can be collected via a database. In addition, special projects can be managed to help develop relevant information. Market research projects might consist of surveys of past clients, prospects, or the competition. Market research should also reveal who likely potential prospects are, as well as major influencers in a city, county, or state. In addition, market research should also keep track of what's new in terms of design, construction material, and what the public is buying. All of this information will be useful for the managers in developing a business direction.

Computers can be a great help with market research projects. However, architects and engineers need not immediately invest in a computer system that provides extensive market research information capability, especially when the investment is not in proportion to the financial structure of the firm. The information that is processed would be of no value to an office not set up to use the data. It is recommended that architects and engineers be aware of the benefit of working toward a database environment as a long-term objective. There are software packages that assist the engineer and architect in many of these areas, and all are available in the IBM® PC and Apple Macintosh® formats. Only the largest international engineering and architectural firms can afford the true mainframe management information systems (MIS). But the average architect or engineer has a wealth of power and information available via a computer system purchased at nominal cost.

A library of current magazines also becomes a valuable market research tool. This will help you keep track of new materials and techniques, as well as provide a wealth of information on what is happening on a large scale. Included in this library should be brochures on all major companies that represent possibilities for commissions. This information is extremely valuable when asked to make a presentation, as it facilitates a better understanding of what the company does. All of this information, kept in an organized fashion, will help you identify opportunities. One person should be responsible for organizing the market research information. One useful technique is attaching a sticky note which the appropriate office staff initials, indicating the material has been reviewed. Suggestions can also be made as to the category to file it under. Thus, everyone who needs to know about something will have a chance to review the new product brochure before it is filed.

Market research is also concerned with feedback from users of your buildings, from prospects, and from people who have esthetic opinions about your work. This is an important part of the market research process as it relates directly to what users think about what you do and how you do it. Besides profit, which is largely a managerial issue, feedback from users is the only way to know what motivates perceptions.

Surveys are useful tools to look at specific target areas. They could be done in house or in conjunction with an advertising agency. Their purpose is to develop information about a variety of topics that will help in almost all areas of the architectural or engineering practice. For example, survey questions could investigate the color and textures of selected materials of a finished project or circulation patterns of the interior spaces. A survey could test whether or not a group of people passing a building knows the architect's or engineer's name. Or a survey could check on the subcontractor's perceptions of how the working drawings addressed the particular area of work. Surveys should be done by marketing professionals who are familiar with the survey process so appropriate survey techniques are used and the results can be properly evaluated with the right perspective.

Value of the architect and engineer

An important part in developing an architectural or engineering practice that includes a well-balanced business methodology is the ability to communicate to the client and prospects the *value* of the architect's or engineer's work. This thesis is the most important strategy in developing a marketing message for any engineering or architectural firm. It is interesting to note that even some of the leading architectural and engineering publications scoff at marketing and competitive tactics during times of economic hardship. This lack of business focus by the literate parts of the profession suggests an elitist attitude that can only hurt those who continue to abide by it. The focus of the total marketing effort is to impart to the prospect the *value* of the service within the confines of a marketing and business solution. When *value* is properly and consistently communicated in light of the company's objectives and mission statement and is done so with the perspective of facing the competition to seek out weaknesses and market niches, that in turn develops programs that satisfy the needs and wants of the target market. Then a positive attitude will develop from the client's perspective. Marketing is when all of this is accomplished within a well-managed, planned effort. The result is that the client will feel comfortable with your expertise, with your ability to manage their project, and with the *value* you offer.

What are the values an architect or engineer can impart to a client? The answer has much to do with how an individual architect or engineer or a firm views the world; however, there are common threads of value consistent in all practices. Each and every firm should examine itself to determine the real values it provides to a customer, then learn to tell the client what it is really getting for the dollars spent. Below are examples that can be used as starting points:

- Good design means more productivity.
- Time savings.
- Dollar savings in construction cost.
- Good design enhances ability to lease a space, and so on.
- An organized bid procedure saves contractual signing problems.
- Contract control through construction management saves time and money.

Unfortunately, for most clients the easiest way to show value is from a monetary point of view. If you can show them they are going to save money by using your services, or additional services you may be proposing, clients have something they can relate to. In other words, when your services can be translated into cost savings or improved profit performance because of your design, there is a realistic chance your services will become important to clients. Design also plays a role, as good design means that people who use the spaces will be comfortable. If it's an office project, good design will contribute to people being more productive.

There are several examples. One example is where a design can be shown to improve the overall profitability of a project. Consider the architect John Portman, who revolutionized the design of hotels by creating lofted lobbies and open spaces within the interior of a hotel complex. Portman's thesis was that a more attractive circulation space would be used and enjoyed by hotel guests and therefore would increase the hotel's profit, which would offset the initial increase in construction expense. The traditional view was concern over all the space going to waste, which would mean lost revenue. In the end, John Portman won, and his ideas for hotel designs became a standard. Portman was able to show *value* for the work through good design.

Another example is proposing that a prospect or client provide lease services for an existing project. You can suggest this by developing the lease drawings from a database that works in concert with a CAD system. There are several benefits that will save the client money. The speed at laying out new lease spaces gives the owner more flexibility in negotiating with potential occupants. Once a project is on the system, it is much easier to get different lease layouts for consideration, as well as accurate accounting of lease space square footages and calculations. Efficiency and accuracy can save the client money. Another case might be an existing building entered into the CAD system and associated database, indicating that existing clients actually have more square footage than the lease records show. The lost square footage leads to an eventual lease rate adjustment that benefits the owner. This same idea can be applied to a new building.

A third example is to show the cost of postponing or delaying construction work in good times and bad times. In rugged mountain country, where year-round building is sometimes not feasible due to the harsh winters, an architect or engineer may be able to convince a client to pour the foundation now, rather than wait until spring. With a foundation in the ground, a jump on next summer's building is gained. If this jump can produce a desirable financial situation in terms of completing construction and providing leasable space sooner, or by gaining a valuable commercial client, or by decreasing the cost of building materials, that should be communicated to the client. Taking an economic interest in the client is a professional attitude and one the client will remember.

There are many ways for architects or engineers to show the *value* for their services within the context of a marketing message. By concentrating on the value of the service and by the marketing messages which provide a substance for the client to identify with, an architectural or engineering office can begin to operate more confidently. This process is not an overnight happening but a long, thought out planning approach that has much to do with changing the public's perception of architects and engineers. By changing the emphasis to the *value* provided by architectural or engineering services and by consistently marketing a firm's attributes, one has a chance at future opportunities.

Marketing Conclusion

This chapter presented a series of marketing tools to help you look at your practice in a logical and creative manner and organize the conclusions into logical patterns of thought that can be used as a basis of analysis and discussion.

Marketing is a set of well-integrated activities that views a firm's resources in light of the competition, the economy, the opportunities and obstacles it faces, along with changing customer needs and technological advances. From this information it sets strategies, or a plan of action, that puts a firm on a course that is in line with its objectives and mission statement and is most often best summarized in the annual business and marketing plan. Marketing creates an environment of acceptance and provides an avenue to communicate the *value* of architectural and engineering services. Advertising agencies can provide valuable assistance with public relations, promotions, and direct mail campaigns. Marketing conditions change, which is the main reason why these activities are ongoing and flexible. Marketing is not static because competition is not static. The resulting business plan offers the only real way to monitor progress with any kind of meaningful conclusions. Balance sheets and income statements tell one story, but without a documented plan of what the firm was trying to do there can be no significance to the conclusions. Expectations of performance coupled with objectives is the only way one can truly suggest corrective actions that are meaningful, realistic, and illuminating.

5

Financial Planning and Implementation

Implementing the annual business plan is basically a response to a well laid out financial plan. The annual business plan includes the financial plan, which contains budgets and other itemized financial goals for the year. It is important to realize that this financial plan is the result of and part of the firm's overall planning by the managers all whom have provided input to next year's activities. The financial plan is necessary in both small and large firms.

This plan is unlike normal budgeting, which takes place without the benefit of the annual plan and is generally a reaction to a request or a need for a budget. It is usually interpreted as putting out another fire and is generally prepared by one manager, allowing other managers to work on other activities. For financial planning to be meaningful, it must be part of the annual planning process; otherwise, the budget will lack the depth and substance necessary in today's competitive and variable economy.

Financial planning and implementation are inseparable, as a good financial plan provides an implicit structure which implementation revolves around. Implementation depends upon managers taking some sort of action. Since managers and architects and engineers have participated in preparing the plans, they are familiar with the ramifications of their budgets and implementation responsibilities in relationship to the plan. The financial plan is the catalyst for the programs to begin and the barometer for measuring performance. Following is a discussion on financial planning and implementation. It is not intended to be an in-depth discussion but an overview that provides a structure for developing a financial philosophy.

Financial Planning

Chapter 2 explained the elements of a financial plan along with the concept of why and how a financial plan is used in relationship to the annual plan. Basically, to be viable the financial plan needs to respond to the goals and objectives and must make sound economic sense. Chapter 3 showed typical financial planning information in the *Sample, Inc.*, annual plan. The economics of *Sample, Inc.'s,* plan is carefully prepared with projections as to where it wants to go and how it's going to get there. The financial aspects of the plan reflect the marketing tactics that have been carefully prepared, the personnel resources that will be needed, and the capital expenditures the firm decided is necessary, along with all the other components of the budget. The plan is for internal use, as well as for guidelines for interested parties, such as banks or outside investors. The plan charts a path that shows how one is going to get there, then shows the forecasted economic consequences of following the desired course of action. When it is all said and done, the product is a plan that meets the approval of those who are ultimately responsible for its success.

Plan concept

The vehicle for organizing and getting the plan off the ground is the budget that follows the financial plan. The concept of working from a budget, or the plan, is all important. The *plan* refers to the approved annual plan for the coming year. Once implemented, the focus of managers will be on the plan and meeting the numbers of the respective departments, or profit and cost centers. The importance here is that in order to maintain control over where you are going, you have to know your relationship to the plan at all times. Hence, the plan provides a benchmark for comparing actual operating results to the budget. Both forecasted revenues and expenses can be compared to actuals. An analysis can quickly tell where you are meeting or not meeting your financial goals. With this knowledge, if necessary, steps can be taken to bring the operation back on track to comply with the plan. The major parts of a plan generally call for the allocation of resources for specific programs. These may be adjusted as the year progresses and as trends are discovered.

The actual implementation of a budget is going to vary from firm to firm depending upon a multitude of factors. Not all firms will recognize the strength of preparing a budget for the remainder of the year. Admittedly, there is work involved in monitoring and managing the information on a monthly basis. However, firms that do follow this course throughout the year are going to be rewarded with knowledge about how they are doing in relationship to the plan and the course that has been charted. A budget does not have to be cumbersome, as it's essentially a projection of the cash flow statement indicating where money is coming from and where it's going to be spent for the year. The budget—prepared, monitored, and managed throughout the year—puts real meaning into the financial plan and the overall business plan.

Much of the necessary information should already be in place in terms of general day-to-day accounting figures, income statements, and balance sheets. The new element that has to be dealt with is the cash flow statement for the year, and particularly the cash flow statement for the current month. There may be more than one person who has a budget, and each one should make a budget request which is reflected in the annual business plan. These are not only for 1 year but are forecasted month by month for the entire year. These requests should be responsive to the plan and to the person's own budget and cost control situation. The resources of cash flow, savings, or bank loan for operating capital should be reviewed; then the whole package should be reviewed and affirmed.

Budgets change during the year. All opportunities cannot be forecasted, and expenses are sometimes higher than forecasted. These situations can be discussed in relationship to the plan at the monthly budget meetings. All surprises are taken into account. The ability to review current budgets and forecasted budgets on a monthly basis gives one the flexibility to counter any unexpected events. In short, the firm is being managed.

Process

As a firm grows and its financial responsibilities grow, there will be a need for one person to be responsible for coordinating these financial activities. In a small office, this can be handled by the principal who has tight control over the finances. In a large office, it can be handled by a business manager who might also be in charge of marketing and administration. In a very large office, a financial planner may be employed who is totally responsible for financial objectives and developing programs for monitoring adjustments to the plans. Just as architecture and engineering has successfully adopted project management as a tool for controlling projects in an office of different scope and stages of completion, business managers and/or financial planners have tools for managing their responsibilities. Many of these tools are available to the smaller offices through the power and productivity of a computer.

At the end of the month there is an operating review meeting where several things happen. First, the current month's operation can be reviewed in terms of what was budgeted for, what was spent, what revenues were collected against what was forecast, personnel levels, current budget requests for the next month, new job prospects and opportunities, and status of current projects on the boards by the project architects, engineers, managers, and so on. At the same time, expenses can be reviewed against what was budgeted and projected. It is now up to the managers to synthesize this information relative to the overall annual plan and its goals and objectives, as well as to what is happening today, and prepare recommendations for the following month's strategy and tactics. These recommendations are reflected in a *budget forecast* for the following month, which reflects all the programs required to keep the firm on track or to get the firm back on track. Although this is not an easy task, the process induces a competitive advantage over firms that do not work with a plan. The premise here is the bottom line: It is profit that allows one to stay in business.

Questions such as the following can be asked and reviewed at the monthly operating review meeting:

Are we on plan or target?

If we're ahead, is the rest of the forecast too conservative?

If we're ahead or on target, did the revenue and expenses occur as we predicted, or did they occur in some unexpected fashion?

If we're behind, where did we fall short?

Did we fall short in revenue or in controlling costs? Or in both?

What is the accounts receivable level?

Is there an unusual bad debt?

If we're behind, what steps must be taken within the guidelines of the plan to correct the situation?

Are there any changes in the financial resources that will require adjustments to manage the business for the following month?

Do we know where the next month's operating budget cash is coming from?

Are there new opportunities we could capitalize on that we should take advantage of?

How do our overall fees relate to the cost of doing the work?

Are the income statement and balance sheet in line with like businesses or as recommended by our accountant?

Are the key business ratios out of proportion?

From a project point of view, are we on schedule with our projects or are we behind?

Do we have any legal problems facing us that can affect the firm financially?

If a number is out of line, what happened to create that situation? What is the solution to the problem?

These questions and others serve to clarify the different business relationships and to build a picture of the short-term goals for the following month and the budgets to carry them out. All of these decisions are relative to the goals and objectives of the overall business plan. And each month's budget meeting offers a chance to correct the course a little bit more, to once again set sights on the end goal of meeting the plan. Meeting the goal is all important. It is this financial operating forum that serves as a platform for implementing the programs of the annual plan. Once this is laid out, management can allocate funds and approve programs and tactics for the next month, and the cycle starts again.

As an example, consider the manager in charge of promotions who has, in response to the annual plan, prepared a program that consists of direct mail and other PR campaigns. This promotion response to the general plan comes with a budget that can be forecasted during the next fiscal year. As the year moves on, implementation requires additional monies spent now, rather than later in the year. Or it may be necessary to increase a campaign in one area. The budget meeting offers a forum to discuss these situations as they occur each month and to provide a corrective action in terms of a new budget forecast. As money is being allocated based upon the plan and the forecast due to the current situation, the budget meeting offers a real opportunity to do something about each situation. This type of operational meeting must occur on a monthly basis, or the thrust of its importance will be lost.

Operational reports and meetings

The actual paperwork involved depends upon the size of the firm and the intensity of the monthly review. As mentioned before, the basics are going to be there, such as the month-end financial statements and balance sheets, forecasts, and project management reports. In addition, the business manager, financial planner, or principal is going to have a suggested budget based upon the plan, money allocation requests, and other business demands, such as loan payments and marketing projects. The analysis should start with an assessment of where the firm is year to date and what was accomplished the previous month. The discussion should outline problems and review current strategies in light of the annual plan. The meeting should also have a portion dedicated to new market intelligence and possible opportunities or losses. In short, this is a real business meeting meant to look seriously at what is happening in terms of trends and to look for whatever corrective measures are necessary to keep on track.

Again, the meeting plan is all important. The plan is made up of individual numbers representing revenues and costs. Harold Geneen, former president of ITT, states the problem clearly: "What you are seeking is *comprehension* of the numbers: what they mean."[17] One has to look behind the numbers to understand what is happening. The above questions and others have to be asked over and over again until answers come forth that make business sense. From this point, plans can be implemented to pursue corrective actions.

The sole proprietor faces a different problem. When there is no staff to share budget responsibilities with, there is also no one to discuss them with. The underlining concept is that any effort expended toward reviewing the budget and resulting consequences on a monthly basis is better than no review at all. A small firm can use all the same financial reporting methodologies to help manage its situation. The minimum the sole proprietor architect or engineer should do is meet with an accountant at least quarterly to go over the financial statements. As the office grows, there will be more opportunities to get input from others.

In any case, whether a firm is small or large, the financial assessment is made by the principal in charge and the staff who participates and have budget or cost responsibility. Additional items that may be discussed are the feasibility of specific projects or how the budget might be better controlled. This is where project management reports which outline the status of individual projects can help bring meaning to the numbers. All that is necessary to give a full understanding of where the firm is and where it's going should be discussed. Table 5.1 is an example of a monthly cash budget report that makes up part of a typical monthly operational report. The report should be backed up by additional budgets and estimates so each number can be addressed as required.

Monthly cash budget.   Many names could be used for the operational report applicable to a particular firm. For the purpose of simplicity and as an example of the process, we will call the working operational report Monthly Cash Budget. It is assumed that accounting consultants will help each firm construct whatever reports are necessary for its individual situation. Financial computer programs can also help you prepare the necessary operational reports. These reports combined with project management reports offer a manageable way to gather information for budget meetings.

For this discussion, the cash budget is divided into four sections. Although other computer programs or spreadsheet plans may have different formats, essentially the same information is communicated. The first section is an analysis of the first month's activity compared to the *plan*. It includes what was planned for January (Jan. plan); what actually happened in January from an income and expense point

TABLE 5.1 Sample, Inc., Cash Budget—January 31, 199 __

	Jan. plan	Jan. (current month to date)	Percent of plan	Plus or minus spent	Jan. FCST	Percent of FCST	Feb. plan	Feb. FCST	Percent of plan	Prior year month (PYM)	Percent of PYM
Financial resources											
Professional fees	32,707	25,846	79	6,861	N/A	N/A	36,796	39,388	107	22,476	115
Additional service fees	11,521	13,875	120	<2,354>			12,962	14,906	115	6,789	204
Reimbursable expense	1,794	1,260	70	534			2,018	2,523	125	945	133
Total cash	46,022	40,981	89	5,041			51,775	56,816	110	30,210	136
Use of cash											
Salaries	20,540	19,781	96	760			22,184	19,781	89	16,825	118
Consultant fees	7,280	12,891	177	<5,611>			7,862	5,727	73	9,608	134
Contract labor	1,145	990	86	155			1,237	1,237	100	345	287
Blueprint/engr. services	1,521	1,790	118	<269>			1,642	1,600	97	1,485	121
Travel	651	555	85	96			703	703	100	890	62
Drafting/CAD supplies	1,560	1,478	95	82			1,684	1,650	98	456	324
Administrative salaries	2,561	1,503	59	1,058			2,765	2,678	97	2,138	70
Accounting	442	440	99	2			478	478	100	269	164
Advertising/promotion	1,518	1,383	91	136			1,640	2,473	151	1,187	116
Office lease	3,025	3,025	100	0			3,267	3,267	100	2,387	127
Payroll taxes	1,189	1,101	93	88			1,284	1,284	100	895	123
Transportation	606	306	50	300			654	654	100	176	174
Capital equipment	1,517	1,517	100	0			1,638	1,638	100	1,187	128
Repairs and maintenance	965	935	97	30			1,042	1,042	100	493	190
Telephone	317	678	214	<361>			342	561	164	476	143
Utilities	335	457	136	<122>			361	361	100	298	153
Legal	744	750	101	<6>			803	803	100	684	110
Licenses	134	130	97	4			145	145	100	111	117
Insurance	2,321	2,321	100	0			2,507	2,507	100	1,900	122
Contributions/subsc.	104	100	96	4			112	112	100	91	110
Postage and freight	250	350	140	<100>			270	270	100	276	127
Misc. expense	340	235	69	105			367	367	100	235	100
Total cash disbursement	49,064	52,714	107	<3,650>			52,989	49,339	93	42,412	124
Opening cash balance	40,363	40,363					37,321	28,630			
Net monthly cash flow	<3,041>	<11,733>	77				<1,214>	7,477			
Closing cash balance	37,321	28,630					36,107	36,107			
Loans	0	0					0	0			
Closing cash balance after loans	37,321	28,630					36,107	36,107			

of view (Jan. current month to date); what the percent of *plan* was (% of plan); and what the correlating balances were (plus or minus). The second part discusses what the month's activities were compared to forecast (Jan. FCST) and (percentage of FCST). In January, there was no forecast, so these two columns are blank. The third part is the Feb. plan and the Feb. forecast. The fourth section compares Jan. figures for current year to Jan. figures of prior year. Also indicated is opening cash position, closing cash position, and whether any loans have been obtained during the month to add to cash reserves.

January budget. The numbers for January (Table 5.1) indicate that revenue was missed by $5,041 and expenses exceeded the *plan* by $3,650. (See the plus or minus column.) This result produced a negative cash flow of $11,733, where a negative cash flow of $3,041 had been projected. The $5,041 the revenue was off is not a lot, but if the trend continued it would result in a $60,000 plus loss in income for the firm on an annual basis. As noted, expenses were also higher than projected, resulting in a negative cash flow. This does not necessarily mean the firm is losing money. A cash flow statement could reflect a negative cash flow, and the firm could still be profitable. For example, cash may be spent in one month for prepaid promotion expenses or capital expenses such as CAD equipment, with knowledge that the monies would be offset the following month. Such situations are easily accommodated in the next month's forecast.

What the cash flow statement does indicate is the firm may not be satisfying the desired profit margin goals. Hence, some corrective actions should be taken to bring the numbers in line with the plan. An analysis needs to be developed to determine what is happening and to produce a budget forecast for February that takes all of the situations into account. Questions such as those listed above or others, depending upon the situation, can be asked. Is the firm growing? Is it declining? Why are the numbers behaving the way they do? Further on in the year, questions can be raised as to whether there is a trend. If there is, it may be that the plan was too ambitious, or the economy was worse than feared, or there was a major problem in the firm affecting production. It is difficult to make a perfect budget each and every time. The important concept is to get a handle on the necessary financial controls that help guide one to the bottom line. The time to address the issue is at the first possible indication that all is not well. That is when one must sit down and look at what created the situation, to ask all of the penetrating questions, and to arrive at a solution that is proactive. Do something—make a decision.

Based upon this information and discussion, a budget forecast for February is adopted. This is a new budget that takes into consideration what really happened last month and what programs have been initiated to correct the situation. This new budget includes corrective measures that bring the firm back to cash positions in line with the *plan*. On the surface it appears an increase in revenue and a decrease in expenses are the easiest ways to achieve the desired results this early in the year. But there is more to it than that. Looking behind the numbers, several conditions present themselves. It has been determined that some accounts payable will be paid in February that will help offset the revenue shortfall. Also, after going through the analysis and inquiring into all the possible reasons why the numbers had not been met, it has been determined the current promotional campaign was not implemented per plan and associated budgets must be adjusted as a corrective action. January figures also show that a large amount was not spent on administrative salaries, which may have had something to do with the slowdown in promotions, such as a direct mail campaign.

Therefore, the advertising and promotions budget has been increased 51 percent, and the telephone budget has been increased. Salaries and consultants and contract labor expenses were minimally decreased in order to get the plan back in line. Consultant fees were higher than budgeted for in January, and it is therefore reasonable that they will be less in February. Since each number is developed from its own budget, such as project managers forecasting consultant fees, it's relatively straightforward to develop reasonable scenarios of what happened. Finally, since different outside companies have different billing cycles which one cannot totally control, this has to be taken into account with the budget.

The monthly operational meeting is also the time to ask the question why. Why was the promotional campaign not implemented on a timely basis as had been laid out in the annual plan? Why were the consultant fees larger than expected? And so on. This is the time to get to the bottom of any problems, to correct them, and to implement plans to improve office functions. So often the budget is not handled with the seriousness a business requires. Although questioning why may be time consuming at the beginning, as one learns and understands the process, the meetings will become some of the more productive staff meetings you will hold.

The last two columns in Table 5.1 indicate the numbers for January a year ago and the percent of the prior year month (PYM). The numbers indicate that *Sample, Inc.,* exceeded last year's numbers by 24 percent. Business increased over last year, however, less than what was forecasted. This gives the reviewer a quick way to determine if the firm is gaining or losing ground. Revenues tend to be cyclical because of elements that could affect construction, such as weather and holidays. Thus, comparing the current numbers to those during the same time a year ago is a fair and reasonable appraisal of activities.

February budget.   Turning to the second example, Table 5.2, the February cash budget, you can see that some progress was made in recov-

TABLE 5.2   Sample, Inc., Cash Budget—February 28, 199 __

	Feb. plan	Feb. (current month to date)	Percent of plan	Plus or minus spent	Feb. FCST	Percent of FCST	Mar. plan	Mar. FCST	Percent of plan	Prior year month (PYM)	Percent of PYM
Financial resources											
Professional fees	36,796	41,742	113	4,946	39,388	106	40,884	44,004	108	36,897	113
Additional service fees	12,962	11,278	87	<1,683>	14,906	76	14,402	15,106	105	12,569	90
Reimbursable expense	2,018	1,490	74	<528>	2,523	59	2,242	2,523	113	1,387	107
Total cash	51,775	54,511	105	2,735	56,817	96	57,528	61,632	107	50,853	107
Use of cash											
Salaries	22,184	19,781	89	2,403	19,781	100	18,897	19,781	105	16,825	118
Consultant fees	7,862	10,872	138	<3,010>	5,727	190	6,698	4,527	68	8,832	123
Contract labor	1,237	1,100	89	137	1,237	89	1,054	827	78	990	111
Blueprint/engr. services	1,642	1,654	101	<12>	1,600	103	1,399	1,100	79	1,462	113
Travel	703	655	93	48	703	93	599	599	100	766	85
Drafting/CAD supplies	1,684	1,278	76	406	1,650	77	1,435	1,255	87	1,123	114
Administrative salaries	2,765	2,394	87	371	2,678	89	2,356	2,678	114	2,278	105
Accounting	478	440	92	38	478	92	407	407	100	380	116
Advertising/promotion	1,640	1,383	84	257	2,473	56	1,397	2,473	177	1,200	115
Office lease	3,267	3,025	93	242	3,267	93	2,783	2,783	100	2,903	104
Payroll taxes	1,284	1,101	86	183	1,284	86	1,094	1,094	100	993	111
Transportation	654	306	47	348	654	47	557	557	100	298	103
Capital equipment	1,638	1,517	93	121	1,638	93	1,395	1,395	100	1,202	126
Repairs and maintenance	1,042	935	90	107	1,042	90	888	888	100	563	166
Telephone	342	678	198	<336>	561	121	292	561	192	532	128
Utilities	361	457	126	<95>	361	127	308	308	100	298	153
Legal	803	750	93	53	803	93	684	684	100	733	102
Licenses	145	130	90	15	145	90	123	123	100	105	124
Insurance	2,507	2,321	93	186	2,507	93	2,135	2,135	100	1,900	122
Contributions/subsc.	112	100	89	12	112	89	96	96	100	98	102
Postage and freight	270	350	130	<80>	270	130	230	230	100	317	110
Misc. expense	367	235	64	182	367	64	313	313	100	265	89
Total cash disbursement	52,989	51,462	97	1,527	49,338	104	45,139	44,814	99	44,063	117
Opening cash balance	37,321	28,630			28,630	100	36,107	31,679			
Net monthly cash flow	<1,214>	3,049			7,477	41	12,389	16,818			
Closing cash balance	36,107	31,679	88		36,107	88	48,497	48,497			
Loans	0	0			0	0	0	0			
Closing cash balance after loans	36,107	31,679			36,107	88	48,497	48,497			

ering lost revenue for the prior month. However, February revenue was only 96 percent of Feb. forecast (FCST), although revenue was 105 percent of plan. Meanwhile, expenses beat FCST by 4 percent but fell short of plan by 3 percent. The Feb. plan, which reflects the annual plan, is where one wants to be; the Feb. forecast is the new plan that includes corrective measures to get there due to January's down month. The task at hand is to review and develop a new budget forecast for March. These and other financial guides are used to help make quick comparisons as to where we are, which leads to discussions as to where we want to go and how do we get there.

The purpose and intent of the cash budget played out on a monthly basis is to reassess the situation, compare the annual business plan reflected by the monthly budget to what is happening, then strategize the accounts to come up with a forecast that is essentially a corrective measure to keep the business on track. The essence of the word *strategize* is to ask why. There is a plan in place; the plan has been well thought out; it has been worked on by everyone and approved by management.

Of course, a cash budget cannot reflect what else is going on in the firm in terms of actual numbers. For example, if a new client just approved a contract for new work, retainers and initial payments might not yet be reflected; however, knowledge that work was coming in would be known in the forecasted budgets for the next month. There also can be other reasons why the income did not match expectations. Some accounts may be behind in paying or holding off for some reason. Reports other than the cash budget report will indicate payments that are 30, 60, and 90 days out. This is the time to address these issues, as income not in the bank means you may have to borrow, which is a double hit. The end-of-month meeting is important from many points of view, and after you become comfortable with the process, it will become a real planning tool.

Operational reports summary.   The cash budget example is one form of accounting control. Another is a budget that includes year-to-date figures for additional comparisons. The information given here is an introduction to financial plans and controls. The important point is that a review process must be implemented on a monthly basis that is used to reflect on the current month's activities and projects. With this information, next month's budget forecast can be planned.

Compare an office that reviews financial data to one that does not. If it does have an income statement, it might indicate the firm is running positive but it would have no way of making comparisons as to where it is. The advantage is with the firm that plans its future using a financial plan backed by a well thought out annual plan which includes a strategic plan for getting to a desired point. No matter what happens, the firm with the plan is going to be in a better position to react to changes in the economy or other impacts to a budget and cash flow.*

Financial planning help.   There is financial help for architects and engineers. One area of help is software that keeps track of what is happening, such as accounting and project management software. A good software package can track all the project management variables and a wealth of additional information. When this information is combined with accounting information, by an in house or outside accountant, the result is a true financial picture. These software tools are reasonable in cost. They provide necessary information and are a good place to begin getting a firm computer oriented.

A second area of help is your accountant who does your taxes and reviews or does your balance sheet and income statement each month. If you simply get statements in the mail, it would be a good idea to take a more aggressive business posture and ask your accountant to review your accounts and offer experienced observations about the financial status of your business. Better yet, have your accountant attend an operational meeting or even help organize the meeting. The accountant may set the tone for future meetings and help convey the message to your staff that this is an important part of an architectural or engineering business.

A third area of help is your local banker. From time to time you may need a short-term loan to meet the monthly cash flow. Asking for a loan the first time you meet your banker is not good banking practice. It is preferable to meet your banker on a quarterly basis, or more often, to review your income sheet and balance statements. These are good times to discuss questions regarding money management and other banking activities. Then, when you do need a loan, the bank knows you and your business and why you need the loan. This relationship can become very valuable in future years as new opportunities develop and you begin to expand your business.

The fourth area is independent consultants who help architects and engineers set up and implement project management, marketing, and other management programs for an office. If your firm is looking at changing the way it approaches business problems and is not sure how to start, consultants offer a way to ease gently into the situation. Many consultants specialize in architectural engineering and contracting (AEC) businesses and have a vast amount of experience in the same problems you are facing.

A fifth area of help is particularly well suited for small firms. It is setting up an advisory board for the sole purpose of making recom-

---

*The above financials and all financials presented have been prepared to illustrate specific concepts. They should not be construed as financial guidelines or accounting advice for an architectural or engineering practice, as every practice is different. See your accountant for information, guidelines, and suggestions.

mendations pertaining to business strategies. Having an advisory board that seriously discusses your strengths and weaknesses and the competitive nature of your practice is advantageous.

Psychological factor

There is a dilemma involved in implementing this kind of accounting process: The kinds of individuals needed to operate at the necessary level are most likely not available in the average architectural or engineering office. Architects are taught to be artists and are forced into management roles only by their success. Yet, one has to start someplace, and it is necessary for the principal who is driving this process to recognize this and take action. For example, business planning methodologies can be learned, and architects and engineers have no trouble assimilating the material. The decisive factor is selecting those who have the attributes for and the interest in management. Many engineers and architects, particularly designers, will not want to work with numbers. But it is essential to do so. The necessary financial numbers skills will come.

Making it work is up to management. The way it starts, the way the first annual plan is done, the way the manager and architects or engineers are motivated are all important to the eventual success. In any case, a firm tends to reflect the personality of the principal architect or engineer. In other words, a conservative architect or engineer goes after projects he or she can readily accomplish in the style that has made him or her successful in the past. On the other hand, the aggressive principal will go out on a limb to try new design ideas. The same style and working characteristics will be used in implementing the new plan and financial constraints. The bottom line is that project managers, architects, designers, engineers, computer people, draftspeople, and staffs will eventually adapt to the leader's decisions. Most, in time, will recognize the importance and the benefit and will be glad that their firm is taking the initiative and striking out in a competitive, businesslike fashion.

Implementation

Once management has written and approved the annual business plan and has prepared the necessary budgets, the next issue is how to implement the ideas in a logical sequence that fosters both motivation and attention to detail. As it has been indicated, many firms do not use a business plan. Many that do have a plan end up shelving it until the following year. This is worse than writing no plan at all, as the effort has been expended wastefully. A business plan has to be implemented to be meaningful; it must be used as a benchmark throughout the year to check progress toward one's goals. Implementation means making decisions based upon the plan from the top down. The plans must be turned into actions and programs that reflect the spirit and intent of the firm.

This is a complicated issue, and each size of firm has a particular set of circumstances that suggests different implementation techniques. Each firm is unique as it is made up of individuals with different skills, different experiences, different interests, and different organizational patterns. For example, a large 100 person office has a different structure than a small 7 person office. And a sole proprietor has yet a different set of problems to face. In addition, all offices use some sort of project management methodology to move a project along through its phases. This process contributes to how a plan is implemented. To complicate the process further, principals tend to contribute on several different levels. And in the case of small offices, principals do everything—from writing the business plan to designing and drafting. One question to consider is, therefore, What is the best way to implement a business plan and track what is happening?

Common sense and communication

First and foremost, the existence of a business plan should not change dynamically what is happening in an office. People still go to work, and they still take lunch and put in overtime. The difference is that an annual plan represents an attempt to safeguard one's future by working toward a profit orientation; this should become part of the thought process. When principals meet with managers, the directions should be an interpretation and communication of the intent of the business plan. In essence, in order for the plan to work, it must be communicated downward. Marketing projects, for example, must be developed as outlined in the business plan, and steps must be taken to make it a real contribution to the office. There is nothing magical about this process. Managers in an office all know what is in the annual plan, and they all know their own responsibilities. Taking a common sense approach in their day-to-day jobs and communicating to their clients and staff, ideas, decisions, and directions that are in tandem with the annual plan is of primary importance. Each manager, from the principal to the project architect or engineer or project managers down to the draftsperson, is charged with a responsibility to do quality work on a timely basis. That is a given. The business plan offers a perspective and a reason why a decision might go one way as opposed to another.

For example, the decision to accept or start one job over another should be decided in favor of the project that most closely interprets the intent of the business plan. This is a managerial decision, and the managers who are involved are charged with the responsibility of interpreting the plan and making the decision based upon it.

An example in the case of *Sample, Inc.,* is if several jobs became available but because of current workload, scheduling, and timing, it is necessary to accept one job and postpone or refuse others. Suppose the jobs were of different scope, say a jail remodel, a custom residence, and a small commercial remodel. In this case, the jail remodel would be favorable, even if the income were less, as it adds to the company's portfolio of correctional work and its long-range development. Of course, every effort would be made to satisfy all job opportunities by thoroughly investigating the client's real timing requirements against the firm's workload; the long-range plan provides a basis for making the final decision.

Thus, common sense and communication play a large role in interpreting and implementing a business plan. Each and every person in an architectural or engineering office has a different role to play, and each person has certain decisions to make that contribute to the plan. The principals communicate downward as to direction and development. Associate architects or engineers talk to project managers, or project architects or engineers, and they in turn talk to designers or draftspeople. Thus the plan can be communicated downward with enough information at each level to make the process work. This in no way replaces or adds anything to the existing communication system. The plan simply exists and is interpreted downward.

Again, it must be mentioned that opportunities arise that are not called for in a business plan; that does not mean one should not consider them. What the business plan does is provide something to which to compare new ideas. It provides a forum for discussion. For example, what if *Sample, Inc.,* were approached by an architectural engineering (AE) firm with the idea that it would like to acquire *Sample, Inc.*? This is not what *Sample, Inc.,* had in mind, but it might open opportunities that can be looked at in relationship to its own plans. The advantage that *Sample, Inc.,* has in this situation is that it has a well-developed, long-range plan. The plan makes it much easier to digest information and opportunities and make reasonable business decisions than for a firm operating month to month. Because *Sample, Inc.,* has considered the possibility of merging with another firm to expand its territorial base, to enhance correctional work opportunities, and perhaps to gain better expertise in construction management, it may very well have the advantage when sitting down at the negotiating table. The minimum it will gain from the encounter is a better understanding of its own needs and the acquisition negotiation process. The small firm has the same ability to manage from strength or from the position of having a business plan. The only difference is that decisions are more centered with the principal, and there aren't as many layers of management to go through.

Strong project management orientation

Architectural and engineering firms manage projects. Every firm uses project management techniques to some degree to manage the quality and flow of work. Each major business sector has some method of controlling different components of the information flow whose sum total equals a completed project or task. Architecture or engineering is no different and has a well-developed project management philosophy. These concepts are well developed in literature distributed by the AIA and are widely written about. The importance of project management techniques as they relate to the business plan is the communication structure the techniques provide for a firm.

Project managers are assigned responsibilities to see that specific projects are completed on a timely basis, are in compliance with contract documents and applicable building codes, and have a certain level of quality. They are also responsible for budgets, scheduling, and monitoring the various systems that support project management. Project managers generally report directly to the different principals and/or coordinating architect or engineer. The important point is there is already a reporting structure in place in most firms that can help implement various attributes of the annual plan. This applies to sole proprietors as well, where the project management application is more concise as there is less communication involved.

Controlling costs and managing the flow of work are very much a part of both project management and business plans, as the costs directly affect the resulting profit. The project manager's task is also impacted by many outside variables. Clients changing the design or the scope of work, hidden site conditions, and insurmountable planning ordinances that take time to review and challenge all complicate the project manager's task. However, the project manager's guide is the business plan and associated objectives that guide the firm to a profitable conclusion. When a plan is well thought out as to cost control measures, problem areas, and so on, the project manager will know or be instructed as to how to react to certain situations properly and in the firm's best interests. The project manager thus manages from precepts and ideology directed at making sure the project is on time and has followed all of the contractual provisions to see that the firm receives proper financial reimbursement in the same proportion it has put out. Again, it is the business plan that provides the guidelines.

Management by objectives

Another implementation technique available to the architect is *management by objectives* (MBO), which is a management tool that provides a structure that allows the delegation of responsibilities and ideas to flow downward through an organization to those responsible for different portions of the work. It works in a large firm and in a small firm. In an ideal situation, the goals and objectives of a company are divided between managers who have specific areas of responsibility, who then delegate downward to all staff levels. When everyone accomplishes exactly what is asked, the plan is accomplished and the goals and objectives are fulfilled. The firm prospers. Of course, this never happens exactly the way it's planned, but having the structure in place allows one the opportunity to review and evaluate at different levels of a firm to seek areas of improvement.

MBO: What is it?   Knowing that it takes common sense and communication coupled with the attributes of a project management system to implement a business plan, management by objectives appears to offer a neat fit into the structured engineering or architectural environment. MBO provides a proven form of managing. *It is a tool or a process, not a solution,* that can be used by engineers and architects to help manage a firm toward directed consequences—the stated goals and objectives of the firm. MBO is not a solution because business is made up of the sum of its parts. If used properly, it can become a valuable implementation and management tool. In most businesses, a business plan is completed, shelved until next year, then taken out, reviewed, and possibly rewritten. Although it is commendable that a plan is written, not to use it as a guide for managing the business defeats the purpose of having it.

What is truly interesting about MBO philosophies is that it's simply a tool which organizes "the things many people are already doing."[18] Studies have shown that using this tool helps lower cost, increase revenues and growth, and produce more profit. It also has the added benefit of providing a realistic picture of what is expected from each employee and his or her contribution to the firm.

A widely used definition of the system of management by objectives is as follows:

> A process whereby the superior and subordinate managers of an organization jointly identify its common goals, define each individual's major areas of responsibility in terms of the results expected of him [or her], and use these measures as guides for operating the unit and assessing the contribution of each of its members.[19]

This definition essentially became the working model for organizations looking for implementation of management functions. As long-range planning strategies became more dominant in the management cycle, another definition of MBO emerged that is particularly useful for design-oriented companies:

> Management by objectives is a philosophy of managing that is based on identifying purpose, objectives, and desired results, establishing a realistic program for obtaining these results, and evaluating performance in achieving them.[20]

This concept is further broken down into nine points that serve to emphasize the steps of effective management[20]:

1. Purpose or mission
2. Environmental analysis

3. Strengths and weaknesses

4. Assumptions

5. Objectives

6. Strategy

7. Operational plans

8. Evaluation and control

9. Individual objectives to lowest level

Note that the breakdown of the MBO definition is similar to a business plan outline previously discussed. MBO philosophies can be viewed as an extension of business planning. The architectural or engineering office, with its project management orientations, offers a tremendous opportunity to use MBO techniques to implement the business plan. Project management techniques are already closely aligned with MBO philosophies. Any time an objective for a task is outlined, then used to evaluate the eventual performance, MBO philosophies are being used. MBO already exists in engineering and architectural offices; it's a matter of understanding and improving upon the standards and implementation.

The major implementation problem is again related to the size of the office and the rather subjective nature of architecture and engineering. In fact, the size of the office is the largest problem when working with and implementing business plans. Small offices do not have the staff and/or the cash flow to implement by delegation and objectives. The reason is that a complete MBO implementation is a complicated managerial task better left to experienced human resource personnel. The answer lies in how the MBO process is used and thought of as opposed to its complete implementation. Many books have been written about MBO methodologies, and this brief discussion is only meant as an introduction. Its intent is to demonstrate that there is a management tool available so business plans no longer have to sit on the shelf but can be integrated into the office. George S. Odiorne aptly identifies the value of MBO with the following four points[21]:

1. If you don't have a goal, you have no idea whether you are on the right road or not.

2. You can't assess results without some prior expectations against which to measure them.

3. You don't know when things are drifting if you aren't clear what goal would compromise "nondrifting" or purposive action.

4. People can't perform with maximum effectiveness if they don't know what goals the organization is seeking (and why), or how well they are doing in relation to those goals.

R. Henry Migliore outlines eight additional benefits to MBO implementations in his book *An MBO Approach to Long Range Planning*[22]:

1. The organization will determine where it's going.

2. It will be able to identify opportunities and risks.

3. All organization members will be forced into a consensus as the direction for the organization is identified.

4. As managers have the opportunity for input into the planning process, they will experience a surge of excitement.

5. Communication in all directions will be instantly approved.

6. Nonproductive persons will fall by the wayside.

7. Increases should be expected in all measurable areas—profitability, productivity, and so on.

8. Within a year, a personal training and development plan will evolve for all persons in the organization.

Reviewing the two above lists, you can see there are major benefits for using the MBO approach. The ideas relate directly back to the purpose of the business plan: If you don't know where you're going and how you're going to get there, how will you know if you're on course or are going to hit the target? In addition, MBO automatically provides the forum for review and contribution by others.

How does MBO work?   There are many managers who have found fault with the MBO system. However, the success of major corporations in managing thousands of people, all of whom contribute to the profitability, increased revenue, decreased costs, and so on, testify as to its potential strengths. MBO isn't easy to adopt completely into an environment; it does require someone who is knowledgeable about MBO planning from a human resources point of view. If the energy behind the plan falls off, if the objectives are unclear, if the plan doesn't have full support of management, if the implementation is weakened as it moves down through the firm, if all are not charged with some responsibility, then the chance for success is reduced.[23] But it must be repeated that some form of MBO is already in every office. Having an annual business plan and a form of implementation which is going to be some form of MBO process doesn't change an office. It offers a structure to a sometimes disorderly environment.

Management by objectives is the delegation of responsibilities through objectives. In a full MBO system, a person's performance is based upon those objectives being met on a timely basis. MBO is simple; it is the implementation that is difficult. In some corporations, MBO is carried all the way through to the performance appraisal of an individual's job; in other words, the measurement that's used to judge whether an objective has been accomplished is also used to judge the performance of the individual and, consequently, the increase in commensuration. Although this is fine for corporations that have the human resource personnel to manage this complicated process, which includes educating the managers in giving fair reviews, performance evaluations are not necessarily the answer for the average engineering or architectural firm.

There are two reasons. The first is that much of architecture and engineering is subjective. A designer's role is difficult to measure objectively in terms of increasing the firm's bottom line and/or profitability and thus falls into a different category for performance review. A second reason is the tasks of architecture and engineering are all interrelated and subject to the whims of many. A client, a bank, a planning commission, or a venture capitalist wishing to have input can all create time delays in terms of changes and constraints. Thus, whereas a set of working drawings can be measured as to whether it was completed on time, there are other factors that affect this kind of evaluation. Hence, it is difficult to implement true MBO appraisals. In the end, it is best to use appraisal techniques that match the job. How then, should one use MBO methodologies in an architectural or engineering firm?

It is important to understand that implementation, as described above, does not necessarily have to be tied to the performance review. Other review processes can be used alone or in conjunction with an individual's objectives. Also, when the objectives of someone are being reviewed as a measure of contribution, the situation should be conducted with fairness and insight. Much has been written about the steps required for review processes; however, if a problem occurs where a manager determines that certain objectives are not being met by an individual, it is important to confront the situation from the following viewpoint[24]:

Am I the problem?   In other words, was the assignment or objectives unrealistic or my expectations unreasonable?

Is the employee the problem?   This requires looking deeper into the employee's performance for trends of a similar nature.

Is there something that no one can control that is the problem?   Often situations develop that create other problems, which no one can be responsible for.

Asking these questions, which should be common to any organization dealing with people, should give one a framework for honest interpretations that are meaningful and realistic. It is important to remember that all change meets with some resistance, and the danger involved is the actual implementation of the plan by someone who doesn't understand the true consequences. MBO offers another way to look at and manage a business.

Summary

Financial planning allows the implementation of the plan to occur with benchmarks to mark the financial goals. MBO allows the programs and tactics to be managed based upon the agreed-upon goals and objectives. MBO is a good, solid management tool; however, there can be undesirable repercussions if the MBO techniques are not managed properly.

Architectural and engineering firms would have a better chance of monetary gains if they developed and used an annual plan. That plan forces them to think about what is happening now, what they would like to happen in the future, what the current environment is, what the strengths and weaknesses of the firm are, and what lies ahead in the form of opportunities. Since a plan is based upon goals and objectives, and since all employees are managed by some sort of objective basis, whether stated or implied, it seems logical that some form of MBO be implemented in an architectural or engineering firm through the project management system that is already in place and that it be surrounded by both common sense and communication. Taking this approach, the implementation of the business plan through the financial plan and downward communication of objectives through a methodological approach such as MBO can only contribute to a better office and a better working environment. It is up to the principal, the "doer" of the firm, to take whatever situation confronts the firm and apply the ideas and concepts to work toward an organized budget and project management.

Chapter

6

Management Perspectives

When preparing to develop an annual business plan, it is important for architects and engineers to step back and view themselves from a perspective that allows a realistic appraisal of what is happening to their professions and how those observations might affect a business plan. Two such observations that add depth and meaning to the overall planning process are discussed here: First, computers and CAD[25] systems are making a large impact on how architecture and engineering are done and will be done in future years. Second, architectural and engineering management is changing from a passive to an active role. Architects and engineers are beginning to manage their own future with more of a commitment to the realities of the business world.

These observations are discussed from the point of view that emphasizes that an annual business plan, and resulting marketing plan and implementation strategies, must have a sense of direction within the context of the architectural and engineering world, as well as within the context of sensible business conclusions.

Computers, CAD, and the Architect and Engineer

Architecture and engineering have experienced a lot of changes in the last several decades. One of the biggest changes has been the blueprint machine, which eliminated the need to employ drafters who simply copied the work of others in order to produce additional sets of drawings. The blueprint machine made reproduction a given and, as a result, firms became smaller as staff size was reduced. It's imaginable that many discussions occurred about the art being lost because drawings were being made to conform to the reproduction process. It's true that the craft that produced the ink masterpieces has, for the most part, faded away. These skills are no longer refined in architectural or engineering schools as they were under the apprentice programs. Schools now have other concerns.

The next development that increased the efficiency of producing drawings was systems drafting. Systems drafting allowed drawings to be combined in different ways, thereby eliminating much of the repetition and helping to reduce the chances for error. Plain paper copiers contribute to this flexibility by combining drawings in a paste-up approach. Systems drafting has generated the use of standardized details from which other details are developed. This process has been carried over to the next development for architects and engineers—computer aided design. CAD provides a real advantage. But for the most part, the majority of small- to medium-size firms still prepare drawings the same way—pencil or ink on mylar or vellum, in some instances combined with reproductive photographic techniques and/or plain paper copiers to produce the final drawing. Some architects and engineers use the large, trained labor pool, as opposed to investing in CAD, to meet their drafting needs. They have not adopted CAD as a technology because of the relatively inexpensive and plentiful labor supply.

CAD helps architects and engineers study and develop the diagrams that describe the work. Again, the same arguments are heard that the art will be lost if architects and engineers use an electronic box instead of hand-produced work. But CAD offers the opportunity to move out of the environment of hand-produced drawings into an arena where high-tech advancements are able to enhance the architectural and engineering services you offer to your clients. Using computers and CAD must be an important business strategy in today's competitive environment.

Computers as a business strategy

New technologies create new ways to produce work, and architects and engineers will need to incorporate these new ideas into their firms. If an architect or engineer is not using CAD, he or she is missing an incredible opportunity to expand creativity and produce efficient, clear drawings. Furthermore, the database created by CAD offers a new way of looking at the design process and the management of information. One cannot pick up an architectural or engineering magazine without seeing numerous references to CAD and database management. The editorial staffs hint that the presence of computers in the engineering and architectural environment is expected in order to remain competitive. Hence, a new burden has been thrust upon the architect and engineer—the integration of CAD and other computer information systems.

Everyone knows of at least one architect or engineer who has successfully integrated CAD and is well on the way to developing an integrated computer-oriented office. On the other hand, everyone also knows architects or engineers who have tried CAD and offer nothing but nightmare stories as to lost time and investment monies. One thing is certain, there is still a lot of fear associated with acquiring a CAD system. But there is also a lot of information and expertise available. It is more a problem of attitude than anything else. Those who have the proper attitude will enjoy receptivity by their staff and clients; those who don't have the proper attitude will be forever looking at the CAD system as a threat.

Computers must first be looked at from the point of view of a business plan and how the management of the firm wishes to integrate them into the business. If the CAD and other computer systems do not have a direction and a goal, they will surely fail. For example, if the office is approaching CAD with a lot of trepidation, the business plan should provide a fair amount of transition time as the office accepts and learns to work with this new tool. Furthermore, CAD drawings should contribute to different parts of many projects during the learning phase, as opposed to being assigned one specific project. Plot plans, where site conditions such as utility lines and setbacks can be generated and plotted at any scale can be the first step. These drawings are extremely helpful to the designer in the early stages. Later, they become the basis for the site plan and other related work.

Other starting places for CAD within an office might be the standard site details that a firm tends to use over and over, such as curb details or tree planting details. As experience is obtained, the CAD system takes on a more dominant role, until design decisions, massing studies, volume studies, square foot analysis, and what if scenarios become common occurrences.

Contrary to this scenario is the office that has the experience and proper personnel and makes a financial commitment to automate almost totally with CAD and project management tools. The two offices are approaching the same problem in different ways, within the context of the business plan that has been discussed and approved.

CAD is a strategy as much as it is a tool. There is nothing that has a greater impact on sales, marketing, production, and the bottom line than a CAD system. Computers are critical to an architect's and engineer's future success. Computers change the way services are rendered and, as a result, create a demand for new services. Architecture and engineering has moved from an information poor to an information rich environment. Managing this information by the acceptance of computers and CAD is one key to competing.

The computer is extremely valuable to the architect and engineer, and its role will become increasingly important as its true advantages are discovered. Architects and engineers have been slow to adapt the computer fully, whether it be CAD or other computer operations. For the most part, they use a computer in much the same way many small businesses do. Besides the obvious advantage of a CAD system, computers offer a way to expedite normal administrative functions from correspondence to bookkeeping, as well as the development of databases for marketing.

There are generally five application areas for the computer within an architect's or engineer's office:

- Financial management and project management
- Word processing and specifications
- Desktop publishing and marketing
- Architect's and engineer's workstation
- Computer aided design

Financial management and project management

From a financial point of view, computers open up a degree of control that before only larger corporations enjoyed. Now accounting software is available in a variety of formats and scope, allowing one to keep track of all necessary information and to produce management reports and budgets. Combined with the help of an accountant, these accounting tools are extremely helpful in managing the plan and day-to-day business functions.

A computer is also essential for the implementation of project management systems. Without a computer, project management becomes a tabulation chore that eventually gets put off, reducing the timeliness and effectiveness of the reporting system. The project management information is important as it is the key to what is happening inside the firm. With a computer, project management truly becomes a tool that helps with the analysis of current jobs and forms a tie between the beginning and end of a project. Architects and engineers should look at a computer as an integrated management system which will track the hours of a particular project versus what was planned for and which is tied directly to a contract. The resulting weekly status reports give management a true reflection of what is happening; if there are problems relating to the budget, it will eventually show up. Used properly, there shouldn't be any surprises at the end of a project, for there will be ample time to make corrective moves.

For example, the designer may have completed the portion of the work within a satisfactory time frame as estimated in the schematic design phase. However, when the job goes into design development, a particular aspect of the work may require additional review for code and/or planning requirements. Additional hours over the planned design development budget may be required to solve the problem. This problem may be magnified if it isn't caught until the construction documents phase. In both of these cases, questions are raised:

Is there any way to make up the difference?

Could we have done something that prevented the problem in the first place?

How is this type of problem reflected in the contract documents?

Is it something unforeseen for which the owner should pay?

The point is that the project management system is tracking the number of hours and activities accurately and generating appropriate reports that can be evaluated and acted upon.

However, if an overage is due to the client, thereby changing the scope of the work, the system provides appropriate documentation as to budget versus changes by the client. Now the problem can be discussed with the client with sufficient supporting material. One of the greatest problems an architect or engineer faces is convincing the client that last minute whims will really change the fee. The tendency is to absorb the additional cost without reflecting a change in fee to avoid an awkward confrontation with the client. It is the we don't want to get the client upset philosophy. Not wanting to get the client upset is fine, but when it's done at the expense of the firm, it's not fine. If the contract negotiations from the onset reflect that all costs, expenses, and changes to the contract will be reflected in some manner as provided in the client and architect or engineer agreement, there shouldn't be a problem. The architect designs it, the contractor builds it, and the client pays for it.

The computer allows accurate tracking through the project management system, giving the project managers and principals a better handle on what is happening. In addition, the financial software is used to record the appropriate debits and credits. The result is an accurate, realistic view of what is really happening, which can now be used as a resource for future planning.

Word processing and specifications

Word processing is the preparation of documentation such as letters, memos, and other forms of written communication. It is referred to as word processing because of the enhanced ability to revise, edit, and move and delete material in an efficient fashion. This process is ideally suited to specifications, where much of the material is either a boiler plate or alterations to existing specs used on former projects. An office might use a dedicated computer, where those who are responsible for the specs share the system. If an office is large enough, the systems might be networked, allowing all those required to participate in the specification writing to access the necessary files. Both the Construction Specifications Institute (CSI) and the AIA produce a master type spec series that can be used as the basis for compiling a specification. Also, in-house specs for the type of work being described might be prepared and used from one project to the next.

Preparing specifications on the computer does not make everyone an expert. Specification writing requires experience combined with more experience. A thorough understanding of the intent of the specs and how the specs are used and interpreted, along with the legal ramifications and connections to other contract documents, is necessary. What the computer does do is make the job easier than the cut-and-paste techniques used in prior years. Now, more time can be spent on the important part of the work as opposed to the production of the final document. Revisions and last minute changes are much easier to incorporate, allowing an easier review process.

Desktop publishing and marketing

Architecture and engineering are graphic professions. Architects and engineers present ideas through graphical means, which are additionally amplified and explained through written communication. Desktop publishing allows the architect and engineer to approach presentations from a graphical orientation. In addition, desktop publishing techniques offer convenience in assembling the work of many people into one final report. With the ability to make transparencies and overheads for presentations, the desktop publishing functions become a valuable presentation tool. The same overheads can be output to laser printers, which further underscores the presentation with clear precise documentation. Desktop publishing is made for the architect or engineer—it can easily change one's entire professional image.

The benefits go on. The desktop publishing systems become the focal point for marketing communications such as newsletters, letters to clients about the work you are doing, and a host of other activities that promote your firm. And it does it with a fresh, professional approach that is as creative as the user of the system.

Another marketing feature of the computer is the ability to create a database of names and information. The lists may include prospects, existing customers, new construction, the competition, and so on. The idea is to develop a way to categorize information, then retrieve it in useful ways. In large corporations this process is referred to as a marketing information system or a management information system (MIS). Through the use of the personal computer systems, small- and medium-size firms can also create ways to manage the information in their environments. Although not as comprehensive as a true MIS system, it is a big step toward managing the information that surrounds an architectural or engineering practice.

This database system collects important information that can then be distributed on a timely basis to assist in marketing and planning activities. It also becomes the focus point for many marketing projects, such as prospecting. This database also provides information for the newsletters, surveys, and other marketing communication material. The computer can easily sort and output this information in a variety of ways, including mail merge for personalized letters and mailing labels. The computer is helpful in developing a marketing program because of its ability to produce a variety of output customized to one's needs.

Architect's and engineer's workstation

The architect's or engineer's workstation (not to be confused with a UNIX workstation) is where each project architect or engineer, or key person, is given a computer to use. Ideally, everyone in a firm should have a computer. There are a multitude of computer applications architects or engineers can use in their daily work, and many who learn to use such a system are lost without it. For example, an architect or engineer can use the system to input the project management information or orchestrate a critical path analysis of a new project so progress can be managed.

Spreadsheets can be developed for everything from tables used in construction documents, legends, and general notes. These can be produced on sticky backs and pasted on the drawings or can be input into the CAD system to become part of the final drawing. The field notes, internal memos, and project notes can be recorded and printed, freeing up secretaries for other work. Beam analysis for preliminary design considerations is available. Specifications can be added through a commercial series or an in-house set. Time management programs can help make each person more efficient. The list goes on and is as long as one is creative. All of these functions complement the person at the board or, it is hoped, the CAD system and allow one to do a better job faster.

The concept of an architect's or engineer's workstation allows each person to use only the software needed to do the job. As more software becomes available and existing packages are improved, there will be more benefits. In addition, as offices expand the use of computers into networked environments, each architect and engineer will have access to the information right from his or her desk. For example, a project architect or engineer may enter the necessary information regarding project management, then bring up the specs that are being written for a specific project, then make notes for others to review. He or she might then type the field inspection notes and output them to the laser printer, where a secretary collates and distributes the notes to the necessary people. Electronic mail can be used for communication. Information such as financial reports can be protected by passwords so only those who have a need to know it will be able to access it.

Not to be confused with the marketing database is the database of products and specifications. It is becoming more and more common for manufacturers to provide product information via the computer. The three most common are a database accessed by a modem, a catalog sent on disk, or a manufacturer providing the software directly. In the area of CAD, the database is particularly useful, as many manufacturers include the diagrams that form the basis for explaining the work. Door and window details are commonly available on disk from the manufacturer. The way information is distributed and how the information is used are changing, and the computer is at the center of these changes.

Computer aided design

Presently, roughly half of the architecture and engineering firms in this country use some CAD system. Many of the systems are underutilized, improperly maintained, and not updated. Management consultants, engineers, architects, and CAD specialists have unanimously agreed that success or failure of CAD depends largely upon the attitude of the management. CAD must be received by an *open* and *enthusiastic* attitude. *A positive attitude by management creates a positive environment for the staff, which influences the success of the CAD system more than the CAD system itself.* By providing the environment in which CAD can be successful, the people who use the system have a chance to meet management's expectations.

The proper environment is a positive attitude coupled with good, sound, practical, and purposeful management. CAD is simply a tool to help make decisions. *People* still make the decisions. Architects or engineers and managers need to understand and emphasize that the sole purpose of the CAD system is to assist in the decision-making process. The CAD system is not intended to replace anyone but to reduce the effort needed to make complex decisions and to assemble diagrams efficiently in the form of construction documents. A properly trained architect or engineer will be more productive than a person on the boards.

Architects and engineers have been slow in adapting CAD technology compared to those in other industries and professions. Because architecture or engineering is so much a graphic profession, the opposite would seem to be true. Architecture is a graphic science; it uses diagrams, perspectives, details, and so on, to describe solutions and designs. With the exception of bidding documents and specifications, for the most part, the final product is a set of drawings, which is a graphical representation of the intended work not a completed building. The contractor is responsible for the completed work and relies on clear, precise, and properly coordinated descriptions of the work. If the design is of high quality, the construction documents are reflective of this, and the proper contractor has been identified through the bidding process, the completed building will be of high quality. What better tool to assist the architect or engineer than a CAD system which provides a way to produce clear, precise diagrams of the work, plus coordinated collateral information.

Another reason why architects or engineers have not fully embraced computers is that they are not used to making capital investments in equipment. Manufacturers spend hundreds of thousands of dollars each year in the acquisition of equipment that is essential for them to remain in business. On the other hand, an architect or engineer can set up a drafting table in a spare bedroom and is instantly in business. One of the greatest challenges besides using CAD is the financial impact of acquiring the hardware and the software. *The tool for softening the effect of CAD acquisition is the business plan, where adequate measures can prepare an office for CAD.* Granted, the first CAD systems were very expensive, and this kept many firms out of the market. However, prices have come down, and lease plans are available to provide for a monthly payment plan with a buy-out amount at the end.

It is ironic that CAD also creates greater competition. For example, when an architect branches out, he or she does work on CAD systems. Now you have a situation where one moonlighting architect can create competitive situations causing problems for other architects. The moonlighting person tends to be newly educated and is comfortable with CAD. The result is that he or she acts as a governor, creating situations where the competitiveness creates a demand for other architects to do their work on CAD. Many large firms have lost jobs to smaller architects who have CAD systems.

Four famous quotes. What is really astounding is what architects and engineers have recently said about why they're not using CAD. The reasons are an indication that CAD is not understood for what it is—a tool that assists the designer in creating more design alternatives, then leveraging this and other information through the use of databases to create diagrams and information about the intended design. The CAD system is not meant to replace anyone or to reduce one's design role.

Following are four statements made by architects about CAD:

1. *CAD limits our ability to draw:* This is an unbelievable statement. If one architect said it, more than one architect is thinking it or, worse yet, believing it. Today, the only way to limit one's ability to draw is to use the drawing board. The CAD system gives you the ability to look at many design solutions quickly and economically. It can save details for later use; it can take sections and elevations and create multiple perspectives for design studies and layouts for perspec-

tive renderings. The above statement is a denial that the profession is changing.

2. *CAD makes our draftspeople lazy:* Any draftsperson who is properly trained on a CAD system will be one of the most productive members of the firm. With background plotting, there is no downtime while a plot is being produced. There are always libraries to update, details to produce, and so on. This quote reflects the attitude that CAD is easy, and if you did it the hard way, you want the people working for you to suffer too.

3. *We're a small office; we can't use CAD:* The misfortune here is not understanding the true competitive nature a CAD system offers. A well-organized and productive system allows one to compete for larger jobs or keep more jobs on the boards at one time. More than one small office has won substantial contracts over larger offices because of CAD. A CAD system can become a competitive advantage.

4. *We do custom work; it doesn't apply to us:* A CAD system allows one to take repetitious designs and repeat them, saving a large amount of drafting time. A good example is a hotel where room after room is repeated. Custom work implies none of these repetitious elements exists; however, the opposite is true. Within any given structure there are hundreds of components that are repeated over and over—from structural steel angles, to wide flange beams, to symbols used to indicate sections and details. Door swings, plumbing fixtures, and lighting symbols are repetitious in every job. Furthermore, the legends, boilerplate notes, and so on, are generally repetitious from one job to the next and much easier to manage in a spreadsheet format.

Architects and engineers have spent hundreds of hours drawing elevations of doors. The way to look at CAD is that you are going to draw this door elevation once, store it in a library, then never draw that door again. By using this method, you can start to build a library that, when used effectively, can save hours on a drawing. In addition, commercial libraries are available as a starting point.

Decisions and productivity. Computers compress the time between decisions. Decisions come three, four, maybe five times as fast. It is therefore important to understand the decision-making process in your office. First, the user should be someone capable of making architectural and engineering types of decisions. A CAD system is not a tool to teach someone to draft. It is important to multiply the efforts of the high producer; the one who has proven him or herself capable in making architectural or engineering decisions that lead to the completion of the project. Second, the office must be ready to receive the information if the CAD system is going to increase the production rate of the office. Sections affect plans, plans alter elevations, and so on. It is the information flow of the decision-making process that must be evaluated. Job scheduling, personnel hour allocations, and project tracking become important issues. As Chief Boyd states, "If you have a badly organized office and you buy a computer to get organized, you are going to be in for a shock."[26]

People claim that CAD is three or four times as fast. CAD is not automatically more productive. The key is that it is more productive when the system is used properly by someone who is experienced and adequately trained, when the system has appropriate libraries the office developed or acquired, the software functions at a high level, the hardware is of sufficient power and capability to take advantage of the software, and the office is set up to use the information being generated. Yes, CAD is more productive, but it is a combination of all these elements working together that increases productivity.

Fee structure.   The implementation of a CAD system will affect the fee structure. If done properly, the annual business plan will have considered any effect on the fees charged by a firm. CAD does affect the cost of doing business, so any discussion about a CAD system should include positions on fee structures. Some architects and engineers set up CAD as a profit center or as a dummy corporation. This fictitious business invoices different projects and bills clients as a cost of providing the service as if the computer department were a consultant. The advantage of this system is there is an accurate record of the hours billed against actual time used. This helps you prepare a return on investment (ROI) analysis regarding the CAD system. Or it will help you estimate CAD time for other contracts which might require a lump sum type of fee structure.

It is also true a CAD system can provide a lot of information to many projects on the boards. For example, the drawings might be used for background plots for consultants, plot plans for new projects, general notes, and legends. Also, CAD services might be offered to other architects or engineers. The downside of the profit center concept is that it tends to take the system out of the drafting room and put it into the hands of more computer-oriented people. Although some people might consider this positive, a CAD system is meant to be used by architects, engineers, and drafters on a daily basis. The profit center concept may serve to alienate the computer people. It is for this reason that implementation is so important, and management must carefully evaluate alternatives and make choices that are best suited for their office. The best place to start is the annual business plan, where many discussions about a wide range of topics can occur.

From a historical perspective, the larger the office, the greater the tendency to have a centralized CAD department. This makes sharing the peripherals and managing the network easier. This does not necessarily mean the location of all CAD equipment is in one area. Due to network technology, computers and CAD systems can be located throughout an office and still be tied together. Hence, whether a firm is horizontal or vertical in structure, CAD and other computer systems can be fit into the existing environment.

Another fee alternative is to put the CAD system into different levels of the organization. Then most offices will use an hourly rate not to exceed type of contract and bill their time at normal office billing rates, plus an additional rate for time on the CAD system. The effect is that certain personnel have two billing rates—one with CAD time and one without.

An idiosyncrasy of a CAD system is the client who states, "You did the job faster, why should I pay the same fee as before?" This is an interesting problem that should be thoroughly understood. CAD affects an architect or engineer in two distinct ways. It allows certain jobs to be completed faster for the same fee you would charge without CAD. The difference in profit is the architect's or engineer's advantage that can be used to pay for the CAD system and contribute to the profitability of the firm. It also allows you to reduce your fee to be more competitive. This is not discounted work but a pricing strategy carefully worked out in advance. The architect or engineer is still entitled to a fair and equitable fee and should not reduce fees just because CAD is used.

What to expect. Another consideration when implementing a CAD system is management expectations. If goals are set too high, there can be disappointment in CAD's productivity. If goals are set too low, the productivity of the CAD system may not be realized. Most users agree that besides eventual increased productivity, other areas of the office are affected. There will be a higher quality of decisions made by the professional staff due to the wider range of alternatives that can be considered. With more data to analyze, the designer is able to reach a more intelligent solution. Design is essentially an evaluation of alternatives, and quality design generally reflects that more than one alternative has been fully explored. This in turn produces a tighter and more rigorous organization for the design process.

An example is a CAD system where the time of year, time of day, and project location can be input. Then the computer can graphically demonstrate the effect of the sun's angle by casting shadows on a perspective view of the project. You can change the date from a summer sun to a winter sun and see the corresponding change on both interior and exterior views. Or you can walk around a project or take a client through a project, room by room. Although this same information is available from charts and graphs, CAD lets you quickly see how the project will look and adjust overhangs quickly, rotate the project, and so on, as you look for the optimum solution. CAD provides a higher level of decision making that leads to a higher level of design than manual methods. CAD is a tool that helps designers produce better quality designs. As expert systems become more common, the computer will actually assist the designer in making decisions, and provide even more information for making decisions.

CAD creates additional services that can be offered to a client. An example is the ability to analyze the combinations of leasing packages available as a ratio of the floor area to the common area for the developer. CAD systems have demonstrated that money is being lost on a particular building because of incorrect square footage calculations, meaning the owner may not be getting the correct monthly lease or rent monies. These and other services do not occur overnight, but it's assured that the traditional scope of architectural and engineering services are changing rapidly and the architect and engineer should be looking for additional services to offer customers. This translates into additional profit opportunities, which should be thoroughly understood and discussed with reference to the annual business plan.

Marketing. Marketing considerations is why CAD has to become an important ingredient of every architectural and engineering office business plan. You might be doing well without CAD now, but who knows what the future will bring. With a successful CAD implementation, the office will enjoy several benefits:

- Better communications
- High-tech image
- Clients who feel that CAD will give them better projects
- Quicker schematic presentations
- More competitive than a non-CAD office
- Greater impact on construction documents
- Contractors who like CAD drawings
- Flexibility of what if scenarios
- Profit orientation
- Opportunities for additional services
- Evaluation of alternatives
- Marketing tool
- Structural analysis

These marketing benefits give the architect and engineer a wealth of advantages to offer clients, and the result is that the firm can create a more responsible and competitive construction environment. The need to address the issue of CAD via strong business planning methodologies is important as architecture and engineering catches up with high technology.

Platforms. One of the most difficult problems is deciding which computer platform to use. There are different applications within an office, as well as different users with different skills and fears. Fortunately, there are safeguards that make the process easier:

1. All competitive CAD software produced by recognized software vendors and used by architects and engineers has third-party packages and seminars and workshops available. These are dedicated to the architectural and engineering environment, so you can't really make a mistake. Again, the attitude and implementation process are at fault for a disastrous or a slow start.

2. Anytime you can get a computer into the office, no matter how, you are better off. If an employee offers to bring in a system, take it. An unknown Russian general once said that quantity has its own kind of quality.

3. The ideal situation is for an office to standardize on one type of system, DOS or Macintosh©, but this is often difficult to do. It is more important to get people to use anything, rather than worrying if they're using the right one.

DOS systems are generally lower in cost, have more software options, and are generally more compatible with other offices. They also typically require more training. Macintoshes© are easy to use because of its graphic orientation, user friendliness, and similarities among its software packages. What's the solution?

The solution is to let it happen. If an office decides to be 100 percent Macintosh©, or 100 percent DOS, that is fine. Or an office might evolve as follows: Its CAD systems tend to be DOS, using Intergraph Microstation© or AutoDESK© software with appropriate third-party application packages. The computers are networked to laser printers, pen plotters, and an electrostatic or direct thermal plotter. There might be one Macintosh system running software that is particularly useful for design considerations, such as Architrion©. Other stations in the office might be DOS or Macintosh, be individual in use, and be closely identified to the architect's or engineer's workstation concept. Eventually, a UNIX workstation might be introduced for added power and networking convenience.

The software and the user's ability will vary, with more exposure increasing the overall ability and comfort with the system. The reason for this mixture is that the two platforms are actually moving closer together. DOS systems are becoming more graphic oriented, particularly with Microsoft Windows© being available, and the Macintosh© is adding more power and compatibility with the DOS side. It's now possible to communicate between the two systems, eliminating many incompatibility issues.

Even in offices that are 100 percent CAD, there is still a need for the designer to be able to sketch initial concepts on paper. This intuitive hands-on approach is the best way to get a feel for the project. But at some point in the early preliminary stages, it starts making sense to input the information and build a database of information that will be used until the project is completed. Some architects and engineers feel that all of it can be done on the CAD system, but for most, the initial stages of design are best left to the drawing board. In any case, preliminary drawings used in presentations are much easier to generate, change, and refine on a CAD system.

Another important point is to realize that a logical starting place with CAD is to impact the drafting portion of the work, where the most monetary advantage can be gained. As you become more comfortable with this part of the system, you can start using a CAD system to help in the design portion of the work, such as site studies and massing or three-dimensional modeling. Implementation is a matter of focusing on a particular problem, such as construction documents, and when that is under control, move on to other levels of use.

It would be nice to have the financial wherewithal to design the best system, all networked appropriately, then have it installed at one time. But this does not happen. Computer systems tend to evolve. Corporations that have the ability to say all DOS or all Macintosh© may simplify the process but risk some potential rewards from not using the other system. It is a difficult call and the primary reason why the question of computers and CAD must be addressed from the perspective of the annual plan. Then and only then can planning be done that is tied together with budgets, expectations, and responsibilities. The only mistake one can really make is not to use a computer at all.

Management Perspectives

Management in architecture and engineering is something that just seems to happen. Most architects and engineers concentrate on their specialty, while minimizing their management effort. Other professions spend more time and energy on management, as they realize good management has a positive effect on a company. Thus, while mainstream businesses (i.e., manufacturing and industry) spend time and money training top business school graduates for management positions, architects and engineers spend time on architecture and engineering. When success does arrive at the architect's or engineer's front door and the practice grows, the architect or engineer is suddenly a manager. With no former education in business concepts compared to those in the mainstream corporate world and with no real in-house preparation, the architect or engineer begins the task of coordination and takes on financial responsibilities. Quite often, it's beyond one's experience.

Thus, not only is business management thrust upon architects or engineers, but they are faced with managing a complex business. New commissions must be carefully contracted for, design problems must be solved, working drawings must reflect economic considerations, construction contracts and construction observation must be made in accordance with prescribed guidelines, additional services must continually be developed into opportunities, and all of this must be tied together with the necessary human resources and expertise to keep the office going. Overshadowing all of these activities is the continual pressure to keep within the client's construction budget and your estimated budget to do the work. This is not only a large task, for many it is an impossible task.

The dilemma of being caught between architecture and management and always having to sweat out payrolls, mortgage payments, consultant fees on a timely basis, and so on, is for some what architecture is all about. There has always been, and always will be, a fraternal aspect of architecture. It is first noticed in school by the long hours spent to meet design problem deadlines. This rite of passage continues, as the romantic image of the architect as the suffering artist.[27] Thus, the management problems the architect contends with are for some an outgrowth of this fraternity and the link to their own image. This is a large part of how architects are thought of by the public they serve.

But times are changing, and architects and engineers are realizing that they must take managerial responsibility for their firm, or the firm will fail in spite of their design prowess. Clearly, the business of business is business. Architecture or engineering is a business and must be managed and directed from that point of view. Success at this level allows one the opportunity to continue to design and to do quality work. Architecture is an art form and will always be judged from an artistic viewpoint. However, a firm must be financially successful, or it will fail. It's that position that points the way toward success.

Where to start?

When an architect or engineer looks at what is needed to know about business, the task suddenly becomes overwhelming. How can you both manage a business at a professional level and still keep track of what is happening with architecture or engineering itself, let alone clients and current construction jobs? The answer is straightforward—the business plan. The business plan is the best starting point for looking at and getting a handle on all the business management aspects with which you have to contend. If you take the time to build an annual plan, with all the proper parts as outlined, it will address all the major issues with which you should be concerned. Necessary conversations with legal counsel and accountants will occur because of the business plan topics that require discussion; budgets will be looked at in relationship to the marketing strategies that have been determined and the resulting programs. All of this is based upon the goals and objectives of the firm, which summarizes the overall direction the firm is taking. The S/W and O/T analysis will be done in light of the problems, challenges, and advantages the firm uncovers and addresses.

Then the plan and the implementation of the plan become the focus points for additional learning. The plan becomes the platform for reading and investigation. If you need to understand cash flow, you can obtain accounting books. If you need a better understanding of marketing and strategy, you can get additional information as background material. The plan serves as a guide, as a light in a dark tunnel, as a tutor, as a messenger. During the year, situations may occur that suggest additional research into specific areas. These can be discussed at the month-end operational meetings. At the end of the year, the *opportunity* presents itself to go through the annual planning process and assess the changes and impact from last year's plan and its implementation. Where do we stand? Did we make the plan? Did the staff perform the way we had projected? The plan becomes the focus point for intelligent business conversations and for banking and accounting relationships. The business plan provides the outline for business achievement and changes and grows as the architect or engineer changes and grows.

The starting point is the business plan. The continued educational process is letting the business plan suggest areas that need further investigation. For example, as a plan is reviewed or at a monthly operations meeting, you might note that a contract problem with a client poses a threat. The client might be claiming that although a contract exists, the architect or engineer had misrepresented the services in the first meeting. The client might also threaten not to pay the entire fee. After discussion, this real and current threat might point out a weakness in how the first meeting was conducted. Upon reviewing the situation, an objective might be set to review the meeting and documentation process for the firm and improve on it.

After meeting with legal counsel, the conclusion might be to send a letter to each new client after the first meeting and before any contract signing, stating what the firm can do, what the firm cannot do, that there are no guarantees on certain zoning or planning requests, that there are no budget restrictions if constant changes are made to the program, and so on. Basically, the letter states whatever the situation requires. This improved client communication limits future liability in terms of client misconceptions.

The letter is a direct result from the analysis done in developing an annual business plan and the resulting goals and objectives. In this case, the situation might be considered a threat to the firm. As one uses the plan concept honestly, it will provide a dynamically changing outline of what is important and what is not important for the business to survive. And it will do this at the level the firm is at in terms of business growth, understanding, and development. Hence, the business plan written today will be different from the one written 3 years from now. Likewise, the contributors will grow, and together they will take on new challenges and attack them at new levels of business sophistication.

The business plan will point out many ideas and concepts to the contributors of the plan, for the plan is like a mirror that reflects ideas back as clearly as it presents them. There is always a new way to look at a subject, and the business plan allows you the latitude to try new ideas in a constructive, organized approach.

As presented at the beginning of this book, architecture and engineering work within a specific environment manifested by many misconceptions about business. Sooner or later these problems are addressed in any honest business plan development. You will find out by working through an annual business plan, from marketing to budgeting, from strategic planning to opportunities and threats, that an architect's or engineer's time is not free; it is a very valuable resource for the firm. You will see that fee cutting is counterproductive to the firm's intent and interest, that marketing is an essential ingredient to a firm's future, that fee collections must be done to ensure a proper business relationship with clients and to maintain a cash position, that a firm must account for cost overruns and seek proper financial remuneration when appropriate to do so, that contracts are the vital link between the architect or engineer and the client and is the main vehicle that outlines commensuration, that liability issues must be addressed to ensure protection of a firm's equity, and that CAD is one of the keys to future survivability. That's just the beginning.

The business plan offers a road map that reflects where the firm has been, where the firm wants to go, and how the firm proposes to get there. Working with this road map is smart and reflects managerial responsibility. Not working with this road map reflects a lack of understanding of how valuable the road map is to the firm's management, employees, and clients, all of whom expect leadership and professionalism. The burden of proof is always on the architect, engineer, or owner to manage effectively; sooner or later, management expertise will prevail. Undertaking the business plan philosophy will produce some interesting experiences. First, you will find out that clients like to do business with architects and engineers who understand business. Clients need design creativity, but they also need to work with architects and engineers who understand business thinking. As you move further into the business arena, you will find that an understanding of finance, marketing, and sales is a clear advantage. The concepts presented in this book are tools. As Buckminster Fuller said, "How tools are used is not the responsibility of the inventor." It's the responsibility of each individual architect and engineer to the profession and to the public he or she serves.

Business Planning Strategies

7

Selecting the Form of Doing Business

When establishing a practice, the architect or engineer must decide the legal form of doing business. Should the architect or engineer operate as a sole proprietorship or as a corporation? Further, as the practice grows, architects and engineers practicing as sole proprietors or as partners should consider whether to reform as a corporation.

Forms of Doing Business

There are three basic forms of doing business: (1) sole proprietorship, (2) partnership, and (3) corporation. Partnerships may be general partnerships or limited partnerships. In most states, corporations may be either general business corporations or professional corporations. In some states, however, design professionals may incorporate only as professional corporations. In addition, under the Internal Revenue Code certain small business corporations may receive favorable income tax treatment by electing Subchapter S status.

A sole proprietorship is a business consisting of a single *owner* who receives all the income from the business, pays all the expenses, owns all the assets, and bears the risk for any of the losses. Further, the business is not incorporated as a corporation.

Architects or engineers who practice out of an office or at home are the prime examples of the sole proprietor. They may not even have employees. However, many such practitioners have a secretary and one or two people working for them. These are usually architects or engineers who receive smaller commissions, although some of them do significant work.

The Uniform Partnership Act, adopted in the majority of the states, defines a partnership as "an association of two or more persons to carry on as co-owners of a business for profit."[28] The partners own the business and divide the income of the partnership among themselves. However, each partner is individually responsible for paying all the expenses of the partnership and each is liable for all the debts and losses of the business.

Partnerships may consist of two or more people. The typical architectural or engineering partnership has less than 10 partners, although some large national design firms have dozens of partners. Some large national certified public accounting firms have hundreds of partners.

A corporation is a distinct legal person owned by its shareholders and formed under the laws of a specific state. The corporation itself receives the income from the business and owns the assets. The corporation, not its shareholders or owners, is liable for the debts and losses of the business. The major difference between a sole proprietorship or a partnership and a corporation is the limited liability of the owners of a corporation for its debts.

What Factors Should Be Considered?

Many factors should be considered by the design professional when deciding which form of business to adopt. These factors are

1. The need to limit the liability of the owner or owners of the business
2. The need for permanence
3. Transferability of ownership
4. Expense of forming the enterprise
5. Number of owners
6. Management
7. Financing requirements
8. Public laws
9. Taxation

Limiting liability

Architects and engineers, like anyone else, prefer to limit their responsibility to pay debts and losses. The major advantage of a corporation is that ordinarily its owners are not personally liable for the debts incurred by the corporation. In a sole proprietorship or a partnership, the owners are personally liable for the debts of the business. They are personally responsible for paying rent, salaries, telephone, mail, and other expenses of the business if those expenses cannot be paid by the proprietorship or partnership due to lack of available cash.

The owner of a business who has substantial personal assets would most likely prefer to protect those assets from having to be used to pay the debts of the business. Thus, an architect or engineer who has a large amount of equity in a house, considerable personal property, and savings in the form of cash, stocks, and other securities may not desire to practice as a sole proprietor or as a partner. He or she would probably prefer to be an owner or a part owner of a practice which is doing business as a corporation.

An architect or engineer who does not have many assets to protect may not care whether his or her liability is unlimited. As an example, a young architect or engineer who is starting a new practice may have no qualms about working as a sole proprietor or with one or two other architects or engineers as a partnership. Further, he or she may be able to protect himself or herself from claims for malpractice by purchasing professional liability insurance.

As a common matter, however, even though architects and engineers have incorporated their practice, they still may be liable for certain of its debts. Banks or other financial institutions ordinarily will not lend money to a small business unless repayment of the loan is personally guaranteed by the owners of the business. Further, as will be discussed in Chap. 9, incorporation may not limit the liability of all the architects or engineers who are owners of the corporation.

Under the law, employees of a corporation who are found guilty of negligence to a third party are liable to that party for damages. The corporation is also liable to the third party if the employee was acting within the scope of his or her duties as an employee of the corporation when the employee committed the negligence. Thus, if the employee is one of the owners of the corporation, the owner-employee may still be personally liable for damages resulting from his or her negligence.

For example, suppose an architect or engineer who is a shareholder or owner of the corporation negligently designs a portion of a building which results in injury to another person. The injured party sues both the architect or engineer and the corporation and recovers a judgment against the corporation and its employee, the architect or engineer. Under such circumstances, both the corporation and the employee, even though the architect or engineer is one of the owners of the corporation, are responsible for paying the judgment. If the corporation has purchased sufficient professional liability insurance covering both the corporation and its employees, both the architect or engineer and the corporation may be protected.

Permanence

A sole proprietorship ceases to exist when the proprietor either decides to go out of business or dies. A partnership ordinarily is dissolved when any partner so desires, when all the partners so agree, when one partner is expelled pursuant to the provisions of the partnership agreement, when the partnership agreement is breached by one or more of the partners, when a partner dies, when one partner or the partnership becomes bankrupt, or when a court so decrees.[29]

Corporations do not face the same limitations on existence faced by sole proprietorships or partnerships. The death of an owner does not result in dissolution of a corporation. A corporation does not cease to exist if either one of its shareholders or it becomes bankrupt. Ordinarily, one owner cannot force the dissolution of a corporation.

If the goal of the founders of a design practice is to continue the practice indefinitely, the corporation is the preferable form of doing business. However, there have been some partnerships that have continued for years, despite the death and retirement of partners and the admission of new partners. Partnerships can continue for decades if they are governed by carefully drafted partnership agreements which handle, among other things, the withdrawal of partners due to retirement, resignation, or death and the admission of new partners.

Ownership transfer

The ability to sell all or part of a business may be advantageous to its owners. A sole proprietorship may be sold by having the proprietor take the necessary legal steps. The proprietorship may admit new investors in the practice either by forming a partnership with the new investors, effectively continuing the business as a partnership, or by forming a corporation, transferring the business of the proprietorship to the corporation and selling shares in the corporation to the new investors.

Ownership of a share of a partnership may be difficult to transfer. Usually, the withdrawal of a partner by the act of selling his or her interest will result in dissolution of the partnership. Sales of proprietorships and partnerships also may be hindered by creditors. With most proprietorships and partnerships, creditors rely in whole or in part upon the ability of the proprietors or partners to pay the debts of the business. Partial ownership in a corporation may be easier to transfer. Ordinarily, all that is required is for the shareholder to transfer all or part of his or her shares of the corporation to a new investor.

Transferability of ownership interest may be extremely important to investors who do not want to participate in the management of the business but would like to earn money from the increasing value of their investment, which they hope is due to the on-going profitability of the business. Such investors or capitalists prefer to invest in a business where their liability is limited to the amount of their investment, where the business is permanent, and where their ownership interest may be easily transferred. A corporation normally fulfills these objectives.

In a small corporation, sale of a part interest in the corporation may not be possible. An investment in a small business usually is permanent until the firm is sold. Many investors do not want to invest in a business whose existence depends upon the management success of one person or a handful of people.

Formation expense

The sole proprietorship is the most inexpensive business to organize. Usually no formal legal requirements are necessary. The proprietor merely goes into business. Of course, doing so may involve renting space for an office, which ordinarily entails a written lease, but there is no need for a written partnership agreement or the expense of incorporation.

Partnerships usually are more expensive to form. Although a partnership may be formed without a written partnership agreement, most architects and engineers find it advisable to retain a lawyer to draft a partnership agreement at the time the business is started or a short time thereafter.

A corporation may be the most expensive form of business organization to establish. A lawyer must be retained to draft articles of incorporation and bylaws. Further, the lawyer must file the articles and bylaws with the appropriate state official and obtain a charter from that official. Annual filings have to be made with the state, and an annual shareholders' meeting must be held.

Fortunately, most states have streamlined their corporate statutes so it is much more simple and inexpensive to comply with the formal legal requirements. Further, many forms required for incorporation and continued maintenance of the corporation are available to attorneys on computer tapes, reducing their work. Thus, the formation and maintenance of a small corporation may be inexpensive for most design professionals.

Number of owners

As a general rule, as the number of owners of a business increases, the corporate form of organization becomes more preferable. Increasing the number of partners indicates that the business will become permanent. As mentioned before, permanency favors the corporate form of business.

Management

Management of the sole proprietorship is easiest. There is only one owner, and he or she can make any business decision without consulting with anyone else. Management of a partnership may be difficult, on the other hand, because each partner is a general agent of the partnership. Technically, a partner may bind the partnership. Even though the partnership agreement may be strict or define the authority of the partners, such an agreement is not binding on the outside world or on those who do business with the partnership.

Management of a corporation is more controlled. The specific authority of each officer of a corporation is delegated by the board of directors or is contained in the articles of incorporation, bylaws of the corporation, or relevant state statutes. Ordinarily, only an officer or employee of the corporation with appropriate authority may bind the corporation.

Financing

Outside investors, who will not participate in the management of the business but are needed to raise capital for the enterprise, may prefer that the business be organized as a corporation. If borrowed funds will be needed for the business, the owners probably will prefer to incorporate in order to limit their liability for the debts of the business.

Public laws

At one time, some states would not permit architects or engineers to incorporate their practices. This limitation has been removed in all states.

Taxation

The profits of both a sole proprietorship and a partner are taxed as personal income under the Internal Revenue Code. There is no double taxation, which may occur when the corporate form of organization is adopted.

Under the Internal Revenue Code, federal taxes must be paid on a corporation's net income. If the owners are employees of the corporation, their salaries and bonuses, along with other expenses, are deducted from revenue to arrive at the net income of the corporation. If any of the net income is paid to the owners as dividends, the dividends are taxed as personal income. In addition, states tax corporate income.

Corporations have to pay a fee or tax when incorporated. Further, some states charge corporations an annual franchise fee.

Corporations also may be subject to federal accumulated earnings tax. Congress was concerned that some corporations accumulate income above the sums needed for the business and not pay out these funds as dividends to the owners to avoid personal income tax. Thus, a federal tax may be assessed against accumulated taxable income. The tax is not due upon funds retained for a reasonable business need, as long as there is a plan for the use of such funds.[30]

Certain small business corporations may avoid double taxation on their income by adopting Subchapter S status. In that case, the corporation does not pay federal income tax on its net income. Instead, the income is passed through to the shareholders, who pay personal income tax on their shares of the net income. Thus, the shareholders pay income tax on the corporation's income as if they were proprietors of or partners in the business.

Use of Subchapter S status is limited to certain small businesses. Further, each shareholder must consent to its adoption. Moreover, the corporation can have no more than 35 shareholders; for purposes of the Internal Revenue Code, a husband and wife are considered as one shareholder.

Sole Proprietorship

The sole proprietorship is the easiest form of business to organize. No special steps are required. The architect or engineer just finds a place to practice and goes into business. He or she provides all the funds for running the business. If there are profits, they belong to the owner. If there are losses, the owner must bear them.

Most design professionals practice as small businesses. At most, they may have one or two secretaries and one to a dozen architects, engineers, or other professionals working for them.

A sole proprietorship terminates when the owner decides to quit or retire or dies. The business may not be easily sold.

The income of a sole proprietor is treated as personal income for federal income tax. The sole proprietor reports the income and expenses from the practice when filing his or her personal income tax return. Any profit from the practice is taxed at the personal tax rates.

The main drawback of the sole proprietorship is that the owner faces unlimited liability. He or she is responsible for all the debts of the business, which includes any damages due to the negligence of the proprietor or any employee.

Another drawback is that certain fringe benefits which may be deductible as business expenses for a corporation are not for a proprietorship. A corporation may deduct medical insurance and certain life insurance premiums for its employees. A sole proprietorship may not.

Since a sole proprietor is considered as self-employed for federal income tax purposes, federal income taxes are not withheld from the owner's income. Instead, the owner must make quarterly estimated tax payments.

Partnerships

There are two basic forms of partnerships: general partnerships and limited partnerships. A general partnership consists of two or more general partners, each of whom has unlimited liability for the debts of the partnership. A limited partnership consists of one or more general partners, each of whom has unlimited liability for the debts of the partnership and one or more limited partners whose liability for the debts of the partnership is limited to the amount of their investment in the partnership.

Most, if not all, architectural and engineering partnerships are general partnerships. Limited partnerships were extremely popular before Congress adopted the Tax Reform Act of 1986. They were then widely used among real estate investors and gas and oil well promoters.

General partnerships

Partners, employees of a partnership, and members of the public usually consider a partnership to be a separate entity, distinct from its partners. This image is enhanced because partnerships usually conduct business from a partnership office, use partnership stationery, and maintain separate books of account. Moreover, clients contract with the partnership to perform design services. In addition, the Uniform Partnership Act provides that real estate may be purchased in the partnership name.[31] Further, the Act acknowledges the difference between "partnership creditors" and "individual creditors" and "partnership assets" and "individual assets."[32]

No particular legal requirements need be met to establish a general partnership. All that is necessary is for two or more people to intend to enter into business with each other as partners. If no written partnership agreement is entered into among the partners, the rights and obligations of the partners are governed by state partnership law.

To avoid potential misunderstandings among the partners and certain problems which may arise under partnership law, most partners sign partnership agreements. The partnership agreement may be amended or replaced as the partnership matures. The concerns of two or three engineers or architects who just formed a partnership, for example, are different from several architects or engineers who have worked as partners for decades and may be facing retirement.

The partnership agreement should cover many subjects. The general partners should be identified, and the name of the partnership should be established. The architects and engineers should agree what type of work they will do, based on their business plan. The location of the business should be identified.

The duration of the partnership should be considered in the agreement. Will the partnership last only as long as all the partners agree or until the death of one of the partners? Or will the partnership continue to exist even though one partner resigns or withdraws from the partnership or dies? Under the Uniform Partnership Act, a partnership terminates when one partner so desires or dies. This rule can be modified by the partnership agreement.

Many design partnerships have continued practicing for decades, during which time partners have resigned, retired, or died and new partners have been admitted. This is possible because of carefully drafted partnership agreements which cover such eventualities.

The relevant provisions of partnership agreements must handle how the withdrawing partner's capital shall be returned. Will he or she get it immediately or will it be repaid over a period of time? These provisions also must state whether the withdrawing partner is entitled to any share of the profits of the partnership for the year in which the partner retired and whether the partner is entitled to any share of the profits in the years after retirement.

The partnership agreement should indicate the amount of the capital investment of each partner. It may also state under what conditions a partner may be required to make additional capital investments. Further, each partner's share of the profits should be provided for in the agreement. The partners need not share equally in the profits.

Draws also should be covered by the agreement. Technically, partners do not receive salaries from the partnership. They usually receive monthly draws against the potential profits of the partnership. It is hoped that the monthly draws of the partners be less than or equal to the annual profits of the partnership. If not, a portion of the draws are being paid from the capital of the business.

Management of the partnership is usually delineated in the agreement. If there are dozens of partners, provisions may be made for a management committee, usually annually elected by the partners, to govern the daily management of the business. In smaller partnerships, the agreement should detail the duties and authority of each of the partners.

Usually, one partner is named the senior or managing partner and acts as chief executive of the partnership. The authority of individual partners to commit the partnership to significant undertakings, such as entering into leases, should be limited. Major transactions should only be entered into by the management committee, duly authorized partners, or a vote of the partners.

For general partnerships with only a few partners, the agreement should contain some means to resolve deadlocks among partners. Should the votes of one or more partners be given more weight than those of the other partners? Should some form of arbitration be mandatory?

Many partnership agreements also state which partners may sign partnership checks, make bank loans, hire firm employees, and determine employee salaries. They also may contain provisions concerning the fiscal year and accounting arrangements for the partnership.

Usually, there are no state fees or taxes for organizing a partnership. However, some states require the partnership to file a document with a county official listing the name and location of the partnership and the names of the partners. These are often called assumed name statutes.

Many small businesses fail because they lack adequate capital. Although a design practice may not require the investment of a retail establishment or a small manufacturing business, it still requires substantial capital. In the initial stages of the practice, as presentations are developed and presented, no income will be coming in from commissions. During this time, operating expenses must be paid and the firm will have to purchase equipment and furniture.

Funds to establish and run a partnership come from three main sources: capital investments of the partners, the partnership, and eventually commissions. Capital contributions are made in the form of cash or other property, such as office furniture and computer equipment. The partners must agree on the value of noncash capital contributions.

There may be disparities among the partners as to their abilities to contribute capital to the partnership. One method of handling unequal capital contributions is to provide for payment of interest at a prescribed rate on the capital contributions of each partner. The interest comes from the income of the partnership. After provisions are made for the payment of interest on capital contributions, the remainder of the profits are distributed to the partners pursuant to the terms of the partnership agreement.

Frequently, a partner may not be able to make any capital contribution, but his or her services to the partnership may be extremely valuable. Or the partnership may be undercapitalized and more capital may be required to conduct the business successfully. In both cases, the partners may agree to withhold certain percentages of income of the partners to build up individual capital accounts. In such instances, the partners for whom the capital contributions are being withheld would have to pay federal income tax on both the amount of the profits paid to them and the amount withheld for the capital contribution.

Loans may be furnished to the partners from financial institutions, other sources, or the partners themselves. If partners lend money to the partnership, the partnership agreement or some other document, such as a promissory note, should state the amount of interest to be paid to the partner. In addition, a method for repayment of the loan should be provided.

One of the major drawbacks of partnership is that each partner is an agent of the partnership. Under the Uniform Partnership Act a commitment made by a partner in the normal course of business binds the partnership, unless the partner had no authority to bind the partnership and the other person was aware that the partner did not have authority to bind the partnership.[33]

Another shortcoming of doing business as a partnership is the unlimited liability of each of the partners. Each partner is personally liable for all of the debts of the partnership. If one of the partners or an employee commits negligence which results in personal injury or damage to another person, the partnership as well as each partner may be liable for the entire amount of the damages.

Retiring partners remain liable for debts the firm incurred before their retirement. In addition, they remain liable for negligence claims if they arose before retirement. A retiring partner is also liable for debts of the partnership incurred after retirement, unless an appropriate notice is printed in a newspaper of general circulation.[34]

Frequently, a partnership will agree to indemnify retiring partners for debts of the partnership, even for those incurred before retirement. Indemnification may be necessary not only to encourage older partners to retire but also to prevent dissolution and liquidation of the partnership upon retirement. However, indemnification may not be fair to the remaining partners. This is true if a sizable debt was incurred while the retired partner was still active in the partnership or if the retired partner committed malpractice resulting in substantial damage to someone. The detrimental effect of the latter event can be minimized if the partnership can obtain adequate professional liability insurance.

New partners in an existing partnership may be concerned about their liability for partnership debts incurred before their admission. Unless otherwise agreed, the incoming partner is liable for preexisting debts of the partnership, but his or her liability may be satisfied only out of partnership property.[35] Thus, at most, a new partner only risks his or her capital contribution to the extent he or she is liable for prior debts of the partnership.

Limited partnerships

A limited partnership only may be formed by complying with the statute. A certificate must be filed with the appropriate state agency containing the specifics of the partnership.

Limited partners may contribute cash or other property, but not services, as capital to the partnership. The liability of the limited partner may not exceed the amount of his or her capital contribution. In order to limit liability, the limited partner must not participate in the management or control of the partnership. If he or she does, liability of the limited partner for partnership debts becomes unlimited.

A limited partnership may be used to entice investors into contributing capital to the partnership without fear of unlimited liability. However, limited partnerships are rarely, if ever, used by architects or engineers.

Corporations

Depending upon the state in which the business incorporates, architects and engineers may incorporate as either general business corporations or professional corporations or have a choice of either one. As an example, architects or engineers may incorporate in Illinois either under general corporation statute or the professional corporation statute. The licensing law of Illinois for architects and engineers does not place any limitation upon the state under which architects or engineers may be incorporated. New Jersey, however, only allows architects and engineers to practice as a corporation if the firm is incorporated as a professional corporation.

The main difference between a general business corporation and a professional corporation is that anyone may be a shareholder of a general business corporation, whereas only a registered architect (or engineer) may be a shareholder of a professional corporation engaging in the profession of architecture (or engineering). Further, a professional corporation may be restricted to a professional practice, whereas an architectural or engineering firm incorporated as a general business corporation may be allowed to engage in a wide variety of business activities.

A design firm can obtain certain benefits if it incorporates and practices under a state general business corporation act. Capital may be obtained from investors who are not architects or engineers. Nonregistered members of the firm can be given or be allowed to purchase shares to reward them for past and future efforts on behalf of the corporation. A top quality marketing director or business manager may be easier to hire or retain if he or she can become a shareholder of the corporation.

Even though Illinois allows architects and engineers to practice as general business corporations, the Illinois corporation may not be allowed to practice architecture or engineering in those states which restrict practice to professional corporations. Under such circumstances, an architect or engineer personally registered in the state must either accept the contract in his or her own name and subcontract performance of it to the Illinois general business corporation or registered architects or engineers who are shareholders or employees of the Illinois corporation must form a professional corporation to accept the contract.

Whether incorporating as a general business corporation or a professional corporation, incorporation of a design practice has several distinct advantages. The major one is the limited liability of the shareholders.

A corporation is formed in compliance with the laws of a particular state. Each of the states has statutes governing the formation, operation, and dissolution of corporations. Many architectural and engineering firms incorporate in the state of the principal place of business. However, some firms may incorporate in Delaware, which has historically had liberal corporation laws.

A corporation is a distinct entity or person. It is separate from its owners. The corporation acts on its own and in its own name. A corporation may enter contracts and buy and sell property. It may hire employees. It may sue in its own name and be sued.

Most states require a minimal capital contribution to form a corporation. When investors make a capital contribution, they are given shares of stock in the corporation and are known as shareholders.

A majority of small business and professional corporations have one class of stock referred to as common stock or common shares. Common shareholders have the right to vote for the directors of the corporation at the annual shareholders' meeting. In addition, certain changes to the corporation's articles of incorporation and bylaws, such as increasing the number of shares, must be voted upon by the shareholders.

Occasionally, a small business corporation will create a second class of stock called preferred stock. Preferred shareholders ordinarily receive a fixed dividend payment on their stock, and their dividends are paid first out of profits of the corporation.

Usually, if the funds are available, the preferred shareholders must be paid their dividends. The common shareholders are paid dividends from the profits of the corporation. The amount of the dividends are determined by the board of directors.

Although corporations must have directors and officers, have by-laws, hold annual meetings, keep minutes, and comply with other formalities, most state laws permit easy methods of meeting these requirements. In fact, in most states a corporation may exist with only one shareholder, who may be the sole director and officer.

Ordinarily, the board of directors of a corporation sets policy for the corporation and selects the officers. The officers of the corporation are charged with managing the daily business of the corporation.

A shareholder may sell his or her interest in a corporation by selling his or her shares of stock. For most small corporations this may be impractical, however, since no effective market exists for the sale of a partial interest in a closely held corporation. Further, the shareholders may agree to restrict their rights to sell their shares to prevent investment by unwelcomed outsiders in the corporation.

As mentioned earlier, one of the main disadvantages of a corporation is that it is subject to double taxation and other forms of taxes not assessed against sole proprietorships or partnerships. The limited liability of a corporation, however, makes it a more attractive vehicle under which to practice architecture or engineering than a sole proprietorship or a partnership.

Joint Ventures

Architectural and engineering firms frequently enter into joint ventures with other firms. A joint venture is formed by two or more entities to carry out a specific project and ordinarily dissolves upon completion of the project.

In the construction industry, two architectural or two engineering firms may form a joint venture to provide the design for a project. Or an architectural firm and one or more engineering firms may form a joint venture to design a project. Or a design firm and a contractor may form a joint venture to design and construct a project.

Joint ventures are common in international business. For instance, design firms from separate countries may form joint ventures to design projects in the host country. Or a foreign design firm may form a joint venture with a host country design firm.

Members of a joint venture may be sole proprietorship, partnerships, or corporations. No formalities are required to form a joint venture, although frequently the parties will agree to a joint venture agreement.

Joint ventures are similar to partnerships, and many aspects of the relationship of the coventurers, such as sharing profits and losses, are governed by partnership law. However, some authorities hold that the authority of a coventure to bind a joint venture is more limited than a general partner's authority to bind a partnership.

Terminating the Business

Not all architectural or engineering practices last forever. The practice of a sole proprietor terminates when the architect or engineer decides to practice no longer on his or her own, retires, or dies. Winding up the affairs of the business is usually simple. All you need do is be sure debts are paid and bills are collected.

Architects or engineers practicing as a partnership or a corporation may no longer desire to practice together for any number of reasons. The practice may not be profitable or a key member of the firm may desire to pursue other opportunities. Frequently, personalities may clash, resulting in the need to dissolve the business or replace one or more of the members. Also, partners or members of the firm may retire or die. Any of these reasons may be sufficient for the members of the firm to dissolve the practice.

If the architects or engineers are practicing as a partnership, the Uniform Partnership Act outlines the steps necessary to terminate the practice. First, there must be a change in the relationship among the partners, such as a death of one partner or the desire of the partners to cease practicing together. This results in a dissolution of the partnership.[36] After dissolution, the partners wind up the business of the partnership.[37] This involves gathering and disposing of the assets of the partnership, such as collecting accounts receivable. Then the bills of the partnership are paid.

If there are any assets left in the partnership after all of the creditors have been paid, those partners who have made loans or advances to the partnership are paid. Next, capital contributions are returned to the partners. Finally, all remaining property is distributed to the partners pursuant to the manner in which profits are distributed.[38]

What if the partnership does not have enough funds to pay all the creditors? In such an event, the partners must contribute additional funds to the partnership. The contributions are based on the manner in which the partners share the losses of the partnership. If one partner pays all of the balance or more than his or her share, then he or she is entitled to indemnification from the other partners.[39]

Dissolution of a corporation occurs when it ceases to exist as a corporation. This happens either voluntarily, such as when the corporation is no longer doing business and surrenders its charter, or involuntarily, such as when the state terminates the corporation's charter for failure to pay the annual franchise fees.

In a voluntary dissolution, the assets of the corporation are sold and the creditors paid before dissolution. Any assets left are distributed to shareholders; preferred shareholders are paid first. If not all debts can be paid, the creditors bear the loss.

If the business is insolvent, the owners may desire to seek the protection of bankruptcy under the federal bankruptcy laws administered by the U.S. bankruptcy courts. A sole proprietor may declare personal bankruptcy. Partnerships also may declare bankruptcy, but the partners are not immune from creditors of the partnership unless the partners declare personal bankruptcy. Corporations also may declare bankruptcy.

Bankruptcy is often a last resort. It usually is less expensive to attempt to liquidate the business without bankruptcy. In that case, the creditors may receive a better recovery—in both amount and speed.

Planning: Legal Strategies

Regardless of the size of a practice, architects and engineers must give some thought to legal problems and issues which may affect the firm in the future. Architects and engineers should not wait for legal problems to arise before addressing them. They need to identify possible legal issues which may arise, as well as what can be done to avoid them.

The typical design firm will face the following legal issues during its history:

From whom should it seek legal advice?

What form of business should it adopt?

What form of professional services agreement should it use?

What steps can be taken to collect sums owed it by a client?

How can the firm protect its clients from potential competitors?

How can the firm protect itself from errors of consultants?

What can the firm do to protect itself from professional liability claims?

Selecting a form of business was discussed in Chap. 7. Insurance is considered in Chap. 9. Professional services agreements will be discussed in Chap. 10. This chapter discusses the remaining topics.

Selecting an Attorney

Regardless of the size of the design firm, the architect or engineer should look for an attorney who is experienced in representing design professionals. Most large metropolitan areas have several attorneys who regularly represent architects and engineers. Such attorneys readily appreciate the unique legal problems facing design professionals and are experienced in addressing those problems.

There are several reasons why the architect or engineer should seek such a lawyer. First, little or no time should be required by the client to educate the lawyer about the client's practice and profession. Because of his or her experience representing design professionals, the attorney should have the necessary background. Second, although the architect or engineer may think a particular problem is unusual, the problem may be routine for an experienced attorney. The attorney may have worked upon a resolution of the issues with other clients. Thus, the attorney will be more efficient, saving legal time and fees for the client. Third, the lawyer will be able to apprise the design professional of legal issues affecting the practice of which the architect or engineer is unaware. Fourth, the attorney will know other professionals, such as insurance brokers, who regularly work with architects and engineers and can help the design professional.

Attorneys who regularly represent architects and engineers also are experienced in defending design professionals in malpractice or professional liability suits. Because they are experienced in this area, they usually are better able to defend the architect or engineer.

The architect or engineer should not only work with an attorney who is experienced in representing design professionals, but also one who can help with other legal questions, such as the form of doing business, estate planning, and employee benefit plans. Because most attorneys tend to specialize and are not proficient in all areas of legal practice, the architect or engineer should look for an attorney who is with a law firm which has lawyers with different expertise or who can refer the client to attorneys with particular specialties.

The architect or engineer should interview an attorney before retaining him or her. The purpose of the interview is to select an attorney who is best suited to represent the architect or engineer regularly, to find an attorney with whom you can work and who is experienced in representing design professionals, and to select an attorney who will be reasonable. Quite frequently, architects and engineers have questions about law pertaining to professional service agreements or construction contract documents that an attorney should be able to answer over the telephone, sometimes after a speedy review of pertinent contract documents or provisions. An attorney who cannot be reached or who does not return phone calls, despite his or her experience, may not be the best attorney for you.

Thus, the architect or engineer should look for an attorney who is experienced in representing design professionals, has access to other legal specialists, and is responsive to your requests for assistance.

The attorney also expects certain things from the architect or engineer. Always be candid with your lawyer when seeking legal advice. If you hold back critical facts, you may not get the best and may even get erroneous advice. Since you may not always be aware of the significant facts, be prepared to explain the complete story to your lawyer.

The architect or engineer should not expect the attorney to know everything about a designer's practice. Even though the lawyer may be familiar with architecture or engineering, no attorney knows as much about the subject as the experienced design professional.

When interviewing an attorney, ask about the hourly rate for legal services and billing practices. Expect to pay more for an experienced attorney than an inexperienced one. The efficiency of the experienced attorney usually outweighs the lower hourly rate of the inexperienced attorney.

Most attorneys prefer to bill monthly for counseling. Occasionally, they will bill upon the completion of a specific project or lawsuit. Normally, monthly billing is preferable for the client because it allows for better control of legal costs.

Finally, what if the architect or engineer cannot locate an experienced attorney in representing design professionals in his or her community? There are several alternatives. First, the design professional may look for an attorney in a nearby community. The expense of long-distance phone calls and occasional trips may be counterbalanced by the assistance such a lawyer can render.

Second, the architect or engineer may be able to locate an attorney in his or her community who regularly represents contractors. Such an attorney may be familiar with the construction process and thus be able to assist the architect or engineer.

Third, the architect or engineer can locate a competent attorney who is willing to learn about representing design professionals. Although efficiency may be sacrificed at first, the attorney may become proficient over time. Further, there are many books, publications, and legal services to help attorneys learn about representing architects and engineers and keep current upon recent legal developments.

Strategies for Collecting Accounts Receivable

A major problem facing architects and engineers is collecting outstanding invoices for fees and disbursements, especially when the economy is depressed. Fortunately, architects and engineers have one tool which can help them collect overdue invoices—the mechanic's lien. Unfortunately, many design professionals fail to use liens effectively to secure payment of their invoices.

The first step most architects and engineers can take to limit uncollectible fees is to select their clients carefully. Just as clients select architects and engineers based upon experience, fees, and design concepts for a particular project, so should the architect or engineer select a client.

What should a design professional look for in a client? First, determine if the client has the ability to pay the fee even if the project is abandoned. You may be able to learn about the client's financial background from a credit reporting agency. Your bank also may be able to obtain financial information about the potential client.

Second, determine that if the client has the ability to pay, does the client have the desire to pay? Some clients can be difficult to collect balances from, even though they have the requisite financial resources. You can probably find out about the client's desire to pay from contractors or other design professionals who have previously worked with the client.

Third, determine how difficult it is to work with the client. Clients who make repeated design changes during the project can be extremely difficult, since they increase the designer's cost and may balk at paying reasonable compensation for design changes. Again, contacting contractors and other architects and engineers may tell you something about the potential difficulties of working with a client.

Fourth, consider the nature of the project. Determine whether the project will be successful for the client. Obviously, a successful project is one ingredient which determines the likelihood of being paid.

Fifth, determine whether the client desires to place any obstacles to payment. As an example, some clients prefer lien-free jobs. Their contracts with the contractors and design professionals may contain provisions waiving lien rights. Such waivers do not help you collect overdue balances.

The design professional's business plan should provide that only after adequate investigation of the potential client and the feasibility of the project should the firm make a decision as to whether to accept commission. Despite such steps, the client still may not be able to pay all or part of the invoices. The plan should therefore provide for a strategy for collecting unpaid invoices. The cornerstone of that strategy should be the use of a mechanic's lien.

A mechanic's lien is a creature of statute, and the statutory requirements for perfecting and foreclosing upon such liens vary among the states. Many states allow design professionals to file liens for service rendered in connection with improvements to a real property. Further, under certain circumstances, a mechanic's lien has priority over mortgages.

Mechanic's lien laws require the architect or engineer to meet certain key dates in order to perfect the lien. These laws usually require that notice be given to the owner and others with interest in or liens upon the property a specific number of days after either the designer has done his or her last substantial work upon the project or the project has been completed. In addition, the statutes require that the liens be filed with a specific government agency within a certain time period and that actions to foreclose upon mechanic's liens be started within a specific time period. Because mechanic's lien statutes require strict compliance with certain time periods, the collection strategy should set up a mechanism to assure these dates do not lapse without appropriate action.

Too often, architects and engineers are reluctant to file a mechanic's lien. Some design professionals think it is unprofessional. Others are afraid the client will become upset. Still others simply fail to file out of ignorance.

If the mechanic's lien is not paid, the designer may file a suit to foreclose the lien. In the suit, the designer seeks an order from the court instructing the property to be sold and the proceeds of the sale to be used to pay the lien.

Occasionally, a designer's right to a mechanic's lien may be time barred. In that case the designer's only resort may be to file a suit against the client to collect the unpaid balance. The architect or engineer proceeds against the client, not the property. If the designer recovers a judgment against the client, the designer may seek to collect payment of the judgment from the property, as long as the client still owns the property.

The business plan should also indicate that before any suit is filed to collect any unpaid fees, the firm should review the project to determine whether the client may have a claim against the firm for professional liability. Often, suits are filed by architects or engineers to collect fees, which result in counterclaims from clients which effectively defeat the claim for fees. The client may be correct and its claim may be valid, but the designer may determine that the cost of defending the counterclaim, even if bogus, exceeds the amount of the unpaid fees.

If the firm is large enough, such a review should be done by a member of the firm who has not worked on the project with the aid of the firm's attorney. This procedure affords some degree of impartiality in determining the likelihood of a claim being made by the client against the architect or engineer in the event a suit is filed to recover the unpaid fees.

Protecting Clients from Competitors

Business practicalities and the U.S. antitrust laws make it difficult, if not impossible, to keep an architect's or engineer's clients from giving commissions to competitors. There are just too many design professionals searching for clients. Also, the U.S. antitrust laws generally bar design professionals from agreeing not to solicit each other's clients or from dividing clients up among themselves.

The most obvious competitors of a design firm are members or employees of the firm who leave to set up their own practice or work for other design firms. The firm may take steps to limit the right of exowners or exemployees to compete with the firm through the use of a restrictive covenant in an employment agreement or a noncompetition agreement.

Generally, under such an agreement, the firm member or employee agrees not to compete with the firm for a specific period of time following termination of employment. Under the law, such agreements must be reasonable or the courts will not enforce them. What is considered reasonable varies among the states.

Usually, restrictive covenants are upheld if they last for only a few years, such as 2 years, and do not cover an unduly wide geographic area. A covenant stating that an architect or engineer who worked in a firm in a particular city was barred from practicing architecture or engineering anywhere in the United States after termination probably would be unreasonable.

The architect and engineer also should consider inserting a trade secrets or confidentiality clause in the employment agreement. Such a provision could be used to bar an employee or exemployee from disclosing sensitive or confidential business information to a competitor.

Contracting with Consultants

The design firm must make a decision as to the breadth of the design services to be offered by the firm. First, will the designer take any projects offered to the firm or will the firm's practice have to be restricted to specific categories of projects? Second, what services will the firm offer for specific projects? The firm must decide whether it will offer only architectural or engineering services or whether it will offer structural, civil, mechanical, electrical, and other design services.

Small design firms usually have professionals from only one or two disciplines. They do not have enough work to justify employing professionals in all areas required for project design. Large design firms can, however, employ full complements of design professionals.

If a firm does not employ all the needed designers for a project, the firm must decide whether it will retain the necessary consultants or whether the owner or other party for whom the firm is working will be requested to do so. Certain types of consultants, such as geotechnical engineers, have traditionally been retained by owners. Owners may also employ all the consultants needed for project design, such as the structural, mechanical, and electrical engineers.

An architectural or engineering firm may prefer to employ the consultants so as to maintain control and coordination of the design. In this case, the firm may be liable to the client or owner for design errors by the consultants.

In order to minimize exposure to claims by the client or the owner for a consultant's negligence, a firm must have a plan or strategy. At a minimum, the plan should require written agreements with all consultants in which the consultant holds the architect or engineer harmless for any consultant errors. Further, the agreement should require the consultant to maintain professional liability insurance of specific monetary limits. Also, if possible, the consultant's insurance policy should state that it is primary to any claims made against the engineer or architect for errors of the consultant and that the architect's or engineer's professional liability policy shall be excess to the consultant's insurance policy.

The architect's or engineer's business plan should require the consultant to provide the firm with evidence of insurance coverage. Usually a certificate of insurance can be obtained from the consultant's insurance broker. The certificate should list the insurance policies purchased by the consultant and the monetary limits of each policy. If the agreement between the architect or engineer and the consultant requires the consultant to have insurance policies with certain provisions for the benefit of the architect or engineer, then the architect or engineer should obtain copies of the insurance policies from the consultant. These policies should be reviewed by the architect's or engineer's insurance broker or attorney to assure compliance with the requirements of the contract with the consultant.

The architect or engineer should appoint one member of the firm's staff to be responsible for assuring the certificates of the insurance are obtained from all consultants. This is necessary so the architect or engineer can verify that the consultant has complied with the terms of the contract.

Professional Liability

The major risk faced by design professionals is claims for professional liability. Architects and engineers are frequently sued by owners for the recovery of damages for alleged design error. In addition, third parties sue designers for recovery of damages for alleged negligence. For instance, construction workers frequently sue architects or engineers, alleging that certain acts of the architect or engineer caused personal injury to the worker.

Even though the architect or engineer may have insurance to cover claims of professional liability made by the owner or a third party, the defense of such claims is still expensive. First, the designer's professional liability policy may contain a deductible feature under which the architect or engineer is responsible for paying the first few thousand dollars of any settlement or judgment. For large design firms, the deductible may be hundreds of thousands of dollars. Many professional liability insurance policies also state that the defense costs or attorney's fees are paid by the insured until they equal the amount of the deductible. Thereafter, the insurer pays the defense costs.

Second, the designer must devote considerable time to working with the designer's attorney and insurance company. Usually the designer is not paid for his or her time. As an example, an architect or engineer may spend time educating the attorney about the facts of the case. The architect or engineer must gather relevant documents, which may be the entire project file, and review the documents with the attorney. He or she must also answer questions the attorneys have for other parties in the suit. Members of the architect's or engineer's staff must prepare for and attend depositions. Finally, if necessary, the architect or engineer must assist the attorney in preparing for trial, attend the trial, and testify at the trial.

Liability for negligence

Ordinarily, an architect or engineer is only liable to his or her client or the third parties if his or her negligence in performing professional services results in damage or injury. An architect or engineer also may be liable for damages for breach of contract, such as if the designer fails to deliver plans and specifications required by the architect's or engineer's contract with the client.

By the early nineteenth century, the concept of negligence had been adopted by English common law and was subsequently accepted by U.S. courts. Negligence is part of the law which covers the rights of people to recover damages for certain harms they have suffered. The right to recover damages for negligence is not based upon a contract.

In applying the law of negligence to a specific case, the courts rely upon the mythical reasonable person. The jury judges the defendant's conduct based upon what it thinks a reasonable person would have or would not have done and compares the conduct of the defendant to the presumed conduct of the reasonable person.

From their experience, jurors determine what a reasonably careful person should or should not do. In an automobile accident case, since most jurors drive or are at least familiar with the operation of motor vehicles, they have a basis for reaching a decision as to what the conduct of the reasonable person should be. Most jurors, however, have no background in technical areas such as architecture or engineering and thus have no basis for determining what the reasonably careful architect or engineer should or should not do. The courts have resolved this dilemma by requiring the plaintiff to present an expert witness to testify as to what a reasonably careful architect or engineer would or would not do under certain circumstances. The expert witness usually is another architect or engineer.

The duty of an architect or engineer often is referred to as the standard of care of the architect or engineer. This is the duty to render professional services with the same skill and care of a similarly situated architect or engineer.

In a recent Minnesota case, the court emphasized that an architect does not guarantee perfection. That court stated that "an architect cannot be certain that a structural design will interact with natural forces as anticipated." The Minnesota court also declared:

> Because of the inescapable possibility of error which inheres in these services, the law has traditionally required, not perfect results, but rather the exercise of that skill and judgment expected from similarly situated professionals.[40]

For decades, the courts held that only someone who had a contract with a defendant could sue the defendant for negligence. This was referred to as the concept of privity of contract. In the early twentieth century, the courts started to limit the applicability of privity of contract in suits filed by a person who was injured by defective products. Eventually, the courts held that a person who had sustained personal injuries caused by the negligence of an architect could sue the designer even though the injured person had no contractual relationship with the architect. Also, people who have sustained property damage due to an architect's negligence may recover damages from the architect, although they had no contract with the architect. In Wisconsin, a shopping center tenant recovered damages from an architect for failing to analyze subsoil conditions correctly during design of the center, resulting in uneven settling of the floor and damaging property of the tenant.[41]

Architects and engineers frequently are sued by construction workers injured in job-site accidents or by the families or personal representatives of workers killed in construction accidents. These suits are filed either as negligence claims against the architect or engineer or under the applicable structural work act in those states which have such legislation.

A negligence case may allege that negligence in the architect's or engineer's design may have been the cause of injury. For example, the plaintiff may have fallen down stairs and may allege that the design of the stairs was defective.

More frequently, the plaintiff alleges that the architect or engineer was either negligent in supervision of the construction or negligent in performing or failing to perform certain safety responsibilities in connection with the construction. Under a structural work case, the plaintiff usually alleges that the architect or engineer was in charge of or in control of the work. In structural work act cases, if the jury finds a person was in charge of or in control of the work, that person becomes liable to injuries suffered by the plaintiff which were caused by a violation of a safety standard contained in the statute.

To determine whether the architect or engineer is in charge of the work under the structural work act, the jury is instructed to look at whether the architect or engineer exercised or had the right to exercise supervision of the construction. Supervision is control over the means and methods of construction. The jury also looks at whether the architect or engineer had any safety responsibilities at the job site.

Injured construction workers usually do not recover damages from architects or engineers for their injuries because the courts have recognized the practicalities of the construction process. Ordinarily, the architect or engineer designs the project and does not supervise the actual construction. The contractor is responsible for constructing the project and the safety of people at the job site. The architect or engineer ordinarily visits the job site to check conformance of the work of the contractor with the plans and specifications and to interpret the plans and specifications for the contractor.

The contract documents usually define the duties of the architect or engineer and the contractor. The construction contract frequently states that the contractor controls the means and methods of construction. The construction contract may also state that the contractor is solely responsible for job-site safety. The architect or engineer has no contractual right to supervise construction. As an example, in most construction contracts, the architect or engineer does not have the right to stop the work.

Thus, in a suit by an injured construction worker, the lawyers first look at the contract documents. The plaintiff's attorney looks to see if the architect or engineer had some control over the actual construction process or had some safety responsibility. The plaintiff's lawyer reviews all the contract documents to determine if they give the architect or engineer the right to stop the work or order the contractor to remove incompetent workers from the project, the obligation to conduct safety meetings, or the duty to assure contractor compliance with the Occupational Safety and Health Administration (OSHA) standards.

The architect's or engineer's attorney reviews the contract documents to be sure they do not give the right to manage construction to any degree or any safety responsibility. The attorney also looks for contractual provisions which place supervision of the construction process and safety responsibility with the architect or engineer. For instance, the attorney will determine if the construction contract makes the contractor solely responsible for safety and compliance with OSHA standards.

After reviewing the contract, the attorneys determine what actually happened during the construction process. Even though the contract does not give the engineer or architect the right to supervise construction or any safety responsibility, the architect or engineer may have done so during construction. The courts hold that if the architect or engineer actually participated in supervising construction or voluntarily assumed certain safety responsibility, he or she may be found liable to the injured worker for negligence which may have caused injury or may be found to be a party in control of the work under the structural work act.

In a 1976 case, an architect was sued for the death of a construction worker who fell through the roof of a building under construction. The jury found in favor of the architect. The jury's verdict was upheld on appeal with the appellate court, which reasoned that the contract did not give the architect any safety responsibility, and the construction contract stated that the contractor would be responsible for safety.[42]

Thus, when planning, architects or engineers should consider the risk of claims and suits filed by injured construction workers or on behalf of workers killed at a job site. They should determine whether any services offered under the plan will increase exposure to such claims and suits. If possible, they should consider the cost of this increased exposure.

The architect and engineer also should consider whether the plan minimizes claims and suits from injured construction workers. Should the plan provide that all contract documents be reviewed to assure that the architect or engineer has no construction or safety responsibility? Should the plan provide that project staff receive periodic training to assure it does not unknowingly assume construction or safety responsibilities?

Another main source of claims made and suits filed against architects or engineers are allegedly defective plans and specifications. These fall into four main categories:

1. Suits by owners or contractors for corrective work during or after construction to repair a defect in construction caused by purportedly defective plans or specifications, such as a leaking roof

2. Suits by owners for a catastrophic failure during or after construction allegedly caused by a defect in the plans or specifications, such as a wall collapse

3. Suits by passersby for injuries supposedly caused by a defect in design, such as a claim for injuries incurred when falling down a staircase

4. Suits by passersby for injuries allegedly caused by catastrophic failure, such as a roof collapse

Business planning can be used to minimize claims for design error. The business plan should provide for quality assurance and quality control aimed at avoiding design errors.

One common method of assuring quality is to provide for an architect or engineer not working upon the project to review the working drawings and specifications for the project. The plan should indicate that this expense be covered by the fee for the project.

The plan should also require documentation of design decisions. For many architects and engineers, a common problem is clients who want a top quality project but can only afford a more simple project. Such clients can be extremely difficult to work with, and a written record containing the history of design decisions can help the designer deal with deflated expectations of the client.

During design, the architect or engineer must consider alternatives and the client's budget to determine which alternative is selected. The designer should not, however, select alternatives without consulting with the client. As an example, an architect may be designing a small commercial office building which requires interior wood trim. The architect can specify oak or specify pine, which is less expensive. However, pine is not as durable as oak and may require more frequent replacements of sections which become damaged during use. If the client decides to use pine, the client's decision should be documented.

A more serious example involves the specifications for mechanical systems for the building. The client may want an optimal HVAC system, but the client may only be willing to pay for a normal commercial installation. If the HVAC system does not meet the client's expectations, the client may complain to the architect or engineer, forgetting that he or she selected the less expensive system. The designer may protect himself or herself in such situations if the designer has adequately documented the design decision or selection.

Documentation may take several forms. For projects involving major budgets, the design professional may submit a lengthy report to the client listing design alternatives, discussing the advantages and disadvantages of each alternative, and making a recommendation. At the other extreme, the engineer or architect may just discuss the alternatives with the client, and have the client make a decision. In such an event, the client's decision should be documented in a letter to the client or a memorandum to the file.

A written record of the design decision is extremely important. It can be used to show the client the history of the role played by the client. It also can be helpful if the client files suit against the architect or engineer for negligent design. It becomes difficult for the client to deny the role he or she played in the design process if there is a written record of his or her involvement.

If the project uses new technology, a written record of the design decision becomes even more important. The documents should describe what was known about the current state of the technology and indicate the risks which were explained to the client.

Most design professionals keep project files for many years after project completion. Maintenance of project files is extremely important, especially if a claim arises after project completion.

Adequate project documentation is extremely important to protect the architect or engineer from client claims in the event the project does not function properly. As an example, a designer recommended to the owner that a certain HVAC system be used to provide optimum building performance. The client, however, elected a less expensive alternative for budgetary reasons. If the HVAC system does not meet the owner's expectations, the architect's ability to defuse any owner complaints or defeat any owner claim may be enhanced if the file contains contemporaneous documentation indicating the owner selected a less expensive HVAC system after the client was advised of the various alternatives and advantages and disadvantages of each.

Architects or engineers face other exposure to claims when they specify equipment or other building components. The design professional's business plan should consider the policy for specifying building equipment and components.

There are three methods of specifying equipment and components. First, the architect or engineer may specify one product by brand name. Second, the architect or engineer may specify several brand names and the contractor selects one of them. These alternatives may be coupled with an or equal provision under which the contractor may request a substitute brand as equal to the specified brand or brands. Third, the architect or engineer may specify a functional or performance specification and rely upon the contractor or vendor to furnish a piece of equipment or a component that meets the specification.

If the designer specifies a particular brand, the architect or engineer may become liable in the event the selected brand does not meet performance expectations. The designer who selected the brand should select one that will do the job. If it does not, the designer may be liable to the owner for the cost of the corrective work.

If the product malfunctions because of a defect in manufacture, the architect or engineer should not be responsible. Ordinarily, the designer is not involved in the manufacture of the product and, accordingly, the architect or engineer does not warrant that the product will be free from defects.

In determining whether a specific product is suited for the project, the designer must rely on performance data from the manufacturer. Usually manufacturers publish details, including performance data, of their products. This is often in the form of product brochures, which may be published in the *Sweet's Catalog*. Sometimes, the architect or engineer must consult with the manufacturer as to whether a specific product is suitable for a particular application. The designer should obtain written confirmation from the manufacturer if he or she advises that the product is right for the job.

Exactly how thorough an investigation the architect or engineer should make is measured by professional standards. What would a similarly situated architect or engineer in the community do? If the reasonable architect or engineer would have relied upon the manufacturer's brochures or catalog sheets, then that is all that can be expected of the designer.[43]

The architect or engineer also should consider the need to issue certificates for progress payments as part of the business plan. He or she should establish a program to review payout certificates to be used on the project. Ideally, the certificates should be reviewed before construction begins so the designer can be assured they do not expand the designer's responsibility as provided for in the professional services agreement.

The wording of payout certificates can present many problems; two deserve special note. First, the certificate may state the work complies with the plans and specifications. That implies that all of the work complies with the plans and specifications, whereas ordinarily the architect or engineer does not observe the construction of all components of the project. Ordinarily, the designer's representative only walks through the project at the time payment is requested to determine whether the work generally conforms to plans and specifications. Certificates which are effectively broad guarantees that all of the work conforms to plans and specifications and should be rewritten.

Second, financial institutions often request the architect or engineer to certify at the time of payout that there are sufficient funds remaining to complete the project. However, no architect or engineer can be expected to give such assurances. The designer does not know whether the client has the funds necessary to complete the project. Further, the designer cannot guaranty that unforeseen problems may not arise upon the project which could increase the cost of construction.

The business plan also should consider the architect's or engineer's policy toward cost estimates. Typically, the owner advises the designer of the approximate amount the owner desires to spend on the project. If the owner does not, the prudent architect or engineer usually asks the owner for the budget for the proposed project or furnishes the owner with a cost estimate at the time the preliminary design is completed. Many architects and engineers do not want to be responsible for the reliability of their cost estimates because they have no control over the bidding process of the contractors and what may transpire during construction.

If the architect or engineer guarantees that the project will not exceed a certain cost but it exceeds that amount, the architect or engineer ordinarily is not entitled to his or her fee. If the designer only gives a cost estimate, the designer is entitled to his or her fee, unless the actual cost substantially exceeds the cost estimate. Thus, the business plan should contain the policy for handling cost estimates. For most architects and engineers, the plan should indicate that no responsibility should be accepted for cost estimates.

The business plan also may consider the architect's or engineer's proposed involvement with environmental projects. Many design professionals avoid undertaking environmental projects because of exposure to suits and governmental regulatory activity. An error in the design of a landfill or an underground tank system can result in serious environmental hazards. Others actively seek such work.

Conclusion

The design firm should not ignore the legal environment. Its owners and managers should keep abreast of legal trends. Further, they should use the services of an experienced attorney. They should not be afraid to consult their attorney just to avoid having to pay legal fees. Time spent with an attorney to avoid future problems is a lot less expensive than hiring an attorney after a problem develops into a lawsuit.

Planning for Risk

Architects and engineers face a variety of risks in their practices. The most common are claims from negligent design by the design professional.

An architect may negligently design roof details for a building, resulting in water during rain storms or snow melting on the roof. The owner may request the architect to pay for work to correct the problem, which was caused by designer negligence. Or a structural engineer may improperly design supporting elements of a structure, resulting in the need to correct the deficiency in order to avoid a catastrophic failure. Again, the owner may look to the structural engineer to pay for the repair costs.

Not only may the architect or engineer face a claim from an owner for negligent design, but the design professional may be sued by a third party. As an example, in the situation where the structural engineer negligently designed the structural elements of a building, the structure may collapse resulting in personal injury to innocent bystanders or damage to property of third parties in the building.

The design professional faces claims ranging from those of minor magnitude to those of immense proportions. Design negligence resulting in a major defect in a structure can be expensive to repair, sometimes costing millions of dollars. Design negligence causing serious bodily injury or death may result in a claim against the designer up to several million dollars, depending upon the nature of the injury and the age and occupation of the deceased.

Risk management involves identifying the risks faced by the architect or engineer, then devising means to minimize those risks. Traditionally, insurance has been the major means for architects and engineers to protect themselves from negligence claims. Other risk management tools, including contractual indemnification and limitation of liability, may also be used by the architect or engineer to minimize risks. Further, the costs of handling risks which materialize may be reduced by using dispute resolution methods other than courtroom litigation.

Insurance

The primary insurance policy for architects and engineers is the professional liability insurance policy, frequently referred to as errors and omission insurance, E & O insurance, or malpractice insurance policies. These policies cover claims made or suits filed against a design professional for the negligent performance of professional services by an architect or engineer.

Besides professional liability insurance, architects and engineers usually purchase general liability or commercial liability insurance, automobile liability insurance, and worker's compensation insurance. Design professionals usually purchase fire insurance or property insurance to cover their office and equipment. Some also purchase valuable papers insurance which covers the cost of reproducing drawings and other documents destroyed by fire or other perils.

Professional liability insurance

There are two main sources of professional liability insurance for design professionals—the CNA insurance program covering architects and engineers, sponsored by the American Institute of Architects and the National Society of Professional Engineers, and the DPIC Insurance Companies. In addition, certain underwriting syndicates of Lloyd's of London have historically marketed professional liability insurance policies to U.S. architects and engineers. Also, numerous other insurers have sold professional liability policies to architects and engineers.

CNA markets its professional liability insurance program through a Washington, D.C., based insurance broker. Each customer or insurance agency must procure insurance through this broker. The DPIC Companies sell insurance to architects and engineers through exclusive agents located throughout the United States. Customers or insureds must purchase their insurance through one of these agents. Other insurers have also established exclusive agents; some do not use exclusive agents and will deal directly with any licensed insurance broker.

Professional liability insurance policies are written to cover all claims made against an architect or engineer arising from the insured's professional practice and for which the insured is legally liable, subject to certain exclusions. Under two common exclusions, the insurer will not cover the design professional for claims arising from warranties or guaranties or from intentional or dishonest acts.

Typically, architects and engineers are not legally liable for warranties or guaranties, unless they agree to warrant or guarantee their work. As stated in Chap. 8, design professionals ordinarily are only liable for their failure to conform to the appropriate standards of practice. They do not warrant or guarantee perfection.

Most professional liability policies do not cover architects or engineers from claims arising from their participation in a joint venture. Insurers will usually cover claims made against the insured for negligence in performing professional services for the joint venture. However, the design professional is not covered under its policy for liability it incurs as a result of the activities of one of the other coventurers.

Because of the limited nature of joint venture coverage available to architects and engineers, the design professional faces a potential gap in insurance coverage. If a coventurer is negligent, each member of the joint venture is responsible for the negligence of that coventurer. Thus, when forming joint ventures, each member should be sure all the other members have adequate insurance coverage and financial resources. In addition, the coventurers should consider whether the joint venture can obtain its own insurance coverage.

Professional liability policies usually afford limited coverage of indemnification or hold harmless agreements. The typical policy only covers such provisions if they do not go beyond the architect's or engineer's common law obligation to render professional services in accordance with generally accepted design standards. Thus, all architects and engineers should closely review indemnification clauses in all contracts with their insurance brokers and attorneys to assure that the provision is covered by their professional liability insurance policy.

Professional liability policies cover claims made against the design professional during the policy period, regardless of when the negligence or the damage occurred. Accordingly, such policies are referred to as claims-made policies. Thus, when the architect or engineer is notified of the claim by a letter, verbally, or by suit papers, it triggers coverage under a professional liability policy. However, many such policies also require the insured to give the insurer notification of facts or circumstances which may give rise to a claim. The policy under which notice of possible claim is made then covers any actual claim arising from those facts or circumstances, even if the claim is made after the policy expires.

Many claims-made policies only cover claims made after a certain date. Some policies provide that only claims made against the insured after inception of the first professional liability policy issued by the insurer are covered. Thus, many insureds under such policies face certain uninsured exposure, since a claim may be made against the insured arising out of professional services rendered years before the retroactive date.

In order to enjoy continuity of insurance coverage under a claims-made policy, the design professional must continue to purchase claims-made policies. If the architect or engineer does not renew a claims-made policy, the design professional will no longer have professional liability insurance coverage; that is because coverage under a claims-made policy is triggered by the receipt of the claim. Some insurance companies have attempted to soften the impact of a termination of claims-made coverage for professional liability claims by providing the option of an extended reporting period under the policy. By paying an additional premium when the policy terminates, the design professional can obtain coverage for a few years for claims made after policy expiration arising from services rendered before policy termination.

In the past, some insurers have sold policies for a one-time premium to cover claims made anytime after policy expiration. These policies were usually sold to retiring professionals who had been insured under claims-made policies. With the payment of one premium, a retired professional would receive coverage for malpractice claims arising from any service rendered before retirement.

Frequently, the design professional's insurance broker can do more to assist the architect or engineer in the designer's practice than procure professional liability insurance. Some insurance brokers specialize in serving the construction industry or architects and engineers. Such brokers review contractual terms to determine if they are insured or insurable. Some offer educational programs aimed at minimizing claims made against architects and engineers, including suggestions on contract provisions which are beneficial to the design professional.

Professional liability insurance is a serious matter for all architects and engineers. Such insurance can protect the design professional's practice from both frivolous and genuine claims. It is often a significant portion of the annual budget. Thus, when procuring professional liability insurance, the architect or engineer should consider the following:

Which broker should be used to procure the insurance?

Should more than one broker be asked to solicit proposals from insurers?

Which insurance companies should be solicited for quotes from the broker?

What should be the limits of the policy? Should it insure for a claim of $500,000, $1,000,000, or more?

What should be the amount of the deductible?

Are coverages required which are not contained in the standard policy form?

Are any changes required in the firm to assure that adequate insurance may be obtained at a reasonable premium?

Answers to these questions may not be easy and can require consultation among the firm's owners, insurance broker, and attorney. The attorney may point out potential areas of liability for which the firm needs insurance.

Commercial liability insurance

Besides professional liability insurance, most architects and engineers purchase commercial liability insurance, which covers other potential business liabilities except for automobile liability. Commercial liability insurance policies cover such claims as those arising when a visitor slips and falls in the designer's premises or the designer is sued for slander or libel.

Commercial liability insurance is referred to as general liability insurance or comprehensive general liability insurance. Such insurance has been sold in the United States for decades. Before 1940, each insurer used individual forms, making it difficult for potential insureds to compare policies and premiums. In 1940, the insurance industry issued the first standard comprehensive general liability insurance form. The form was called comprehensive because it insured against all perils, unless specifically excluded. Before that, most insurance policies only insured against specifically named perils.

The standard form was redrafted, and revised versions were issued in 1966 and 1972. In the early 1980s, the standard form was rewritten. The impetus for the revision was the insurance industry's desire to limit coverage for pollution liability claims and to meet the challenge of increasing product liability claims.

Initially, the insurers' new standard form did not cover any claim arising from pollution, including product liability claims arising from products containing toxic materials. Many insurers declined to use the broad-form pollution exclusion and issued amendments or endorsements to their policies that covered pollution claims.

The insurers also desired to limit their exposure to product liability claims by proposing a claims-made policy as an alternative to the traditional occurrence policy. The early standard comprehensive general liability insurance policies provided coverage on an occurrence basis. Coverage for the claim was triggered by the policy in effect at the time of the occurrence giving rise to the claim, regardless of when the claim was made. In the mid-1980s, many insurers thought that the use of claims-made policies would limit their exposure to product liability claims. So many insureds objected to the use of the claims-made policy that most insurers never adopted it.

The current standard form of commercial liability insurance has three main coverages:

A. Bodily injury and property damage
B. Medical liability
C. Personal injury liability

Coverage for bodily injury and property damage resembles traditional general liability insurance. It is for claims arising from bodily injury and property damage, defined as physical damage to property. A product manufacturer or seller would pay the extra premium to purchase products liability coverage. A contractor would pay the extra premium to purchase completed operations coverage. In such circumstances, the coverage insures the product manufacturer and seller from claims that a person was injured due to a defect in a product. The policy insures contractors against a wide variety of claims such as suits filed after construction is completed by people injured due to defects in the structure.

Standard commercial liability insurance contains many exclusions. For design professionals the most important exclusion is the architect and engineer exclusion, which says that the insurer will not cover claims arising from professional services by the insured. Thus, architects and engineers should procure both professional and commercial liability insurance policies.

Coverage for medical liability insures certain medical payments regardless of fault. Under this coverage, medical payments incurred by people injured on the insured's premises are covered even though the insured is not legally liable. The purpose of this coverage is for the insured to maintain the goodwill of visitors to the architect's or engineer's premises.

Coverage for personal injury liability insures against certain false imprisonment, invasion of privacy, slander, libel, and advertising liability claims. Ordinarily, architects and engineers do not need such insurance coverage. There are, however, cases in which design professionals have been sued for libel or slander.

Automobile liability insurance

Most design firms maintain some form of automobile liability insurance. Such policies usually insure the business for claims arising from accidents during the course of business involving owned, nonowned, and hired vehicles.

Umbrella and excess liability insurance

Basic or primary professional and commercial liability policies are for claims of a certain monetary limit. Usually, primary insurance may be purchased for $100,000, $500,000, or $1,000,000. If the firm desires more insurance, the insured must obtain umbrella or excess liability insurance.

In the past many large design firms have had layers of umbrella and excess insurance, sometimes for $50 million or more in coverage. In recent years, however, at times even large design firms could only obtain limited insurance coverage above their primary professional liability insurance policies.

Owner's protective insurance

The owner frequently may require the contractor to provide owner's protective liability insurance. Such insurance protects the owner from claims arising from accidents during construction. The policy is similar to a commercial liability policy, but the premium is paid by the contractor and the owner is the insured who benefits from the policy.

Builder's risk insurance

Most construction projects require builder's risk insurance, which is usually purchased by the owner. This insurance covers damage to the project under construction due to perils such as fire, explosion, windstorm, or vandalism. Builder's risk policies do not cover damage caused by defective work by the contractors or negligence of the architect or engineer.

Builder's risk policies normally insure everyone connected with the project, including the owner, the contractors, architect, and engineer. The policy typically ends when the structure becomes occupied.

Worker's compensation insurance

Employers are required by state law to have worker's compensation insurance, which covers their employees for personal injuries arising during the course of employment. Benefits are paid to the injured employees or survivors of a deceased employee according to a schedule established by the state. The employer is required to pay the employee's medical bills and a certain amount a week while the employee is unable to work due to a work-related injury.

Worker's compensation insurance policies cover other claims made against the employer. These are claims filed against the employer by a third party who is being sued by the employee for injuries arising during employment. As an example, an injured employee may receive worker's compensation benefits for a work-related injury then sue one or more other people connected with the project, alleging that their actions caused or contributed to the injury. The third party in turn may sue the employer, alleging that the employer's actions wholly or partially caused the injury. The employer's liability part of the worker's compensation policy would cover such a claim of a third party.

Property insurance

Most design professionals have office furniture, computers, and other equipment. The architect or engineer must determine whether such items should be insured against damages from such causes as fire. In addition, the architect or engineer may have work in progress and must consider whether drawings and other documents should be protected by valuable papers insurance.

Self-insurance

During business planning, the design professional must determine what risks to insure and what risks not to insure. The architect or engineer, for example, may desire to insure only against risks likely to result in claims. They may insure against professional liability claims because they know the chances of being sued for malpractice are high. They may not insure certain equipment from loss due to fire or peril because the equipment may not be valuable.

One major decision the design professional must make is how to handle professional liability risks. Many firms insure against such risks; many firms do not because of the relatively high cost of professional liability insurance.

A survey of 1764 consulting engineering firms by the American Consulting Engineers Council (ACEC) indicated that in 1990 21.6 percent of those firms did not have insurance. Further, the cost of professional liability insurance for the firms which did have it was 3.98 percent of billings. The reason for most firms not having malpractice insurance seemed to be the relatively high premiums.[44] The ACEC survey also indicated that smaller engineering firms are less likely to maintain professional liability insurance than larger firms. Forty-three percent of firms with less than five employees had no malpractice insurance; only 9 percent of firms with more than 500 employees did not have professional liability insurance.[45]

Although the architect or engineer may save the cost of the insurance premium, the designer should consider what could happen if the firm has no insurance. If there is a lawsuit, even though the architect or engineer may be found not guilty, the expenses can be financially burdensome. Paying an attorney to defend a design professional in a malpractice suit can exceed $50,000. The architect or engineer also may have to hire experts to testify on the designer's behalf, which may add thousands of dollars to defense costs.

By practicing without insurance, the firm places its own assets at risk and may even place the personal assets of the owners at risk. If the claimant receives a judgment in his or her favor, he or she may collect the judgment from the assets of the firm, including its accounts receivables. If the firm is a partnership, the judgment is payable from the personal assets of the general partners. If the firm is a corporation, any employee of the firm who was negligent may be sued.

For self-insured firms (firms which are not insured), under federal tax law litigation expenses and payments for settlements or on judgments are deductible when paid. Insurance premiums are deductible when paid.

Firms which do not have insurance may account for professional liability risks in one of three ways. First, litigation expenses and payments for settlements and on judgments may be treated as business expense when incurred. Second, the firm can make an expense charge every year and transfer the expense charge to a reserve fund. The expense charge would be an estimate of litigation and liability payments upon an annualized basis. Third, the firm can establish the reserve account and fund it with cash or other assets.

Under the second and third methods, litigation and liability payments are charged against the reserve as incurred or paid and only would be used if the firm's accounting is on an accrual basis. Thus, the firm's financial statements would not be affected by an abnormal, nonrecurring, or nearly nonrecurring charge.

The use of a sinking fund has some merit. Under this method, the firm puts aside a certain amount of cash annually which is available to pay litigation costs and liability payments that could be expensive and extremely burdensome if they had to be made in a relatively short period of time.

Being self-insured requires discipline. With the firm's own assets, and perhaps its owner's personal savings at risk, it must be careful about the assignments it accepts. Marginal work should not be taken. Projects which may be risky should be avoided. Projects for certain clients may not be acceptable. Marginal developers may become involved in a project which fails, resulting in a meritless lawsuit against the architect or engineer as the developer attempts to recover all or part of the losses.

Transfer Risks via Contracts

By procuring insurance to cover certain risks, the architect or engineer passes the potential economic impact of those risks to the insurer. Besides using insurance, the design professional may transfer certain risks by contractual means. There are three common methods of passing risk by contract:

1. Indemnification
2. Limiting liability
3. Procuring insurance

Indemnification

Under indemnification, the architect or engineer is held harmless for the design professional's own negligence or someone else's negligence, such as the owner, general contractor, or subcontractor. By using contractual provisions which limit liability, the architect or engineer limits the potential damages the design professional may owe to the other party to the amount stated in the contract. In addition, the design professional may agree with another party that that party shall purchase certain insurance for the benefit of the design professional.

Indemnification provisions are commonly used in construction contracts. Sometimes, the owner may require the architect or engineer to hold the owner harmless from claims made against the owner due to the negligence of the design professional. As an example, after completion of construction the owner may be sued by a visitor who is injured on the owner's property. The visitor may allege that a certain architectural feature may have been negligent. The owner could use an indemnification provision in the professional services agreement with the architect to tender the defense of the lawsuit to the designer.

Indemnification provisions are also common in contracts with general contractors. Although the architect or engineer is not a party to the construction contracts, such contracts contain provisions for the benefit of the architect or engineer, such as indemnification provisions. Under such provisions, if the architect or engineer is sued by a construction worker injured at the job site, he or she should tender the defense of the lawsuit against the design professional to the contractor.

A simple indemnification provision of a construction contract for the benefit of an architect could read:

> Contractor agrees to indemnify, hold harmless, and defend the owner and the architect from any claims, lawsuits, and expenses, including attorneys' fees arising, or allegedly arising, from any personal injury, death, or property damage occurring during the performance of the work by the contractor.

As a general rule, the courts will narrowly interpret indemnification provisions and will refuse to enforce them for minor reasons. Thus, the courts usually state that a person cannot be indemnified against his or her own negligence, unless the provisions specifically so provide. Thus, if the owner and the architect desire to be indemnified for their own negligence, the above provision could be rewritten to read:

> Contractor agrees to indemnify, hold harmless, and defend the owner and the architect from any claims, lawsuits, and expenses, including attorneys' fees arising, or allegedly arising, from any personal injury, death, or property damage occurring during the performance of the work by the contractor, *whether any negligence of the owner or the architect contributed thereto.*

In states in which such an indemnification provision would be enforced, the contractor would have to indemnify the architect or engineer even though the injury or damage was the sole fault of the designer. Many contractors consider this unfair, especially where it impinges on the cost of their insurance. As a result, in many states contractors have been able to convince legislatures to pass statutes declaring that indemnification provisions in construction contracts under which one is held harmless for one's own negligence are void and unenforceable.

In business planning, the design professional must make two basic decisions regarding indemnification: First, the firm must decide whether, as a general policy, it will indemnify its clients. If so, it should then decide what type of indemnification it will provide for its clients. Second, the firm should decide whether it will be expected to be indemnified by the contractor. If so, it should determine what type of indemnification it desires from contractors.

In its dealings with its clients, the firm should be careful that the indemnification provision is not too broad. It should avoid agreeing to indemnification provisions under which it would hold its client harmless for all losses sustained by the client. At most, the firm should only indemnify its clients for negligent acts or omissions of the firm. Further, the firm should only agree to indemnification provisions which will be covered by its professional liability insurance.

For contractors, most design firms either use standard contract documents drafted by professional organizations such as the American Institute of Architects, which contain indemnification provisions, or develop their own standard general conditions, which contain indemnification provisions. Such provisions usually require the contractor to hold harmless both the owner and the design professional. Further, many general conditions require the contractor to procure insurance covering its obligation to indemnify the owner and the architects.

Limiting liability

Risk may be transferred to another person by limiting that person's right to recover damages from the designer. This is referred to as limiting liability or limitation of liability and may be done by contract.

Exculpatory agreements are used to prevent any transfer of the risk. Membership contracts for health clubs often contain exculpatory provisions. Such provisions usually state that the member bears all risk of using health club facilities, even if the health club is negligent, such as with the maintenance of the equipment.

A design firm would prefer its clients to exculpate it from any negligence which results in damage to the client. As a practical matter, however, no design firm can expect any of its clients to do so. However, many clients may agree to provisions in professional service agreements to limit the liability of the architect or engineer.

Limitation of liability provisions have been used for thousands of years. Phoenician shipowners and shippers agreed that the owner's liability for damage to the shipper's cargo would be limited to the value of the vessel. In recent years, limitation of liability provisions have become more prevalent in contracts in the United States, especially among design professionals.

There are several advantages for a design firm to use limitation of liability provisions in its professional services agreements. First, the amount of damages that would have to be paid by the firm if it is negligent is limited. It is hoped that no claim would result in damages which would be paid by the firm that would make it insolvent. Second, if the damages paid by the firm's insurers are limited, the firm's insurance premiums may be lower. Third, the amount of damages which may be incurred due to a design error may bear no reasonable relationship to the amount of the fee. For instance, a structural engineer may do the structural design for a few thousand dollars, but the cost of correcting a structural design error may be several hundred thousand dollars.

Although there are many limitation of liability provisions, they take certain basic forms, some of which may be used in combination with one another. Liability may be limited by (1) excluding liability for certain types of damage, (2) the amount of insurance coverage, (3) the amount of the fee, (4) some stated monetary amount, or (5) agreeing to redo any negligent design work for no additional fee.

Under the first method, the design firm and the owner may agree that the firm shall not be liable to the owner for consequential damages. Although consequential damages have no precise definition, they usually are viewed as those damages arising from physical damage to the property but not the cost of repairing the property. Damages arising from the loss of use of damaged property would be consequential damages. For example, if the negligence of the design firm resulted in the owner being unable to use all or part of the building designed by the architect or engineer either due to catastrophic failure or the need to do corrective work in the building, the owner's need to rent additional space would be a consequential damage.

Provisions denying the owner the right to collect consequential damages are prevalent in the electric utility industry. Most utilities agree that if the negligence of a design firm results in it being unable to use an electric power plant, the utility is not entitled to consequential damages such as the cost of purchasing power from other electric utilities.

Under the second method, the design firm's liability is limited to the amount of its insurance coverage. Sometimes the provision is interpreted to mean the monetary amount of the firm's professional liability insurance, even though the claim may not be covered by the policy.

Accordingly, some provisions are written to provide coverage for damages covered by valid and collectible insurance.

The third method is becoming more common. Under this method, the architect's or engineer's liability is limited to the fee or some percentage of it.

Under the fourth method, the design firm is responsible for a fixed monetary sum, such as the cost of the project or a percentage of it. Occasionally, the owner and the design professional may agree in the contract to limit the designer's liability to a fixed sum, such as a million dollars.

The fifth method is not used as frequently as the other four methods. Under this method, the design firm agrees that if any of the work is negligent, the firm will redo the design. Sometimes the owner agrees that the design firm would not be responsible for the construction cost of the corrective work.

The design firm should consult with its attorney about the use of limitation of liability provisions and their specific form and language. Many firms which have adopted some provisions have developed standard wording which they try to use in all their professional services agreements.

Many clients will object to the use of limitation of liability provisions or to specific wording. Bargaining power and skill in negotiation will determine whether the completed professional services agreement contains a limitation of liability provisions.

Procuring insurance

Another method of transferring risk is for the architect or engineer to arrange for another firm to procure insurance covering the design profession. As an example, the architect or engineer may want the owner or contractor to purchase professional liability insurance for the design engineer. As a practical matter, this usually is not done. However, the design firm may be able to have the owner or contractor procure certain insurance for its benefit.

Some insurance companies now offer project-specific policies which afford professional liability insurance coverage for all design firms working on the project. Because of the nature of the policy, the design firm may be able to arrange for the owner to pay the premium for such a policy.

For some major construction projects, owners have implemented wrap-up insurance programs. Under such a program, everyone associated with the project is covered for certain claims under a general liability policy and a worker's compensation policy. Such policies usually cover the owner, the architect, the engineers, the general contractor, all subcontractors, and all vendors. The aim of the wrap-up program is to have all claims defended under these insurance policies using one law firm. Thus, if a construction worker is injured and sues certain people associated with the project, each of these people would be defended under the same insurance policies by the same law firm. The efficiency of such a program is apparent.

Under wrap-up programs, claims against architects and engineers are covered unless they arise from errors or alleged errors in the plans and specifications. The design professional still must maintain professional liability insurance to cover such claims.

The design professional also may be covered under the general or commercial liability insurance policy of the contractor. Frequently, construction contracts require the contractor to list the owner and the architect or engineer as additional insureds under its commercial liability policy. Unfortunately, the standard commercial liability insurance policy excludes coverage for professional liability claims against architects and engineers. Thus, if the suit alleges that the plaintiff was injured due to the negligent performance of professional services of the architect or engineer, the contractor's insurer may deny coverage to the design firm.

Similarly, the construction contract may require the contractor to purchase an owner's protective policy insuring both the owner and the architect or engineer. However, the owner's protective policy may also exclude coverage for professional liability claims made against an architect or engineer.

Because of the complexities which may arise when the design firm requests another person to procure insurance for its benefit, any proposed program should be reviewed by the firm's insurance broker or an insurance consultant. Exclusions in certain standard insurance policies could negate the benefit of any such programs to the design firm, unless those exclusions are deleted or modified.

Controlling Litigation

Unfortunately, most architects and engineers will be defendants in professional liability lawsuits one or more times during their professional careers. Small firms usually face suits that do not involve much alleged damage, frequently $100,000 or less. Nevertheless, the cost of defending such a lawsuit can be significant to the firm.

Both large and small firms occasionally are defendants in lawsuits in which the plaintiffs seek recovery of substantial amounts of money as damages, often exceeding $1 million. Attorneys' fees and disbursements may amount to hundreds of thousands of dollars.

Many firms maintain professional liability policies to protect them from their potential exposure and to pay the legal fees and other defense costs. Generally, however, such policies have deductibles, frequently $10,000 or more for small firms and $100,000 or more for large firms. Professional liability policies insuring architects and engineers usually provide that the insured pays all or part of the attorney's fees and other defense costs until the deductible is exhausted. Accordingly, the firm may have to pay significant sums of its own cash to defend a malpractice suit.

Defending a lawsuit also produces hidden costs for the architect or engineer. In assisting the attorney, the firm must devote the time of its staff. When the lawsuit is first filed, the attorney will have to spend time with the design professional's staff to determine the facts and devise a defense strategy. The staff will have to gather documents to explain the background of the lawsuit. As the lawsuit progresses, the staff will have to expend more energy in assisting the attorney.

In defending most lawsuits, the firm must call upon its own staff to support its attorney. As a result, the staff's time is taken away from on-going projects for which the firm derives income and is devoted to the lawsuit for which the firm receives no payment. Accordingly, the firm should take steps to minimize both the direct and hidden costs of litigation.

For small firms which are infrequent targets of lawsuits, no formal business plan for defending such suits need be established. However, the large firm should plan ahead for defending lawsuits to minimize costs and to maximize the probability of a beneficial outcome to the firm.

Many large design firms have formulated plans which have certain common elements. First, a senior staff member is designated responsible to the firm for defense of the suit. He or she usually knows the firm and how it works and has years of design experience, which will make assistance to the attorney more effective. Large firms with in-house legal staffs place this responsibility upon the law department. Other firms select a senior design professional who has prior litigation experience.

All requests for aid usually pass from the defense counsel to the staff member responsible for litigation. The staff member then coordinates the work required to gather information and documents sought by defense counsel. Designating one staff member to coordinate the internal staff effort results in efficiency. There is no need for defense counsel to engage in lengthy discussions and education projects with the staff member. The staff member also responds to defense counsel in a manner easy for the attorney to understand.

Most large firms designate one law firm to coordinate the defense of the suits filed against them. Firms with national practices which may be sued in different locales frequently find it more efficient to have their regular attorneys work with local counsel in defending suits. Under such circumstances, requests for assistance from the firm usually are made to the firm's regular attorneys, who then work with the firm's staff member responsible for litigation to obtain the required help.

Some large firms designate one law firm to handle all their litigation throughout the United States. It may be more economical to deal with one law firm which regularly works with their firm and knows the details of the design firm's professional practice and method of working.

Alternative Dispute Resolution

When planning for litigation, the design firm should consider whether it will prefer some form of dispute resolution other than court litigation. For years, the American Institute of Architects and other design groups have promoted arbitration as an alternative to court resolution of disputes. The standard contracts published by the American Institute of Architects and the Engineers Joint Contract Documents Committee contain mandatory arbitration provisions.

A nationwide program for arbitration of construction industry disputes is conducted by the American Arbitration Association. Its Construction Industry Rules contains the guidelines for such arbitration.

In arbitration, the parties agree to submit any disputes between them to a panel of arbitrators, who makes a final and binding decision. The arbitrators make their decision after hearing presentations by each person.

Arbitration may have several benefits. First, in construction industry litigation under auspices of the American Arbitration Association, the arbitrators usually have some construction expertise. The arbitrators may be architects, engineers, contractors, or lawyers who regularly represent clients in the construction industry. The expertise of the arbitrators may be the main advantage of arbitration. Decisions are not left to judges and jurors unfamiliar with construction and with no technical expertise.

Second, arbitration may be less expensive than litigating in a court. Ordinarily, the parties do no discovery in arbitration, which can lead to significant savings. Third, arbitration usually is more expeditious than litigation. Usually, extensive pretrial legal work is avoided. Fourth, the decision of the arbitrators is final. The parties are not entitled to any appeal to a higher tribunal. Fifth, the rules of evidence need not be followed by the arbitrators. Proponents of arbitration argue that the rules of evidence often preclude consideration of relevant evidence because of minor technicalities.

Arbitration does, however, have certain shortcomings. First, the arbitrators need not follow the law in reaching their decision. Over the years, the courts have developed specific rules governing the rights and duties of people in the construction process. The arbitrators may ignore those rules.

Second, the people need not present experts in an arbitration proceeding. Many do in order to help the arbitrators and increase the chance of success. However, the arbitrators still may find against a design professional.

Third, the arbitrators may not have enough or the right type of expertise for a particular proceeding. Many arbitrators are lawyers who may have no training in architecture, engineering, or construction. Arbitrators who are architects or engineers may not have the correct expertise for the matter they are hearing.

Fourth, arbitration may not be significantly less expensive than litigation. Arbitration of complicated matters can involve many days of hearings, and some hearings may really be taken up with discovery which would not occur before a trial in a court of law.

Fifth, the people have no right to discovery. Without the use of depositions, interrogatories, and requests to produce documents, the people may not be able to prepare for the arbitration proceeding adequately.

Sixth, the arbitrators do not have to follow the rules of evidence. This can result in hearsay and irrelevant and unreliable testimony being heard by the arbitrators.

Seventh, the people involved have no right to appeal to a higher court. In the judicial system, people may appeal rulings of the judge and findings of the jury they think are erroneous. The parties to arbitration do not have such a right. Thus, a clearly erroneous finding of the arbitration cannot be set aside, except in certain limited circumstances such as fraud committed by the arbitrators.

In recent years, mediation has arisen as another alternative way to resolve disputes. Mediation may take several forms. Under one method, the people involved undertake nonbinding arbitration. The arbitrators issue a decision, then the people use the arbitrators' findings as a basis to conduct settlement negotiations.

The minitrial is one form of nonbinding arbitration. In a minitrial, the people present summaries of their cases to a judge or jury. The judge or jury then issues a decision, which is used to begin settlement discussions.

More frequently, the people agree upon a mediator who meets with them and attempts to have them agree to an amicable settlement. The mediator listens to everyone's positions and encourages a compromise.

Conclusion

Both an experienced insurance broker and a competent attorney can be extremely helpful to the design firm that is intelligently planning for future risks. Insurance brokers and attorneys who regularly work with architects and engineers are aware of the hazards they face in daily practice. Insurance brokers and lawyers are resources which should not be overlooked.

Negotiating the Professional Services Agreement

Many architects and engineers do not give sufficient thought to the importance of the professional services agreement. Design professionals ordinarily contract with the owner or another architect or engineer. In the latter situation the principal design professional, usually an architect, will contract with engineers to furnish structural, mechanical, and electrical design for a project. Then the principal design professional will contract with the owner to furnish all the design services for the project.

All architects and engineers should develop a specific policy toward contracting for professional services. The stakes are too high not to do so. The professional services agreement establishes the obligations of the people to the contract. Either knowingly, but more often unwittingly, architects and engineers frequently agree to contract provisions which expand their traditional responsibility. As an example, a services agreement written by an owner may obligate the architect to guarantee a perfect result or exact cost estimate.

The design firm should develop a written business policy for negotiating all professional services agreements. Provisions should be made to assure that the written policy is followed.

All architects and engineers should be familiar with professional services agreements. This is a function of education and experience. The business plan should provide for acquainting key staff members with a general background of the law affecting professional services agreements.

Various alternatives are available for educating staff members about the intricacies of professional services agreements. Some of the alternatives are as follows:

1. Staff members can attend seminars and programs put on by the professional organizations such as the American Institute of Architects.

2. Staff members can read books and other literature about professional services agreements that have been written for architects and engineers.

3. Staff members can participate in educational programs of insurers who issue professional liability insurance covering architects and engineers.

4. Staff members can attend in-house seminars. These seminars are usually most helpful if the firm's attorney and insurance broker also participate.

The firm also should make a decision as to whether it should adopt a standard professional services agreement. Many design firms use the standard forms published by the American Institute of Architects or other professional organizations. Other firms have developed their own standard professional services agreement. When selecting a standard form, the firm should consult with its attorney, explore options to various provisions, and consider the potential areas of liability of the firm.

Although the firm's clients may not want to accept the standard professional services agreement, it can be used as a basis for negotiations. Changes suggested by the owner can be analyzed by the firm and its attorney to determine whether they may increase the firm's liability exposure.

The firm should carefully review any owner-drafted professional services agreements. Often, such documents are not acceptable to design professionals. Owner-generated agreements frequently contain provisions detrimental to architects and engineers. Some provisions, such as guaranties or warranties, may not be even covered by the designer's professional liability insurance policy. For example, the National Association of Attorneys General (NAAG) issued standard construction documents forms which contained onerous provisions for architects and engineers.[46] The NAAG form for design services would increase the liability of any design professional who agreed to it. It required the design professional to supervise construction. Since architects and engineers are not contractors, they avoid assuming any responsibility for the methods or means of construction. Also under the NAAG documents, the designer enforced "faithful performance" of the construction contract by the contractor and was to suspend work by the contractor under certain circumstances. Again, these are responsibilities which architects and engineers have traditionally not accepted. The NAAG forms also increased the responsibility of the designer for the cost of the project and imposed an absolute warranty of perfection upon the design professional. Either undertaking may not be covered by the architect's or engineer's professional insurance policy.

Because of protests from architects, engineers, and professional insurers, the NAAG forms were withdrawn from use. However, these forms are a perfect example of how design contracts tendered by the owner to the design professional may contain unacceptable terms that greatly expand the designer's liability exposure and ignore the traditional role played by the architect and engineer in the design and construction process.

Once a standard form is adopted, the firm must decide how the proposed professional services agreement will be presented to the client and how any modifications will be negotiated. For small firms, one of the principals can handle the negotiations involved in drafting the agreement.

Larger firms have two alternatives: First, the principals involved with the client may handle the negotiations. Second, the firm can have one principal or key staff member handle negotiations for all professional services agreements.

The first alternative results in continuity because the same people from the firm are involved throughout the relationship with the client. However, this alternative presents potential hazards. The principals soliciting the commission have a vested interest in securing the work and may not be the best negotiators for the firm. Also, spreading negotiations among all the principals may not result in developing the best expertise for negotiating professional services agreements.

Although the second alternative introduces a critical temporary participant in the negotiating process, it does have advantages. First, through repeated exposure to professional services agreements and the problems which may arise in negotiating their terms and conditions, at least one staff member will develop significant expertise in this area. He or she should learn which provisions to avoid in the professional services agreement and be able to spot situations when legal counsel should be consulted. Until the negotiator becomes proficient in this area, he or she should frequently consult with the firm's attorney. It is hoped that after a short period of time of working with the firm's counsel, the negotiator should be able to work relatively independently.

If the first alternative for negotiating a professional agreement is adopted as firm policy, the firm should require that all such agreements be reviewed by one specific principal or key staff member before execution. Through a review process, the firm may be able to stop the negotiating teams from agreeing to contractual provisions which may be detrimental to the firm.

Whichever alternative is used by the firm, not only should the firm consult with counsel when appropriate, but the firm also should consult with its insurance broker about contractual provisions. The insurance broker should be consulted to assure that key contractual provisions will not bar insurance coverage in the event a claim or lawsuit arises from performing services under the agreement. The firm should want the contract covered by its professional liability insurance.

Working with Consultants

When planning, the firm should decide whether it will contract with the necessary consultants to render design services required for the project or whether the owner should contract directly with the consultants. If the architect or engineer contracts with the consultants, better coordination of the overall design effort may be achieved. However, by contracting with the consultants, the firm may become liable for the professional errors or omissions of the consultants. If the consultants contract directly with the owner, the firm avoids this liability exposure.

If the firm decides, as a matter of business policy, to retain all or any consultants for projects it will do, it should adopt certain policies for consultants. First, it should develop a method for prequalifying consultants. The firm should not enter into contracts with consultants with whom it is not familiar or in whom it has little or no confidence. The firm should avoid entering into contracts with consultants based upon price alone.

Second, the firm might develop a standard written contract to be entered into by its consultants. Several professional organizations, including the American Institute of Architects, have written such forms. However, these forms do not necessarily cover all the problems which may arise while working with a consultant.

The contract should specifically describe the amount of money to be paid to the consultant for its services and when the consultant will be paid. The firm also should consider whether the contract should contain a provision stating that the consultant will not be paid by the firm until it is paid by the owner for the consultant's services.

The contract should describe the scope of services to be provided by the consultant. A well-defined scope of services not only delineates responsibilities, but clarifies who may be ultimately liable for a design error or omission of the consultant. A well-drafted scope of services also should minimize claims for extras from the consultant.

The agreement should also provide that the consultant will indemnify the firm, and perhaps its client, from claims or lawsuits arising from the performance of services of the consultant. The firm does not want to end up having to pay for a consultant's negligence.

The agreement should specify the insurance policies to be maintained by the consultant and the amount of insurance for each policy. At a minimum, the consultant should be required to have a professional liability policy which, among other things, insures the provision of the consultant indemnifying the firm.

Further, the contract should require the consultant to furnish a certificate evidencing his or her insurance coverage. Such certificates are usually issued by the consultant's insurance broker. The firm may also ask the consultant to provide copies of his or her insurance policies. These steps are required so that the firm can assure itself that the consultant has adequate insurance coverage.

A policy should be devised for assuring that certificates of insurance are received from all consultants and are updated or renewed as required. Some mechanism should be established to determine which projects require certificates of insurance from consultants. Then a procedure must be adopted to assure certificates of insurance are received as required. One method of assuring that consultants furnish the necessary certificates is to not pay them until the certificate is received.

The firm should establish a business policy outlining who will negotiate consultant contracts. Again, this may either be the project team, with a review of the agreement by a designated staff member, or one specific person not affiliated with the project team.

Specific Contractual Provisions

As part of planning for the professional services agreement, the design professional should establish a policy for each of the major provisions of the agreement. The architect or engineer should consider the good and bad points of specific provisions and select alternatives which meet the requirements of the design professional. Moreover, by thinking about these provisions beforehand, the design professional should be better able to respond to objectionable provisions made by the client.

The complexity of the professional services agreement depends upon the nature of the project. Smaller, less-complicated projects may not require an exhaustive agreement. As an example, a contract for a mechanical engineer to review an existing HVAC system to determine whether any of it needs to be upgraded could be described in a simple letter. The mechanical engineer could send a letter to the client, briefly outlining the services to be performed and the manner and method of payment. The client could then be requested to sign a copy of the letter and return it, indicating that the letter is a binding contractual agreement.

If the architect or engineer is going to use letters for contract documents, he or she should consider including certain standard provisions in the letter. Such provisions designed to protect the architect and engineer are discussed in this chapter.

An agreement for a larger project may be more complex. Numerous provisions may be necessary to describe the responsibilities of both the design professional and the client, although this may not always be the case.

Scope of services

The professional services agreement should clearly describe which services are to be performed by the architect or engineer. It also should state what services are not to be performed by the design professional. As an example, the client may have hired several design professionals, such as an architect, a structural engineer, and a mechanical-electrical engineer, for a project. In this case, the agreement should state that the architect will not provide any structural, mechanical, or electrical services. If the architect is to coordinate these other services, however, the agreement should say so and describe the expected coordination effort. Will the architect assure that there are no interferences in the design of the professionals working upon the project? Will the architect be responsible for incorporating the drawings and specifications of the other consultant in the bid and contract documents? Will the contractor furnish all working drawings and submittals to the architect for all the professionals working upon the project?

A well-defined scope of services also benefits the architect or engineer if the designer makes a claim for extra work. If the scope of services is properly drafted, the justifiability of the claim for extras should be apparent to the client.

The standard form for professional services of the American Institute of Architects contains a detailed description of the services to be performed by an architect. The description of these services is broken down into the schematic design phase, the design development phase, the construction documents phase, and the construction phase.

A description of design phase services may be relatively easy to state. For example, the agreement may simply state that the architect is to design a building of so many square feet and so many stories to be located at a particular site. The description may also contain a projected cost for the building.

The scope of services for the design phase may be more detailed. Particular materials to be used, such as prestressed concrete, may be stated. Also, particular systems, such as a specific HVAC system, may be specified.

The scope of services performed by the architect or engineer is limited by design decisions made by the client. Although the architect or engineer is responsible for the design, the client's decisions have an effect on that design. For instance, the owner's budget for a project defines the design alternatives of the architect or engineer. A limited budget means that certain expensive materials or systems may not be used.

A description of the services expected by the design professional during the construction phase can be difficult to draft. An architect or engineer usually performs four basic services during construction:

1. Interpret the contract documents.
2. Observe the progress of construction to determine if the work complies with the plans and specifications.
3. Certify payouts to the contractor.
4. Review contractor submittals, such as shop drawings and samples of material.

Writing a provision stating that the architect or engineer will interpret the contract documents is simple. The design professional should, however, consider whether the contract should say more. For instance, the design professional should decide whether it is necessary to state whether his or her interpretation of the contractual documents is conclusive and binding upon the contractor.

Drafting a provision covering the design professional's responsibility for on-site observation services is more difficult. Most standard industry forms do not state how many visits the architect or engineer is expected to make to the construction site. For many projects, architects or engineers normally visit the site only when payout requests are submitted by the contractor. When payout requests are received, the architect or engineer walks through the project to determine the quality of the work and whether the observed work conforms to the plans and specifications.

Unfortunately, it is extremely difficult, if not impossible, to state what exactly the architect or engineer should observe when examining the progress of construction to determine whether the work conforms to the plans and specifications. The client wants the architect or engineer to note every deviance from the design, which would make the design professional a guarantor of the contractor's performance. The architect or engineer usually does not want to warrant that all construction defects will be noted, especially since he or she cannot have an on-site observer overlooking the work of all the tradespeople all of the time. Moreover, the client would not be willing or could not afford to pay for 100 percent inspection of all of the contractor's work. Only for certain types of construction, such as nuclear power plants, has the construction industry come close to 100 percent inspection of a contractor's work.

Accordingly, the drafting of the on-site observation provision usually results in a compromise. Typically, the design professional agrees to observe the progress of the work at certain intervals to determine whether the construction conforms to the plans and specifications. The client agrees that the architect or engineers may not notice all construction defects and is not a guarantor of the performance of the contractor.

The courts have considered the architect's or engineer's obligations in connection with examination of the work. Unless altered by contract, the architect or engineer only is expected to act reasonably and is responsible for the failure to notice a defect in construction if he or she was negligent as determined by relevant professional practice. Thus, if a reasonable architect or engineer would have noticed the defect, then the one observing the progress of construction should have noticed the defect.

Architects and engineers frequently are obligated to visit the project site to review the progress of construction in connection with payout requests of the contractor. As part of the process, the design professional issues a certificate for payment stating that the work has progressed as stated in the payout request and indicating that he or she has examined the work to determine whether the construction conforms to the plans and specifications. Some certificates provided by clients request the design engineer to certify that the work complies with the plans and specifications. Such broad language may be interpreted to indicate that all the work conforms to the plans and specifications and may make the architect or engineer the guarantor of the contractor's performance. Many design professionals refuse to execute such broad certificates and prefer to execute a certificate stating that "to the best of my knowledge the work conforms to the plans and specifications."

The professional services agreement should contain a statement as to the architect's or engineer's responsibilities for certifying requests for construction payouts or progress payments. This provision also should clearly state the design professional's responsibility for observing the work and indicate that the architect or engineer does not guarantee that the contractor has complied with the plans and specifications in all respects.

The professional services agreement also should outline the design professional's responsibility for reviewing shop drawings. Ordinarily, the architect and engineer prepare drawings indicating general design concepts. The project cannot be constructed from those drawings. The contractor must produce shop drawings from which the building components will be fabricated and constructed. The architect or engineer reviews the shop drawings to determine whether the building, as constructed, will conform to his or her design. However, the design professional does not verify the dimensions on the shop drawings and does not review the engineering done by the contractor in connection with the production of the shop drawings.

The owner may expect the architect or engineer to make a detailed review of the design and engineering of the contractor. However, such duplication of effort adds cost to the project and usually is unnecessary. Accordingly, the contract should contain a provision clearly stating the design professional's limited responsibility in the shop drawing review process.

Standard of care

Many design firms include a statement of the standard of care expected of them in performing services for the project in their professional services agreements. A clearly written professional responsibility provision should help the engineer or architect in any disputes with a client over the adequacy of the design.

Normally, design professionals do not guarantee a perfect result. Rather, they are obligated to perform their services using the same degree of skill and care as any architect or engineer would in a similar situation. Many clients, however, do not understand this concept of professional responsibility and often tender professional services agreements to the architect or engineer containing absolute guaranties. Most design professionals will not accept such provisions because they broaden their traditional professional responsibility to the client and the public. Moreover, many professional liability insurance policies covering architects and engineers will not insure such guaranties.

Firms should, therefore, consider the advisability of including a statement of the standard of care expected in all professional services agreements. As an example, the statement could read:

> The architect or engineer shall render services in accordance with the standard of care regularly followed by architects or engineers in this community.

Method of the work

Architects and engineers do not ordinarily supervise or control the construction process. The contractor is responsible for constructing the project. Many clients do not understand this distinction and assume that the architect or engineer actually supervises the work of the contractor, especially after a contractor error delays construction or results in a catastrophic loss. Accordingly, many design contracts, including standard agreement forms published by professional organizations, state that the design professional shall not be responsible for the methods or means of constructing the project.

The firm also should consider including a provision indicating that it shall not supervise construction of the project for another reason. Construction workers are frequently injured at the project and often file suits to recover damages for their injuries. Such suits are common in states that have structural work or scaffolding acts and hold anyone found to be "in charge of" the work liable for injuries sustained by a worker. One of the factors the court or jury weighs when determining who is in charge of the work is whether a defendant has any right to supervise construction. Thus, many design professionals find a statement indicating that they are not responsible for supervising construction helpful in limiting their exposure to lawsuits filed by injured construction workers.

Job-site safety

Job-site safety is extremely important. No one wants to see anyone injured at the work site; moreover, accidents result in construction delays and lawsuits. Architects and engineers have avoided becoming involved with job-site safety, except for their own employees. They do so for several reasons.

First, most architects and engineers do not have any training or experience in job-site safety. If they cannot adequately perform the task, it does not make sense for them to assume such responsibility. Second, job-site safety is closely intertwined with the method of doing the work. Thus, rationally, the contractor should be responsible for job-site safety. Third, those responsible for job-site safety also may be liable for damages in suits filed by injured construction workers. In states with structural work or scaffolding acts, those who are responsible for job-site safety may be found to be in charge of the work and hence liable. In other states, those responsible for safety may be found negligent and thus liable for the injuries sustained by the injured worker.

Most design professionals use service agreements which state that they will have no responsibility for safety. Again, it is important that the architect or engineer not voluntarily accept any safety responsibility because it could result in the design professional being found liable either under structural work or in negligence.

Owner's responsibilities

A firm should determine whether its professional services agreement should have a provision detailing the owner's responsibilities. Such a provision should help minimize any misunderstanding with the client as to what is expected. As an example, if the owner is to furnish a survey or a soil report, the agreement should so provide. Many standard form services agreements published by professional societies, such as the American Institute of Architects, contain statements listing the reports and information to be furnished by the client.

Payment

The firm should consider business policies which will assure it is paid for the work it performs. Too often, architects or engineers do preliminary design work for projects which do not go forward, resulting in nonpayment of invoices.

In the boom portion of the construction cycle, numerous developers appear with often speculative projects for office, commercial, residential, and multiunit housing projects. Typically, the architect or engineer is not paid until construction financing is funded. As the construction cycle turns into the "bust" phase, many design professionals are not paid because their developer clients can no longer obtain construction financing.

Although architects and engineers must live with the construction cycle, there are certain steps they can take to minimize unpaid bills. The firm should weigh credit checks for all new clients. It should review reports from credit agencies and information from financial institutions to determine whether the design professional should enter into a business relationship with a new client.

The firm also should consider a continuing review of the financial resources of its existing clients. The design professional should be alert for signals that a client may be depleting its resources and ability to obtain construction financing. The firm should be on the lookout for signs of overbuilding in its market. If such signs become prevalent, the firm should seriously weigh whether it still wants to be involved in speculative projects.

The firm should attempt to get paid as much as it can as soon as it can. Although design professionals traditionally do not ask their clients for retainers, the firm should consider such a possibility. Are there clients who would be willing to pay a portion of the design fee before the preliminary design phase begins?

The firm also should encourage periodic payments. It may not be wise to work on a lump-sum basis, paid when the design is completed, especially where design may take several months or longer. Under such circumstances, the firm should consider whether it should be paid as certain design phases are completed.

If invoices are unpaid, the firm should consider a policy for collecting them. A follow-up system should be in place to determine when payment of invoices is overdue. In addition, some policy should be adopted about contacting clients about overdue payments. The firm should also consider a policy for collecting payments after its efforts prove unsuccessful. Should the invoices be placed with a collection agency or an attorney? Too often, architects and engineers are reluctant to pursue unpaid statements vigorously.

In many states, design professionals have an option for collection of unpaid bills. As discussed in Chap. 8, the architect or engineer may file a mechanic's lien against the real property upon which the project is or may be placed.

Clearly, overdue bills are a serious matter and the firm should develop policies to deal with this problem. In establishing its policy, the firm may want to consult with its attorney, accountant, and banker.

Cost estimates

In developing its business plan, a firm should consider how to handle its responsibility for cost estimates. Owners desire to construct projects within budget; this goal, however, is not always obtainable.

The designer has no control over the prices of vendors or contractors. A contractor deals with many variables when putting together a cost proposal. If the specifications permit the contractor to install one of several materials or systems, the price of each material or system usually varies. In addition, the labor cost for installing specific materials or systems may vary. Further, if the contractor receives proposals from subcontractors the price quotations of subcontractors in the same trade usually vary.

Contractor cost proposals also vary with the state of construction activity. If construction activity is down, many contractors and subcontractors will make price concessions. Moreover, the designer has no control over inflation. The amount of inflation and the contractor's assumption about future inflation influences the contractor's proposed cost. Further, the designer has no control over wage rates. In many areas of the country, the construction trades are heavily unionized. For long-term projects, the designer may be unable to estimate future wage rates.

Because of the many variables involved in the cost-estimating process, many design firms do not assume any responsibility for the accuracy of cost estimates. Most of these firms disclaim any liability for inaccurate cost estimates in the professional services agreements.

The standard professional services agreements published by the national design professional organization contain such disclaimers. AIA Document B141, the standard professional services agreement form of the American Institute of Architects, includes a detailed description of the cost-estimating process and specifically states that the architect has no liability if the contract bids vary from the architect's cost estimates. Similarly, EJCDC Form No. 1910.1, published by the Engineers Joint Contract Documents Committee, contains a disclaimer of the reliability of cost estimates prepared by engineers.

Code compliance

When drafting professional services agreements, most design professionals do not give any thought to problems which may arise from code compliance. Many architects and engineers are willing to enter into professional services contracts under which they agree the design will meet the requirements of all applicable laws, regulations, and codes. For ordinary building projects, such an undertaking may not be objectionable since designers are usually familiar with laws, regulations, and codes in the communities in which they practice. However, for a complex project which requires sophisticated engineering, the designer should consider other alternatives. As an example, the architect or engineer may find it advisable to list the laws, regulations, and codes which will apply to the design of the project.

The design firm also should consider another possible source of conflict. Occasionally, a local building inspector may require a certain design detail even though it is not required by the building code. The firm should consider whether the professional services agreement should provide for the client to pay any additional cost resulting from differing interpretations of the building code by the building department and the architect or engineer.

Indemnification

Chapter 9 discussed the use of indemnification to allocate risk among those involved in the construction process. When doing its business planning, the design firm should weigh the desirability of obtaining indemnification from the others involved with the project. Further, the firm should consider under what circumstances it will indemnify others working on the project and whether its agreement to indemnify anyone else should be limited.

Any design professional would like to be held harmless from any liability arising from his or her negligence. But no client or contractor would ever agree to give an architect or engineer complete indemnification for negligent design or field services. Contractors have, however, been willing to indemnify architects and engineers for certain risks.

Traditionally, contractors have agreed to indemnify owners, architects, and engineers for damages resulting from the contractor's performance of the construction contract or from the contractor's negligence. Further, contractors usually will agree to hold harmless the owner and design professionals even if the negligence of one or more of them contributed to the damage. Unfortunately, as discussed in Chap. 9, the contractor's ability to indemnify may be limited.

Accordingly, the drafting of a hold harmless provision in a construction contract and the insuring of it becomes a complex matter. State law clearly affects the drafting of the provisions, and the adoption of any particular provision should be undertaken with advice from the design firm's attorney and insurance broker.

Not only do design firms seek indemnification provisions in construction contracts, but frequently they are requested to hold the owner or client harmless. Clients prefer that the architect or engineer indemnify them against damages caused for any reason by the designer. However, as pointed out in Chap. 8, a design professional is only liable for damages resulting from his or her negligence and is not a guarantor of a perfect result. Further, professional liability insurance policies covering architects and engineers usually do not cover guaranties or warranties of the designer. Thus, when agreeing to indemnify the client, the design firm should only hold the client harmless for claims arising from the firm's negligence.

Limiting liability by contract

When doing business planning, the design firm also should consider including limitation of liability provisions in its professional services agreements (see Chap. 9). Many firms regularly use such provisions to minimize exposure to potential claims from clients. For many projects, a professional error or omission of the design could result in a major catastrophic failure, such as a wall collapsing, or substantial corrective repair, such as to avoid a wall collapse.

The architect and engineer should be aware of one shortcoming of limiting liability provisions. Since such provisions are creatures of contract, they only bind or apply to those for whom the contract applies, usually the designer and the client. Limitation of liability provisions do not limit or affect the claims of third parties, such as innocent bystanders or construction workers, who are not parties to the professional services agreement.

Insurance

During business planning, the design firm should consider what forms of insurance it should carry and what forms of insurance it should expect its clients to provide. For instance, the design firm may have decided that it will maintain professional liability insurance of certain limits. It also may want its clients to purchase insurance for the protection of the project, such as all risk builder's insurance. If so, the firm should decide whether the professional services agreement should specifically state what insurance policies each should purchase.

In addition, the firm should determine whether to obtain certificates of insurance from the client and owner to show if the required insurance has been purchased. If the firm is to be insured under the insurance of any other party connected with the project, such as the client or contractor, it should require that certificates of insurance be sent to it. Further, the firm should set up a mechanism to assure it receives the certificates of insurance and that they are kept current.

Document ownership

When business planning, the firm should establish a policy for ownership of the documents it generates. Ordinarily, documents, including designs, prepared by a design professional become the property of the client when the fee is paid. Many design professionals, however, state in the contract that the ownership of the documents remains with them.

Akin to the concept of the ownership of the documents is the right of the client to reuse the documents for other projects. Most architects and engineers wish to avoid reuse of their documents for other projects without their consent. Accordingly, some design professionals now bind the client by contract to either obtain their written permission before reusing the documents or to hold them harmless from any damages resulting from the unauthorized reuse of the documents.

Arbitration

Chapter 9 discusses the benefits and detriments of arbitration and other forms of alternative dispute resolution. During business planning, the firm should adopt a policy toward arbitration.

Planning for Fringe Benefits

Owner and employee compensation is a major component of a design firm's expense. An important part of compensation is fringe benefits, which frequently run between 30 and 40 percent of cash compensation.[47] Because of the impact of these expenditures on its budget and profitability, every design firm, from its founding and throughout its existence, must plan for fringe benefits.

Fringe benefit plans, including retirement plans, are governed by several federal statutes. The Employee Retirement Income Security Act of 1974, commonly referred to as ERISA, regulates pension plans and describes the type of plans which may be used, how the plans are funded, how employee interests become vested, how funds are to be managed, how payments are to be made to retired employees, and how plans may be terminated. ERISA covers a wide range of employee benefit plans, such as retirement plans and health plans.

Besides ERISA, other federal laws affect the implementation of the employee benefit plans. Among these statutes is the Civil Rights Act of 1964, barring discrimination in employment based upon race or sex. Thus, sex cannot be used as a basis to distinguish between the amount of distribution made to an employee under a plan.[48]

The Pregnancy Discrimination Act of 1978 amended Title VII of the Civil Rights Act of 1964 and prohibits discrimination because of pregnancy. Accordingly, health plans may not place limits upon the amounts of benefits purely because of a plan participant's pregnancy.[49] The Older Americans Act and the Age Discrimination in Employment Act bar discrimination among employees based upon age and affect the provisions of various employee benefit plans.

Because of the complexity of the federal laws and regulations covering benefit plans, design firms should regularly consult with an experienced employee benefits attorney. The attorney should draft the plan documents or review documents for master plans in which the firm wishes to participate. For example, the firm may not want to establish its own retirement program but rather to participate in a retirement plan program available from an insurance company or bank. The insurance company or bank may have a master retirement plan, approved by the U.S. Department of Labor, which the firm may adopt.

The firm also should consult other experts when implementing and operating its benefit plans. If the firm will manage its own retirement plans, it may need to work with an actuary. Or it will have to consult with an insurance broker to establish a group health insurance plan for its employees. Further, the firm should consult with its accountant about the cost of various plans and the effect each will have on its income tax obligations.

Once the plans are established, the firm should periodically review them with its benefits lawyer. The statutes and regulations covering benefit plans are constantly changing, so plans must be reviewed to assure compliance with legislative and regulatory changes. In addition, the firm should ask its attorney to keep it posted of any statutory or regulatory changes which may affect any of its plans.

The firm also should periodically review the effectiveness of each of its plans. As an example, the performance of investment managers of retirement funds varies. The firm should assure that its investments are receiving a favorable rate of return. If not, it should consider changing investment managers. Also, health insurance plans must be constantly reviewed because of the ever-increasing costs of health care.

Due to changes in the Tax Reform Act of 1986, there are no longer any distinctions among corporations, partnerships, or sole proprietorships in the effect of employee benefits plans. Before the Tax Reform Act of 1986, corporations had distinct advantages over partnerships and sole proprietorships, but those distinctions were eliminated by the Act.

Selecting Fringe Benefit Plans

There are several factors to consider when deciding whether to adopt fringe benefit plans and how to operate them:

1. What plans do other employers have?

2. Which employees does the firm want to benefit?

3. What are governmental limitations upon each of the plans?

4. What will the firm's contributions to the plan cost?

5. What will it cost to establish and administer the plan?

Employers must offer certain fringe benefit plans in order to attract and keep employees. Traditionally, welfare benefit plans have been viewed as helping or improving employee morale. Today, however, benefit plans offered by competing employers may be a prime determinate of the plans a firm must maintain.

In determining which employees should benefit from a plan, the firm needs to consider three groups of employees: owner-employees, key employees, and all other employees.

The owners of many design firms regularly work in the firm; they may be sole proprietors, partners, or shareholders of a corporation. When planning for owner-employees, several factors should be considered in developing fringe benefit plans. First, the financial condition of the owner-employee, along with future financial needs, should be analyzed. If the owner-employee has substantial assets, he or she may not want or need a retirement plan. However, the owner-employee may require estate planning to minimize estate and inheritance taxes upon his or her death. If the owner-employee is facing future substantial expenses, such as college tuition, he or she may want to maximize future income at the expense of fringe benefits. If the owner-employee does not have substantial assets, a retirement plan which maximizes retirement benefits may be advisable.

Second, the owner-employee may be supporting a spouse or a child with a chronic medical problem requiring significant expenses, some of which may not be covered by health insurance. If the expenses are not covered by health insurance, the owner-employee should determine whether a benefit plan could be devised to limit the financial burden of these expenses.

Third, the age of the owner-employee should be weighed, along with his or her assets. Retirement planning for younger owner-employees is different from such planning for older owner-employees. Younger owners have many years to accumulate a retirement fund. Older owners who do not have substantial assets may only have a few years to accumulate a retirement fund.

A small- or medium-sized design firm may have one key employee to whom they may want to make attractive fringe benefits available. Some medium- and large-sized design firms may have several such key employees. The income, assets, and needs of key employees should be examined just as those for owner-employees.

Employees may be awarded for past service. More frequently, however, they are offered benefits to retain them as employees. Under such circumstances, programs offering deferred compensation or an ownership interest in the business should be explored.

In considering the benefits needs of employees who usually are not paid as much as owner-employees or key employees, the firm should consider the impact of certain government programs, such as Social

Security and Worker's Compensation. Usually, employee benefit plans are established so they are received under a company's fringe benefit programs.

A firm's contribution to a proposed benefit plan is a factor used to determine whether the plan will be adopted. Many design firms work with limited budgets, so they may be unable to afford all available plans. Medical plans can result in substantial premiums or costs. Frequently, firms limit these plans to control costs. As an example, many firms do not have dental care coverage because of the relatively high cost of plans with this feature.

Costs of administering a plan also should be considered when deciding whether to implement it. The firm should not adopt a plan with marginal value and burdensome administrative costs. For a design firm with limited financial resources, the administrative costs of employee benefit plans could be burdensome, especially during a period of business slowdown.

Compensating Employees

Employees are compensated by the firm paying either present benefits or future benefits. Present benefits are pay or wages, granting an ownership interest in the business, and certain fringe benefits. Future benefits include deferred compensation, granting a right to an ownership interest in the future, and retirement plans.

Wages and salaries are the main means of employee compensation, although for many companies fringe benefits have become a substantial part of the employee's compensation. Giving employees increased pay in lieu of certain fringe benefits, however, has benefits to the firm. First, administrative costs of maintaining plans are eliminated. Second, the cost of establishing a plan is avoided. Third, the firm is not necessarily wedded to the plan, which may require regular contributions in future years. Thus, the cost of terminating a plan which may no longer be advisable is avoided.

Employees have an economic incentive to trade pay for certain fringe benefits, such as health and life insurance programs. Usually, premium costs are reduced by participating in group insurance programs, which is beneficial to the employee. Moreover, if an employee buys an individual health policy using his or her pay, the premium payments are not deductible from the employee's personal income tax. Thus, the employee has incentives for the employer to pay for certain fringe benefits.

Giving an employee an ownership interest in the business may be desirable for several reasons. First, employees who become part owners of the business may have more incentive to be productive. Second, it may be necessary to make key employees part owners of the business in order to keep them. Third, ownership in the business may result in more income for the employee.

Deferred compensation used to be an important fringe benefit for employees. Before the changes in the tax rates, employees preferred to defer payment of certain compensation until after retirement, when they would be in a lower tax bracket. Because of the lower maximum tax bracket, however, deferred compensation is no longer as popular as it had been.

A company may promise to make an employee an owner of the business in the future. This can take the form of a promise of stock options or the granting of stock options by a corporation. Partnerships can enter into agreements with employees to make them partners at some time in the future.

Retirement Plans

Retirement plans are a popular fringe benefit. An important distinction must be realized about retirement plans. They can be either qualified or nonqualified plans. Qualified plans are the most common type. They meet the requirements of the Internal Revenue Code, and therefore the employer's contribution is tax deductible as a business expense but the contribution is not taxable income. Employees only pay income tax upon distributions under the plan. They do not pay income tax on income made off of the investment of the assets of the retirement plan.

Qualified plans have significant tax advantages. However, they can be expensive to establish and maintain. Complying with the federal law governing qualified retirement plans may take many hours of a lawyer's time. Further, the company has to make substantial contributions annually for the employees covered by the plan, manage the funds, and make periodic reports to the government and its employees.

The expense of operating qualified plans may be minimized if the design firm adopted either a prototype or master plan approved by the Internal Revenue Service. A prototype plan is a standard plan used by individual employers. A master plan is the same as a prototype plan except the funds are managed by a single financial institution or group of financial institutions.

A nonqualified plan does not meet the regulatory requirements of the Internal Revenue Code. Hence, it does not produce the tax benefits of a qualified plan. However, it may be possible to cover fewer employees under a nonqualified plan than a qualified plan. Under a nonqualified plan, the employer may deduct its contributions to the plan in the years in which the employee must report the contribution as income.

Retirement plan funds are held by a trustee who is responsible for maintaining and investing the funds. The trustee may be the company which has established the plan or be a financial institution, such as a trust company or an insurance company. The trustee administers the fund pursuant to the document establishing the plan.

There are two basic types of retirement plans: the defined benefit plan and the defined contribution plan. Under a defined benefit plan, the participant is paid a fixed sum as a pension as determined by the schedule of benefits for the plan. Usually, pension payments are determined by a combination of salary history and years of employment with the firm. Under a defined contribution plan, contributions are made to the plan according to the plan agreement. Frequently, contributions are a certain percentage of employee pay. The employee's retirement benefit is based upon the value of the employee's vested share in the plan at the time of retirement.

For defined benefit plans, the company must determine current and future obligations under the plan and make payments to the plan to meet those obligations. Most defined benefit plans require regular review by an actuary to establish current and future payments due under the plan. The actuary usually considers a number of factors, such as fund income, turnover, retirement age, and pay scales.

Benefits to be paid under a defined benefit plan are certain only if the plan is fully funded. A fully funded plan has enough assets to cover obligations for past service and future service. The government has established complex regulations governing funding. These regulations allow an employer to fund over a certain period of years but requires certain minimum funding. The government also has regulations governing overfunding. Compliance with these regulations requires the services of an actuary, an accountant, and a lawyer.

Because of the cost of complying with regulations covering defined benefit plans and the relatively high cost of fully funding a defined benefit plan, such plans are not too popular with small businesses. In addition, some large employers have terminated defined benefit plans because of the large sums necessary to fund such plans fully.

For a small design firm, a defined contribution plan may be the best alternative. Administrative costs of such a plan are lower. Further, the firm's contribution is easily determined, since most firms provide for contribution to be based upon a percentage of employee salary.

The success of the trustee in investing the assets of a defined benefit plan is a major factor in determining the company's contributions to the plan. Ill-advised investments can severely damage a plan and make an employer's contributions extremely burdensome.

For defined contribution plans, the participants are not guaranteed a specific pension or benefit when they retire. When the employee retires, he or she is entitled to receive his or her share of the plan. This amount depends in part upon the success of the trustee in investing the plan's assets. Most defined contribution plans provide that upon retirement, the employee may either take his or her share out of the plan or the trustee will purchase an annuity for the employee, which determines monthly payments the employee will receive until death. If the participant elects to take his or her share of the plan in cash upon retirement, the employee may roll over the lump-sum payment into an IRA to avoid paying income tax upon the payment and to continue to accumulate income without income tax liability.

Some employers have adopted target benefit plans. Under such a plan, certain assumptions are made to arrive at specific benefits for plan participants upon retirement. However, the actual retirement benefit depends upon the market value of the assets in the individual employee's account. As an example, if the plan's assets are not as successfully invested as the actuarial assumption, then benefits would be reduced.

Under a target benefit plan, the employer's contribution is fixed at the initiation of the plan, which removes the problem of uncertainty of the future for the employer. However, the benefits to be paid under the plan are not fixed and hence uncertain.

There are two basic alternatives for plan operations. The first is the trust fund method of operation. The owners of the firm may be the plan's trustees and either handle the entire administration of the plan or delegate certain aspects of the plan administration to others. The plan can also delegate a third person, such as a trust company or an insurance company, to be trustee.

If some of a firm's owners are to be the plan's trustees, they must make basic decisions regarding the investment of the assets of the plan. Frequently, they consult with a stockbroker or financial adviser about plan investment decisions. Many plan trustees invest plan assets in specialized investment accounts established by trust companies similar to mutual funds; other trustees invest plan assets in mutual funds.

Many defined contribution plans provide for plan participants or employees to determine how their share of the plan assets will be invested. As an example, a plan may allow participants to select to invest various portions of their share of the fund in an aggressive common stock, a balanced stock and bond fund, or income funds managed by a trust company. Some plans may even allow employees to select specific stocks and bonds in which their share of the funds will be invested.

The second method of operation is the use of insured plans. Under such plans, the employer pays its contributions to an insurance company, which invests the contributions and makes distributions to participants pursuant to a schedule of benefits. Insured plans have two basic funding options. First, cash value life insurance or deferred annuities are purchased for each employee as contributions are received. Second, the funds can be allowed to accumulate and be managed as a trust plan. Upon retirement, annuities are purchased for retiring employees. If an employee terminates before retirement, payments are made pursuant to the schedule of benefits.

Some insurance companies allow an employer with 10 or fewer participants to use individual insurance policies for funding. Usually, one of the firm's owners or employees is designated as trustee of the plan and receives employer contributions and pays premiums on the individual insurance policies. Generally, cash value insurance policies are purchased by the trustee for each plan participant.

Employers may also use group permanent or cash value life insurance, group deferred annuities, and deposit administration plans to fund insured plans. With the first two plans, the life insurance or annuity contract is purchased as contributions are received. Under the deposit administration plans, contributions are invested as a trust plan and upon retirement deferred annuities are purchased for the retiring participant.

Types of Retirement Plans

There are five basic types of qualified retirement plans:

1. Profit-sharing plans
2. Stock bonus plans
3. Pension plans
4. Annuity plans
5. Cash or deferred plans

Profit-sharing plans

U.S. Treasury regulations define a profit-sharing plan as "a plan established and maintained by an employer to provide for the participation in his [or her] profits by his [or her] employees or their beneficiaries."[50] A profit-sharing plan is a form of a defined contribution plan.

A profit-sharing plan can provide for either contributions to be made each year or to be made each year at the discretion of the employer. Most profit-sharing plans follow the latter alternative and indicate that at a certain time the employer or the board of directors in the case of a corporation will determine how much of the firm's profits shall be contributed to the plan, usually a percentage of employee compensation.

Upon retirement or termination in participation in the plan for another reason, such as termination of employment or death, the employee's interest in the plan is determined by the amount of contributions made on behalf of the employee, the forfeiture of former terminated employees who were not fully vested in the plan at the time of termination, and success of the investments of plan assets by the trustees. Since a profit-sharing plan is a defined contribution plan, the employee's benefits under the plan are not fixed until retirement or termination.

There are noncontributory and contributory profit-sharing plans. Under contributory plans, employees are required to contribute a certain portion of their compensation to the plan. The employer also may allow employees to make voluntary contributions to the plan, which are deducted from wages and salaries.

Profit-sharing plans may allow for loans to be made to a participant from his or her account. There are strict government regulations governing such loans. The loan may not exceed $50,000 or the value of the employee's account and loans must be repaid in 5 years. Profit-sharing also may provide for certain incidental benefits; these are life, accident, and health insurance.

Profit-sharing plans are attractive to many employers. They can be written to provide for contributions only in those years in which the firm has profits. Further, the plan may be written so the amount of the contribution is determined by the employer. Many design firms may find profit-sharing plans appealing because of profit vulnerability due to the ups and downs of the construction cycle.

Stock bonus plans

Stock bonus plans are similar to profit-sharing plans, except employer contributions need not depend upon profits and benefits are distributed in stock or shares of the employer. Stock bonus plans may only be used for corporations.

Employee stock ownership plans, or ESOPs, are governed by ERISA. An ESOP is a stock bonus plan, and may provide for stock bonuses and the right of employees to purchase employer securities through their contributions to the plan.

Although there are differences between stock bonus plans and ESOPs, the Internal Revenue Code requires both to have certain provisions. Under certain circumstances, voting rights in securities held by the plan must be passed on to the employees. A participant may be able to demand an employer's securities when distributions are made, and an employee may require the employer to buy back employer securities which are not publicly traded. Distribution of securities must start not less than 1 year after retirement, death, or disability, and the distribution must be completed within 5 years after distributions begin. The plan may provide for cash distributions at the employee's option.

The plan may provide for employer contributions to be made in cash, appreciated property, or employer securities. If the employer contributes stock to the plan, the employer receives a tax deduction for the fair market value of the contributed stock.

ESOPs can be an effective tool for transferring ownership of a corporation to its employees. As an example, a major shareholder may wish to retire but does want to continue being an owner of the business. Certain employees may want to purchase the shares of the retiring owner but may not have enough personal resources to pay for the shares. The corporation could use an ESOP to purchase the shares. If the ESOP did not have enough assets, it could borrow the money to buy the shares. The U.S. Treasury Department has issued stringent regulations governing the use of loans by ESOPs to purchase employer securities.

ESOPs also may provide that certain participants in the plan may elect to have up to 25 percent of his or her account balance in the plan invested in nonemployer securities. These are people who are 55 years or older and have participated in the ESOP for at least 10 years. Participants 60 years or older and who have participated in the plan for at least 10 years may elect to have 50 percent of their account balance in nonemployer securities. Diversification of retirement savings may be preferred by many who do not wish to put all their eggs in one basket.

Stock bonus plans and ESOPs have certain advantages. Employees who own company securities in such a plan may be more loyal and less prone to leave the company for other opportunities. Such employees may think of themselves as part owners of the business and be more willing to devote their energies to the success of the business. As mentioned above, an ESOP may be used to borrow money necessary to purchase the stock of a major shareholder, keeping control of the company in the hands of those who have worked many years to make the business successful.

Stock bonus plans and ESOPs do have some drawbacks. The amount of each employee's account in the plan is directly tied to the success of the business and the value of the employer securities in the plan, although the plan must provide for older participants to have the right to elect to diversify a certain portion of their account balances. Further, a long-time employee of a small corporation who may have a relatively sizable distribution due him or her may elect to take the distribution in employer securities. As a result, a large block of company stock could end up in the hands of an employee or the employee's descendants, whose interests may be radically different from those of management.

Pension plans

A pension plan is a retirement plan which provides "systematically for the payment of definitely determinable benefits...to employees over a period of years, usually for life, after retirement."[50]

Under pension plans, retirement benefits are usually determined by length of service and compensation; company profits are not used to determine employer contributions to the plan. Accordingly, pension plans are defined benefit plans. A pension plan may require either employer or employee contributions or both.

Although many employees prefer pension plans over other forms of retirement plans, pension plans have a major drawback. Inflation erodes the buying power of retirees receiving benefits under the plan. Under the law, the plan may provide for cost-of-living adjustments, but most pension plans do not provide for such adjustments due to the difficulty of predicting future inflation.

A money purchase plan is a pension plan which has the employer make predetermined contributions to the plan. Usually, the contribution is a percentage of an employee's compensation. The contribution is made regardless of the firm's profitability. Otherwise, money purchase plans are similar to profit-sharing plans and are a form of a defined contribution plan.

A pension plan also may provide for incidental benefits, if certain regulatory requirements are met. These benefits are life insurance, disability benefits, and medical benefits.

Annuity plans

An annuity plan is "a pension plan under which retirement benefits are provided under annuity or insurance contracts without a trust."[51] In an annuity plan, the employer will usually purchase an annuity for an employee when he or she becomes eligible to participate in the plan. The employer pays the premiums for the annuity until the employee retires.

Annuities are usually issued in the name of each employee participating in the plan. However, the annuity may be held in the name of a trustee until the employee retires. Also, master contracts are sometimes used under which the general provisions of the annuity are contained in the contract and the employee receives a certificate indicating his or her participation in the plan.

The primary benefit of annuity plans is that most of the administrative burden is transferred to the insurance company. After the insurance company receives the premiums from the employer, the insurer manages the money and does the necessary actuarial analysis. Further, annuity contracts usually are sold with a guaranteed rate of return. Thus, the problems of investment experience do not affect the employer. In essence, an annuity plan is a pension plan under which the employer's contribution is fixed by the amount of the premiums which must be paid every year.

Cash or deferred plans

Certain profit-sharing and stock bonus plans allow the employee to have the employer's contribution paid in cash. This option may take various forms. As an example, the employee may have a certain portion of his or her profit-sharing bonus go to the plan, with the balance paid in cash.

In some plans, the employer will match or partially match the sum the employee contributes. As an example, for every dollar the employee defers or contributes to the plan, the employer may contribute $1 or some lesser sum on the employee's behalf.

A cash or deferred plan could be written to favor highly compensated employees. Accordingly, the U.S. Treasury Department has written complex regulations limiting the amount of contributions which may be made to such plans. Cash or deferred plans also may allow employees to make voluntary after-tax contributions. However, the amount of these contributions is limited by the Internal Revenue Code.

A cash or deferred plan also may allow an employee to receive a cash distribution to meet a pressing financial need, such as medical expenses of the employee, spouse, or dependent children; a down payment for a principal residence; tuition for college or other post-secondary education of the employee, spouse, or dependent children; and funds required to avoid eviction or mortgage foreclosure on the employee's principal residence.

Stringent rules govern from which portion of the employee's account a hardship distribution can be made. Other regulations govern hardship distributions, including a certificate from the employee justifying the need for the distribution.

Selecting the Retirement Plan

When a firm does its business planning, it should decide whether it will adopt a retirement plan. In its early years, the owners may not want to adopt a retirement plan because of business start-up costs. Further, the firm's income may not be sufficient to support a retirement plan. However, when and if the firm decides to initiate a retirement plan, the owners must make a basic decision: Do they want a defined contribution or a defined benefit plan?

Defined contribution plans include profit-sharing, stock bonus, money purchase pension, and target benefit plans. Profit-sharing plans or a stock bonus plan under which the employer has the discretion of making retirement plan contributions may be attractive to design firms because of the cyclical nature of the construction industry and the profits of those firms.

Cash or deferred plans, either part of a profit-sharing or a stock bonus plan, may be preferred by some employees. Under this option, the employee can decide whether to take a part of his or her bonus in cash, or in some cases all in cash, which may help the employee meet personal living expenses.

ESOPs have certain advantages, especially when the firm desires to purchase the shares of a major shareholder. For privately owned design firms, ESOPs have some drawbacks. For instance, the firm must be prepared to purchase stock from the ESOP in the event a terminating employee elects to take his or her contribution. In difficult financial times, such a demand from a major participant in the plan could severely test the financial strength of the firm.

Employees may prefer defined benefit plans (pension and annuity plans) because their retirement benefits are fixed upon retirement, although this seeming security may be offset by future inflation. With defined benefit plans, the employer's contributions are fixed and must be met, regardless of the firm's profitability.

A defined benefit plan may be advantageous to a firm if its owners are nearing retirement and do not have a retirement plan. Relatively large contributions would have to be made to the plan to fund the future retirement benefits of older owner-employees or key employees who are not owners.

Defined contribution plans may allow flexibility in investments. Further, they may be written to allow participants to control the investment of their account balances.

Finally, the firm may have a combination of defined contribution and defined benefit plans. The use of two such plans may be more effective in meeting the retirement needs of owner-employees and other employees.

Individual Retirement Options

If a firm elects not to adopt a retirement plan, its employees still must plan for retirement. The Internal Revenue Code allows employees not covered by a retirement plan to invest in an individual retirement account, or IRA. Under an IRA, a person can contribute $2,000 a year (or $2,250 in certain instances) to a trust, custodial, or annuity account and deduct that amount from his or her income on the individual income tax return. In addition, certain non-tax deductible contributions may be made to an IRA. The income earned on the funds invested in the IRA is not taxed.

A person may draw all or part of his or her funds in an IRA in the year he or she reaches 59½. The funds are subject to individual income tax as they are withdrawn. The holder of an IRA must begin drawing funds from the IRA no later than April 1 of the year after the year in which he or she reaches 70½.

Under the Internal Revenue Code, an employer may establish a simplified employee pension arrangement, or SEP. Under the SEP, the employer may contribute up to 15 percent of employee compensation to the plan not to exceed $30,000 for any one employee. The contributions are paid into IRAs set up for each employee.

SEPs may be used if the employer has another qualified retirement plan, subject to certain limitations. Also, for firms with 25 or fewer employees, a SEP may contain a provision allowing employees to receive certain amounts of the SEP contribution in cash.

Group Insurance Plans

Most firms offer group insurance for their employees. Group insurance policies are less expensive than individual policies because there is no need to underwrite individual policies. Further, commission rates to the insurance broker or agent are lower. In addition, since the employer administers part of the program, the costs of the insurer are lower. Finally, since premiums for group insurance usually are an ordinary and necessary business expense of the employer, the cost to the employer is lower than for that of an individual policy where the premium is paid with after-tax dollars.

Usually, group insurers prefer the group to be large enough to minimize the chance of adverse results and to lower administrative costs. In recent years, however, the size of groups have become smaller so many design firms may now qualify for their own group plans. Small firms may also look at another insurance alternative rather than group policies for the firm. Many professional organizations now offer group insurance plans for their members and may cover employees of member firms. Small firms can also investigate the possibility of purchasing individual insurance policies for its owners and employees.

Group insurers require mandatory participation of all employees in plans where the employer pays the entire premium. For plans where the employees pay part of the premium, group insurers usually require participation of 75 percent of the employees in the plan.

Underwriters of group insurance plans look to the insurability of the group, not to the insurability of the plan participants. Their aim is to develop a plan so that the group may be covered with insurance. Group insurance plans are subject to governmental regulations. Usually, all or certain provisions are proscribed for group plans.

Group life insurance

Under some group plans, the employer selects the benefit levels of life insurance. Other plans permit the employees to select benefit levels within certain limits. Neither employers nor insurers want employees in ill health to be permitted to select relatively high benefit levels.

Group life insurance policies are usually written on an annual basis. Generally, the policies allow newly eligible employees and other eligible members to be added during the year. Employee dependents are covered under most plans, although perhaps at a lower benefit level. Some plans also provide for benefits for retired employees.

Group health insurance

Group health insurance is written to cover employee medical expenses arising from illness and off-the-job accidents. Work-related accidents and illnesses are covered by worker's compensation insurance.

Group health plans usually provide a variety of coverages, such as disability income and accidental death and dismemberment. Other plans provide coverage for nursing homes, birthing centers, and hospice expenses.

Other Benefit Plans

Design firms should consider the need for other benefit plans. Some of these plans, such as dependent care plans, have evolved because of the changing working environment.

Death benefit plans

Some employers may pay death benefits to the beneficiary or the estate of a deceased employee. These benefits are paid by the company, not the insurance policy. Ordinarily such benefits would be taxable to the beneficiary. However, under the Internal Revenue Code, an employer may take up to $5,000 as a tax-free benefit.[52]

Nonqualified deferred compensation

Nonqualified deferred compensation plans lack the tax advantages of qualified plans, but they may be adopted by employers for certain reasons. Sometimes they are used to minimize an employee's taxes. The deferred compensation is paid after the employee retires and is in a lower tax bracket.

There are many forms of nonqualified deferred compensation plans. The amount of deferred compensation may be determined by the performance of the employee or the success of the business. Or nonqualified deferred compensation may be used in conjunction with retirement benefits to be paid to the employee under a qualified plan. Such payments may be necessary for highly compensated employees.

Dependent care plans

The Internal Revenue Code contains provisions that allow employers to deduct employee dependent care expenses as an ordinary and necessary business expense, subject to certain limitations. The allowable amount may be as much as $5,000, subject to the amount of the employee's income.

Cafeteria plans

Cafeteria plans let employees select from various benefit plans based upon his or her needs. These plans let employees select among cash payments and qualified benefits.

Worker's compensation

All the states have laws requiring employers to pay worker's compensation benefits to employees whose injuries or illnesses are work related. Most firms cover worker's compensation payments with insurance.

Loss of Owner or Key Employee

The loss of an owner or key employee due to death can be extremely detrimental to any design firm. For one thing, it may result in increased cost of operation to replace that person. An executive search firm may have to be employed to locate a suitable replacement, and the new employee may request certain economic incentives to change jobs. Moreover, the firm's expenses still have to be paid until a replacement is found, and revenue may be down.

In the case of a sole proprietorship, the owner may consider buying insurance upon his or her life to provide funds to run the business until a new owner is found or to provide for orderly winding up of the affairs of the practice. With any sole proprietorship, a new owner must be found immediately, or the firm may have to be dissolved.

With partnerships or corporations, the owners may want to purchase key person insurance on the lives of each of the owners. The proceeds of the insurance could be used by the firm to buy out the ownership interest of a deceased partner or shareholder.

For partnerships, each partner could take out a life insurance policy on the other partner. Firms with several or more partners could purchase the life insurance policies instead of the individual partners. Although the premium payments may not be taxable, proceeds from the policy should be enough to buy out the equity of the deceased partner.

A corporation may find it advisable to purchase life insurance, although it is not deductible from the firm's income tax. If the corporation is in a lower tax bracket than the shareholders, the shareholders would be economically advantaged if the corporation paid the premiums.

Whether a partnership or a corporation, some method should be devised to value the ownership interest of deceased owners of the business. In a partnership, a provision covering this topic can be placed in the partnership agreement. For corporations, this topic can be dealt with in a shareholder's agreement.

Because of the difficulty of evaluating the worth of a small business, many partnership and shareholder agreements set the book value of the firm at a certain date as the amount to be paid to the heirs or estate of the deceased owner. Some agreements provide for certain additional payments to the estate or heirs, such as payment of monthly draws or salary for a period of months. Such temporary payments can be of immeasurable assistance to the deceased's family, since it may take them several months before they can collect upon the proceeds of life insurance. Also, such temporary payments may assist the family during the period of time the deceased partner's estate is being probated.

12

Planning for Ownership Transition

Design firm owners should consider the continuation of the practice after the current owners retire and the need for transfer of ownership. For small design firms, sale or transfer of the ownership of the practice may not be practical. Therefore, the owners can liquidate the firm when they decide to retire. Outstanding accounts receivable are collected, assets are sold, and debts are paid.

Selling a firm's assets may not yield much cash; desks and equipment are old and without much market value. However, many small design firms have two assets which may be valuable to new owners or other design firms. The first is drawings owned or retained by the firm. A value can be placed on the drawings depending upon the volume of business generated from projects such as regular remodeling of or changing large buildings or specialized structures. Another valuable asset of a design firm may be its client list. A competitive design firm may be willing to pay money to the owners of the firm being liquidated for the firm's client list.

Some small design firms may be able to sell their practice without the need for liquidation. Possible purchasers include competitive firms or even employees. Several years before retiring, the owners of a small firm may discuss selling the practice to one or two key employees. If no key employee is able to buy or is interested in buying the firm, the owners can consider hiring a new professional with the understanding that he or she will have an opportunity to purchase the practice when the existing owners retire.

Whether the owners are able to sell the entire practice or certain key assets, such as its inventory of drawings for completed projects or its client list, the owners should be prepared to work for several years after the sale of the business. The new owner or owners may need the former owners to introduce him or her to existing clients and otherwise assist during the transition period.

Medium- and large-sized design firms have more alternatives available for ownership transition. The owners can sell the business to employees who have been trained to take over the practice. Or the firm may be sold to a publicly or privately held firm.

A publicly held business is a firm whose stock is traded on a stock exchange or in the over-the-counter market. Usually, there is a ready market for the stock so that its value may be determined daily. The owners of a medium- or large-sized firm may want to trade the business to a large, publicly traded firm in exchange for marketable stock.

If a merger is worked out under the Internal Revenue Code, the owners of the firm being acquired will receive shares from the buyer, and any gain in the transaction will not be subject to income or capital gains tax at the time of the sale. Further, the owners of the acquired firm receive marketable stock, which any of them may sell when they desire to do so.

If the owners of the acquired firm take shares in a publicly held corporation as part of a merger, the value of their investments becomes subject to the value of the stock in the market. However, this contingency can be avoided by selling the stock.

The owners of a medium- or large-sized firm can also sell their practice to a privately held corporation. In some instances, the sellers may prefer a merger with the buyer. In such cases, the sellers usually receive shares in the buyer, but because the buyer is privately held the shares are not readily marketable.

If the firm is bought, usually in exchange for money or some other consideration, the sellers probably will incur certain tax liability at the time of the transaction. The selling owners may prefer this alternative because it gives them cash, which they can invest as they choose.

Frequently, if the buyer purchases the seller outright, the buyer may have to finance all or part of the transaction by borrowing money. The buyer may be unable to obtain financing from a bank or other sources or the interest rate for borrowing the necessary funds may be too high. Under such circumstances, the buyer may request the sellers to finance part of the purchase.

The sellers must look at the strength and future prospects of the buyer to determine whether they will help the buyer finance the sale. If the sellers are amenable to helping the buyer, there are certain alternatives available. The buyer can promise to pay a certain portion of the purchase price at a later date or make periodic payments over a specific time. The sellers may want a promissory note and security agreement granting them a security interest in certain assets of the buyer.

In some instances, the buyer may agree to issue debentures or bonds to the sellers, which pay a regular interest rate and are payable upon a certain date or dates. Or the buyer may be willing to issue preferred stock to the sellers. Preferred stock provides for stated dividend payments, which only can be suspended if the corporation is not profitable. Usually unpaid preferred stock dividends accumulate until the corporation is profitable again, at which time the accumulated preferred dividends are paid before any dividends are paid upon the common stock of the corporation.

As mentioned in Chap. 11, the owners can form an ESOP, transferring their ownership in the corporation to its employees. Using such a transaction, the owners may receive more from their ownership in the practice than by selling the firm to an outside corporation.

The sale of a business is frequently considered only a few years, at most, before the owners sell the business. If the owners are contemplating selling the business, however, they may want to look at how the decision impacts business planning. As an example, the owners may want to maximize profits in those years immediately before the contemplated sale of the firm in order to make the business look more attractive to potential purchasers.

Many medium- and large-sized design firms find that profits are maximized, along with ownership interest, if a mechanism is provided for promoting future owners from within the firm. These firms hire young architects and engineers from professional schools or other firms and promote them within the firm until some of them become owners of the practice when existing partners or shareholders retire. If the firm decides that promotion from within is in the best long-term interest of the firm and its owners, the business plan must provide for the recruiting, training, and development of staff and transition of ownership from the retiring partners to the new partners.

The business plan can be used to determine future staffing needs of the firm. The plan should provide a guide for future business during the short and medium term. From the estimate of future revenue, management can determine the need for additional professionals. Further, a breakdown of needs for inexperienced and experienced architects and engineers may be formulated. Then management can plan for recruiting new professionals.

The firm's budget can allocate funds necessary for recruiting. Visiting and interviewing at college campuses can be expensive. Not only does the firm incur travel and lodging expenses for its interviews, it also loses time from ongoing projects. If necessary, the budget must also provide for recruiting experienced professionals. In addition, the firm must decide whether it will use its internal resources, an agency, or a combination of both to hunt for experienced staff.

As new staff members are hired, the firm must plan for their training. The firm should decide whether all or some recent college graduates will rotate through various departments of the firm to give them experience in the different activities. A rotation program may help both the individual and the firm decide where the person can be used most profitably in the practice.

The firm should develop some policy about continuing education to assure that both relatively inexperienced staff and experienced professionals keep current with recent developments in the various design disciplines. The plan and budget should therefore consider whether training should encompass continuing education programs offered by the local chapter of the American Institute of Architects and other professional groups.

Next, the firm must plan for management development. Not all professionals are capable of becoming good managers. Some architects and engineers may be outstanding in their fields but do not have the desire or capability to become good managers. The firm should develop a policy for spotting young designers who may become good professional managers. From this group of architects and engineers, the firm can select its future partners or owners.

When developing future managers, the firm should consider the need for diversity. A good designer may be or may not be able to function in other areas, including the management of other designers. A good administrator may not be a good marketer. The firm has to look at its current staff of managers and owners and estimate when each of these key people will retire. Then it should develop a mechanism to identify the skills it will need in future managers and owners to replace key staff members as they retire.

For example, one partner or owner may be especially successful in marketing. The loss of such a person due to resignation, death, or retirement can be detrimental to the continued success of the firm unless steps are taken to identify and develop younger professionals who also may excel in business development.

The firm also should make a decision as to how widespread ownership will be. Will the firm aim toward a relatively large number of partners or owners with a managing partner and/or management committee running its affairs? Or will the firm limit ownership to a few design professionals?

Some firms find that opening ownership to a relatively large number of professionals encourages employee retention. Many professionals covet the prestige of being part owner of a design firm. Other firms find that competent employees may be retained without the need to offer every qualified person an ownership interest in the firm. They are able to grow successfully with only a few key staff members who are also owners. Somewhere, however, the firm should develop a policy about ownership succession.

Once the firm decides that its future owners will come from within the firm, it must adopt a policy as to how ownership will be transferred. Some design firms have adopted a policy of infrequent changes in ownership. For instance, a design firm may have from 5 to 10 owners active in the practice. Every 5 or 10 years, a few of the owners may retire. At that time, certain key employees are selected to replace the retiring owners. Under such a policy, significant ownership shifts can result within the firm every 5 to 10 years.

Other firms adopt a more gradual change in ownership. Every year or so, certain key employees are selected to become partners or owners, even though a current owner may not be retiring. These firms think that by regularly making certain key employees owners or partners, other employees are encouraged to stay with the firm and work productively in the hopes of being promoted.

Whatever approach is adopted, the firm must develop a policy for buying out retiring or terminating partners or owners and the economic basis for admitting new owners. The partnership agreement or agreement among shareholders, if the firm is a corporation, should state this policy.

Some firms have developed a two-tier partnership or shareholder approach to ownership: firm level and senior level. After a certain number of years of experience, key design professionals are considered for the firm level of partnership or ownership. In partnerships, this person may become an associate or income partner. In corporations, the person may become a nonvoting shareholder. The firm level partners or nonvoting shareholders receive a regular draw or salary and at the end of the year may receive a bonus. The bonus may be determined by the senior owners of the firm or be based upon an objective standard, such as a certain share of the profits.

The senior level of owners are the real owners of the practice. They are the partners or shareholders who can vote on firm policy and operations. They are the owners whose income is determined by their share of the equity in the business.

The firm policy, as evidenced by the partnership or shareholder agreement, should determine how terminating or retiring owners are paid for leaving the practice. Most firms usually provide that these persons will receive back their equity in the business. The owner may be able to withdraw his or her investment upon termination or retirement or his or her capital may be returned in periodic payments.

Some firms provide for a buy-out of retiring owners. Under this approach, the retiring partner receives a certain payment in addition to the return of his or her equity. As an example, the retiring owner's average annual pay for the last 5 years before retirement may be used as a basis for the payment.

A buy-back has several advantages. First, it is a form of payment to the retiring partner or owner for his or her contribution to the goodwill of the firm which is not compensated from the return of capital upon retirement. Second, the payment compensates the retiring owner for assistance he or she may lend the firm in transition following retirement. Third, the payment, along with a covenant not to compete, buys the retiring owner's continued loyalty and prevents him or her from working for a competitor upon retirement.

Ownership succession is important to any design firm. The firm should have a definite policy toward ownership succession which should be part of its business plan.

Conclusion

The owners of a design firm should carefully plan for ownership transition. Both accountants and lawyers can aid owners planning for transition. Further, consultants are available who also will work with the firm's owners in developing strategies for ownership transition.

Making Your Own Business Plan

I. Fill-in-the-Blanks Business Plan

II. Alternative Business Plan Outlines

I. Fill-in-the-Blanks Business Plan

One of the hardest parts of business planning is how to begin. Starting, it seems, is an overwhelming task as evidenced by the many architects and engineers who do not have a plan. Once you begin and experience the process, however, you will see it is not difficult and is extraordinarily beneficial. To help you get started, a fill-in-the-blanks business plan is included. This will help you think along the lines of business planning. You may use this as a starting point, then develop a full plan such as shown in the *Sample, Inc.,* example. Or you may just use this plan. Having something written down on paper, even in an outline format, is better than having nothing. It is a starting point, just like the first spade of dirt turned over on a new construction site. You have to start someplace.

Executive overview

The executive overview will be filled in last. It is essentially a summary of what a reader will find in the heart of the plan. It is meant to give direction and establish parameters for the readers.

_____

_____

_____

_____

_____

_____

_____

_____

_____

_____

_____

_____

_____

Mission statement

The starting point for any business plan is the company's mission statement. This statement is a summary of the overall direction of your company. As the economy and your practice change and new people join the firm, the mission statement may change. The following is an example of a mission statement:

> To improve the profits of *Imaging Architects* by developing our expertise in construction management, thereby allowing our client developers to be more profitable in the construction sequence. To provide a quality, timely service that becomes recognized throughout the county and state for its excellence.

You can write your company's mission statement here:

Company Name: _____

Mission Statement: _____

_____

_____

_____

_____

_____

_____

_____

Market characteristics

In the space below, indicate the characteristics of the marketplace in which you practice.

1. _____

_____

2. _____

_____

3. _____

_____

4. _____

Describe your market

Geographic: _____

_____

_____

Demographic: _____

_____

_____

Competition

List the major competitors with whom you compete or who represent a threat to your firm. List their *features*, *advantages*, and *benefits*:

Name	Features	Advantages	Benefits

1. _____

_____

2. _____

_____

3. _____

_____

4. _____

_____

**List your company's features,
advantages, and benefits**

	Features	Advantages	Benefits

1. _____

_____

2. _____

_____

3. _____

_____

4. _____

_____

Opportunities and issue analysis

On the situational analysis form, list the opportunities and threats (O/T analysis) and the strengths and weaknesses (S/W analysis) of your firm. Also indicate the resulting issues that are facing your firm.

Situational Analysis

	Current		Future	
	Strengths	Weakness	Opportunities	Threats
Developing issues:				

Objectives

The next step is to list the company's objectives. Objectives are the focus points of what needs to be accomplished in order for the company's mission statement to be implemented. An objective is a specific statement of what a company is trying to accomplish. Objectives are often classified into financial objectives, marketing objectives, and human resource objectives. A partial list of objectives for *Imaging Architects* might be as follows:

Financial Objective: Restructure the financial reporting system to include construction management services.

Marketing Objective: Develop a program where the special skills and talents of *Imaging Architects* will be identified by prospects as saving time in their construction projects and, hence, making them more profitable.

Human Resource Objective: Develop a sense of an office identity that provides a place where people want to come to work and work hard to stay here.

List your company's objectives based upon the mission statement and the direction you wish your firm to take.

Financial Objectives

1. _____

_____

2. _____

_____

3. _____

_____

Marketing Objectives

1. _____

   _____

2. _____

   _____

3. _____

   _____

Human Resource Objectives

1. _____

   _____

2. _____

   _____

3. _____

   _____

Goals

The next step is to outline the goals. Goals expand the objectives into parts, which make them easier to address. Goals and objectives also address the specific issues important to your firm as developed through the S/W and O/T analyses. Goals help interpret objectives as time-measurable items. For example, a financial objective of *Imaging Architects* can be interpreted through goals in the following manner:

Financial Objective: Restructure the financial reporting system to include construction management services.

Goals:

1. By February 15, begin the evaluation on new construction management and project management software.
2. By March 15, order and install the selected project management software.
3. By April 15, merge all ongoing construction management projects on to this system and begin producing off-line reports.
4. By May 31, produce the first end-of-month report for each current construction management job and prepare a summary for the end-of-month review meeting.

In the spaces below, list each one of the financial, marketing, and human resource objectives, along with their associated goals. Photocopy this page to provide more space as required.

Objective

1. _____

_____

Goal 1

_____

_____

_____

_____

_____

Goal 2

_____

_____

_____

_____

_____

_____

Goal 3

_____

_____

_____

_____

_____

_____

Goal 4

_____

_____

_____

_____

_____

_____

Marketing strategies

Another aspect of the annual business plan is the marketing strategies that position the firm from a marketing perspective. There can be many marketing strategies; each firm will have different strategies and emphasize different ideas. The marketing strategy encompasses all the issues, as well as the goals and objectives, facing the firm. As a starting point, here is an outline of what should be addressed from a minimum point of view. Add to this list as the situations require.

Marketing strategy statement

Target market

_____

_____

_____

_____

_____

Positioning

_____

_____

_____

_____

_____

Services offered

_____

_____

_____

_____

_____

Price structure

_____

_____

_____

_____

_____

Market research

_____

_____

_____

_____

_____

Contractual

_____

_____

_____

_____

_____

_____

Promotion

_____

_____

_____

_____

_____

Action plan

The action plan is the final step in the planning process. It is usually done by managers who have been assigned specific objectives and/or goals. The action plan is usually done after the business plan has been accomplished. These are not the same as the company's goals and objectives but are more individual. At this level, a goal or objective is a measurable item, and steps are required to complete it. Often these steps are not done by the same person. Therefore the action plan breaks down objectives into actions that are assignable and are to be completed by a certain date.

Objective and goal

_____

_____

_____

_____

_____

_____

	Action	Responsibility	Date
1.			
2.			
3.			
4.			

Financial statements

Financial statements round out the plan and give it depth and meaning. For the outline format, income statements, balance sheets, and budgets can be attached as the minimum information provided. In addition, a complete financial overview should be prepared with the help of an accountant or experienced business manager. The importance of financial planning cannot be underestimated in the architectural and engineering world.

Conclusion

Every plan must have a conclusion, even if it seems obvious what it is. This gives the author a chance to summarize the important points so a reader is properly informed of the intent, purpose, and conclusion.

Below, state the conclusion of your plan.

Conclusion

_____

_____

_____

_____

_____

_____

_____

_____

Now you can write the executive overview. Having done this, you will have a working guideline of an annual business plan for future reference and use. Building upon this by developing your own plan will help you plan your business future.

II. Alternative Business Plan Outlines

There is no magic formula for the *right* business plan outline. The one for *Sample, Inc.,* was the best plan outline for that given situation. Plan outlines will change based on the problem and issues being addressed and the information available. After reading the business plan for *Sample, Inc.,* and comparing it to the outlines in this appendix, you will see that the content is essentially the same and the information is roughly in the same order, but the words change. For example, positioning and situational analysis are essentially the same, but you may feel more comfortable with one word than the other. You can customize your plan, using the plan method discussed in this book.

Who are we?

Where do we want to go?

How do we get there?

Following this guideline, you will be able to produce a plan that is both individualistic and informative. If you see something you like, take it, modify it, change it to your liking, and make it yours.

Alternative outline I

      I. Executive Overview

     II. Situational Analysis

       Positioning

       Regional market area analysis

       Market opportunities

       Competitive environment

    III. Marketing Objectives

       Strategic objective

       Sales

       Market share

       Profitability

    IV. Marketing Strategies

       Target market

       Description of services

       Pricing and profit goals

       Obstacles and risks

     V. Marketing Tactics

       Additional services

       Implementation

       Financial summary

    VI. Conclusion

   VII. Appendix

Alternative outline II

I. Executive Summary

II. Positioning

Transition

Objectives

Parameters

III. Obstacles and Risks

IV. Opportunities

New markets

Existing markets

Additional services

V. Marketing Strategies

Objectives

Strategies

Communication system

VI. Financials

Market share

Income statement

Balance sheet

Promotion plan

Financial projections

VII. Conclusion

VIII. Appendix

Alternative outline III

    I. Statement of Objectives

      Objectives

      Executive overview

    II. Substantiating Objectives

      Positioning

    III. Assumptions

      Market

      Competition

      Operating environment

    IV. Present Method

    V. Proposed Method

      New target market

      Staffing

      Computer applications

    VI. Financial Analysis

      Present income statement and balance sheet

      Pro forma income statement and balance sheet

    VII. Conclusion

    VIII. Appendix

References

1. Robert A. Howell, *How to Write a Business Plan,* American Management Association, New York, 1982, Chapter 1, p. 4.
2. Robert P. Howell, *How to Write a Business Plan,* American Management Association, New York, 1982, Chapter 1, p. 2.
3. Sun Tzu, *The Art of War,* "A Treatise on Chinese Military Science Compiled about 500 B.C.," Graham Brash (Pte) Ltd., Singapore, 1982.
4. Peter F. Drucker, *Managing for Results,* Harper & Row, New York, 1986, p. 206.
5. Philip Kotler, *Marketing Management,* Prentice-Hall, Englewood Cliffs, N.J., 1984, Chapter 2, p. 4.
6. Philip Kotler, *Marketing Management,* Prentice-Hall, Englewood Cliffs, N.J., 1984, p. 68.
7. E. Jerome McCarthy, *Basic Marketing: A Managerial Approach,* 7th ed., Richard D. Irwin, Homewood, Ill., 1981, p. 42.
8. *American Heritage Dictionary,* 2nd ed., Dell Publishing Company, New York, 1983.
9. W. R. King and D. I. Cleland, *Strategic Planning and Policy,* Van Nostrand Reinhold, New York, 1978, p. 133. From *Strategic Planning and Management Handbook,* Van Nostrand Reinhold, New York, 1987, p. 65. The diagram represents the basic structure of planning pyramids and is used with a slight word change for clarification.
10. Kenichi Ohmae, *The Mind of the Strategist,* McGraw-Hill, New York, 1982, pp. 91–92.
11. Al Reis and Jack Trout, *Marketing Warfare,* McGraw-Hill, New York, 1986, p. 7.
12. Kenichi Ohmae, *The Mind of the Strategist,* McGraw-Hill, New York, 1982, p. 36.
13. Kenichi Ohmae, *The Mind of the Strategist,* McGraw-Hill, New York, 1982, p. 38.
14. Kenichi Ohmae, *The Mind of the Strategist,* McGraw-Hill, New York, 1982, p. 57.
15. Henry Assael, *Marketing Management, Strategy and Action,* Kent Publishing Company, Belmont, Calif., 1985, p. 699.
16. Philip Kotler, *Marketing Management,* Prentice-Hall, Englewood Cliffs, N.J., 1984, p. 194.
17. Harold Geneen with Alvin Moscow, *Managing,* Avon Books, New York, 1984, p. 202.
18. George S. Odiorne, *MBO II: A System of Managerial Leadership for the 80's,* Fearon Pitman Publishing, Belmont, Calif., 1979, p. 54.
19. George S. Odiorne, *MBO II: A System of Managerial Leadership for the 80's,* Fearon Pitman Publishing, Belmont, Calif., 1979, p. 53.
20. Henry R. Migliore, *An MBO Approach to Long Range Planning,* Prentice-Hall, Englewood Cliffs, N.J., 1983, p. 2.
21. George S. Odiorne, *MBO II: A System of Managerial Leadership for the 80's,* Fearon Pitman Publishing, Belmont, Calif., 1979, p. 58.
22. Henry R. Migliore, *An MBO Approach to Long Range Planning,* Prentice-Hall, Englewood Cliffs, N.J., 1983, p. 4.

23. Henry R. Migliore, *An MBO Approach to Long Range Planning,* Prentice-Hall, Englewood Cliffs, N.J., 1983, p. 8.
24. George S. Odiorne, *MBO II: A System of Managerial Leadership for the 80's,* Fearon Pitman Publishing, Belmont, Calif., 1979, p. 69.
25. In this book, CAD refers to computer aided design and/or computer aided drafting, which is sometimes referred to as CADD.
26. Chief Boyd, stated in a CAD seminar at an AIA convention.
27. Thomas Fisher, Editorial: "Patterns of Exploitation," *Progressive Architecture,* 1991, p. 9.
28. Uniform Partnership Act, Sec. 6.
29. Uniform Partnership Act, Sec. 31.
30. Internal Revenue Code, Sec. 531–537.
31. Uniform Partnership Act, Sec. 8(3).
32. Uniform Partnership Act, Sec. 41.
33. Uniform Partnership Act, Sec. 9(1).
34. Uniform Partnership Act, Sec. 35(1)(b)(jj).
35. Uniform Partnership Act, Sec. 17.
36. Uniform Partnership Act, Sec. 29.
37. Uniform Partnership Act, Sec. 37.
38. Uniform Partnership Act, Sec. 11.
39. Uniform Partnership Act, Sec. 12.
40. *City of Mounds View v. Waligardi,* 263 N.W. 2d. 420,424.
41. *A.E. Investment Corp. v. Linle Builders, Inc.,* 62 Wis. 2d 479, 214 N.W. 2d 764 (1974).
42. *Brown v. Gamble Construction Co.,* 537 S.W. 2d 685 (Mo. App. 1976).
43. *South Burlington School District v. Calcagni-Frazier-Zajchowski Architects, Inc.,* 138 Vt. 33, 410 A. 2d 1359 (1980).
44. "Design firms 'go bare' due to high cost of liability coverage," *Engineering News Record,* December 10, 1990, pp. 19–20.
45. "Trends," *The Midwest Engineer,* January 1991, p. 3.
46. National Association of Attorneys General; Model Design and Construction Documents: A Model Form of Agreement between the Owner and Design Professional; A Model Form of Agreement for Construction between the Owner and Contractor, and Standard Form General Conditions of the Contract for Construction, Washington, D.C., December 1988.
47. Robert I. Mehr, *Fundamentals of Insurance,* Richard D. Irwin, Homewood, Ill., 1986.
48. *In City of Los Angeles, Dept. of Water and Power v. Manhart,* 435 U.S. 702 (1978), on remand 577 F2d 98 (9th Cir. 1978), appeal after remand 652 F.2d 904 (9th Cir. 1981), judgement vacated 461 U.S. 951 (1983) and in *Arizona Governing Committee for Tax Deferred Annuity and Compensation Plans v. Norris,* 463 U.S. 1073 (1983) appeal after remand 796 F.2d 1119 (9th Cir. 1986).
49. *Newport News Shipbuilding and Dry Dock Co. v. EEOC,* 462 U.S. 669 (1983).
50. Treas. Reg. § 1.401-1(b)(1)(iii).
51. Treas. Reg. § 1.404(a)-3(a).
52. IRC § 101 (b).

Bibliography

American Heritage Dictionary, 2nd Ed., Dell Publishing Company, New York, 1983.

Assael, Henry. *Marketing Management, Strategy and Action.* Kent Publishing Company, Belmont, Calif., 1985.

Drucker, Peter F. *Managing for Results.* Harper and Row, New York, 1986.

Fisher, Thomas. *Progressive Architecture Editorial: Patterns of Exploitation.* Penton Publishing, 1991.

Geneen, Harold, with Moscow, Alvin. *Managing.* Avon Books, New York, 1984.

Howell, Robert A. *How to Write a Business Plan.* American Management Association, New York, 1982.

King, W. R., and Cleland, D. I. *Strategic Planning and Policy.* Van Nostrand Reinhold, New York, 1978. From *Strategic Planning and Management Handbook.* Van Nostrand Reinhold, New York, 1987.

Kotler, Philip. *Marketing Management.* Prentice-Hall, Englewood Cliffs, N.J., 1984.

McCarthy, E. Jerome. *Basic Marketing: A Managerial Approach,* 7th Ed. Richard D. Irwin, Homewood, Ill., 1981.

Migliore, R. Henry. *An MBO Approach to Long Range Planning.* Prentice-Hall, Englewood Cliffs, N.J., 1983.

Odiorne, George S. *MBO II: A System for Managerial Leadership for the 80's.* Fearon Pitman Publishing, Belmont, Calif., 1979.

Ohmae, Dr. Kenichi. *The Mind of the Strategist.* McGraw-Hill, New York, 1982.

Reis, Al, and Trout, Jack. *Marketing Warfare.* McGraw-Hill, New York, 1986.

Tzu, Sun. *The Art of War,* "A Treatise on Chinese Military Science Compiled about 500 B.C.," Graham Brash (Pte) Ltd., Singapore, 1982.

Index

Accounts receivable, collecting, 8, 177–179
Accugraph, 152
Action (or tactics), 34
Action plan, 258
Advisory board, 58–59, 87, 129–130
Age discrimination in Employment Act, 222
Agreements:
  consultants, 180–181
  noncompletion, 179–180
Alternative dispute resolution, 205–206
American Institute of Architects (AIA), 8, 144
American Management Association (AMA), 11, 18
Annual operating business plan, 63–85
Arbitration, 205–206
Architect(s):
  as an artist, 3, 11, 154
  as businesspeople, 7
  and engineers:
    image, 106
    value of work, 115
  image, 7
  training of, 3
Architrion, 152
Attorneys, 10
  selection, 175–177
AutoDESK, 152

Bankruptcy, 174
Benchmarks, 5, 16, 43, 86, 119
Brochures, 8, 107–108
Business, architecture as a, 4
Business plan, 18
  annual plan, 22

Business plan (*Cont.*):
  as a communication tool, 13
  biased opinions, 60
  conclusion, 52, 259
  degree of measurability, 12
  guidelines for stability, 5
  implementation, 130–131
  methodology, 19–20
  model, 54
  names, 18
  outlines, 23, 260–263
  success, 24
Business strategies, 12
Business termination, 173–174

Chief Boyd, 149
Competition, 28–30, 248
Competitive advantage, 13, 96–101
  aggressive initiatives, 99
  annual plan, 153
  business plan, 11
  key factors for success (KFS), 97
  relative superiority, 98
  strategic degrees of freedom (SDF), 100
Computer-aided design (CAD), 11, 14, 146–153
  business planning, 11
  fee structure, 149
  management expectations, 150
  marketing, 150
  platforms, 152
  productivity, 152
  software, 152
Computers, 11
  as a business strategy, 140

Construction:
  documents, 6
  observation, 6
Construction Specification Institute
  (CSI), 144
Consultants, 124, 210–211
Contract labor, 4
Contracts:
  AIA, 10
  application for payment, 8
  letter form of agreement, 10
  no contracts used, 10
Corporate employees, negligence, 161
Corporations:
  consumer stock, 171
  formation, 171
  general business, 170–171
  preferred stock, 171–172
  professional, 170–171
  taxation, 165
  termination, 173

Desktop publishing, 144

Employee benefit plans:
  cafeteria plans, 237
  death benefit plans, 236
  dependent care plans, 237
  group insurance, 235–236
  master plans, 226
  master retirement plans, 223
  nonqualified deterred compensation, 236
  nonqualified plans, 226
  prototype plan, 226
  qualifed plans, 226
  retirement plans, 226–233
    annuity plans, 232–233
    cash plans, 233
    deferred plans, 233
    defined benefit plans, 227–228
    defined contribution plans, 227–228
    pension plans, 232
    profit sharing plans, 229–230
    selecting, 233–234
    stock bonus plans, 230–231
    target benefit plans, 228
  selecting, 223–225
Employee Retirement Income Security
  Act, 222
Employee stock ownership plans,
  230–231

Employees, compensation, 225–226
Environement, 3
ERISA, 222
ESOP, 230–231, 234, 241
Executive overview, 261
Executive summary, 25
Existing business plans, 59

Fee cutting, 6, 7
Fee structure (CAD), 149
Fees:
  lack of collection, 9
  real estate agents, 7
Financial:
  bottom line, 37
  budget, 119–120
  cash flow number, 37
  cash flow projections, 51
  detailed budget, 51
  financial resources, 52
  five-year income statement projection, 50
  image number, 37
  management, 142
  objectives, 36
  overview, 49
  planning help, 129
  pro forma balance sheet, 50
Financial statements, 257
Financial strategies, 14, 48
Forms of business, 159
  financing, 164
  formation expense, 163
  limiting liability, 160
  management, 164
  number of owners, 163
  ownership transfer, 162
  performance, 162
  public laws, 164
  taxation, 164
Fringe benefits (see Employee benefit
  plans)

Goals, 40, 253
  and objectives, 9, 14–15, 17, 33–35

Human resource objectives, 38–39
  quality of work-life, 39

Indemnification, 199–200, 219–220
Insurance:
  automobile, 195

Insurance (*Cont.*):
  builder's risk, 196
  claims made, 192–193
  commercial liability, 194–195
    bodily injury, 195
    medical liability, 195
    personal injury liability, 195
    property damage, 195
  employer's liability, 196–197
  errors and omission, 6, 10
  excess, 195–196
  occurrence, 194
  owner's protective, 196
  procuring, 202–203
  professional liability, 10, 191–194
    claims made, 192–193
    exclusions, 191–193
  property, 197
  umbrella, 195–196
  worker's compensation, 196–197
Intergraph MicroStation, 152
Internship, 4
IRAs, 234–235
Issues and risks, 31

Joint ventures, 172–173

Key employee, loss, 237–238

Liability:
  exposure, 6
  limitation, 220
  limiting, 200–202
Limited partnerships, 170
Litigation, management, 203–205

Management by objectives, 133–138
  definition of, 134
Management perspectives, 153–156
Management responsibility, 154
Market characteristics, 27, 248
Marketing, 102–117
  advertising, 8
  defined, 43
  lack of, 8
  needs and wants, 103
  objectives, 37
  plan, 18, 22
Marketing communications, 107–113
  advertising, 111
  brochures, 107

Marketing communications (*Cont.*):
  direct mail, 108
  newsletters, 109
  publicity, 110
  social contacts, 112
Marketing mix, 44
Marketing research, 13, 113–114
Marketing strategies, 15, 42–43, 255
  list of, 46–47
Marketing strategy, 44
Marketing strategy statement, 45
Mechanic's lien, 178–179
Mediation, 206
Minitrial, 206
Mission statement, 26–27, 247
Monthly cash flow budget report, 123

Negligence:
  guarantee, 183
  liability, 182–189
  standard of care, 182–183
Negotiation, 7–8

Objectives, 251
  human resource objectives, 252
  financial, 251, 253
  marketing, 252
Odiorne, George S., 135
Ohmae, Dr. Kenichi, *The Mind of the
    Strategist*, 93
Older American Act, 222
Operating review meeting, 120–123
Opportunities, 31
  and issue analysis, 14–15, 30
  and threats, 249
Owner:
  loss, 237–238
  transition, 239–244,

Partner:
  agreement, 167
  capital, 168–169
  personal liability, 160
Partnership, 160
  draws, 167
  formation, 166
  general, 166
  limited, 166
  loans, 169
  management, 167–168
  partner authority, 169

Partnership (*Cont.*):
  partner liability, 167
  termination, 167, 173
Performance review, 137
Plan, the, 119
Plan implementaion, 47
Planning pyramid, 90–91
Portman, 116
Positioning, 14–15, 26, 28
Preconceived ideas, 55–56
Pregnancy Discrimination Act, 221
Principal, time is free, 5–6
Professional liability, 181–189
Professional service agreement:
  code compliance, 218–219
  cost estimates, 218
  document ownership, 220–221
  indemnification, 219–220
  insurance, 220
  limiting liability, 220
  method of the work, 215–216
  owner's responsibilities, 216
  payment, 216–217
  safety, 216
  scope of services, 212–215
  standard of care, 215
Profit, 5
Project management, 129
Promotions, 41
Purpose statement, 19

Quality control, 185–186
Quality design, 5–6

Reis, Al and David Trout, *Marketing Warfare*, 96
Risk, 32–33
  planning, 190–191

Sample, Inc.:
  business plan for, 63–85
  profile of, 61
Scope of work, 6
  changes in, 9
Self-insurance, 197–198
Services rendered, 8
Situational analysis, 250
Slogans, 41–42
SMART, acronym, 35
Sole proprietor, 12, 43, 50, 58–59, 87
Sole proprietorship, 173
  defined, 159
  formation, 165
  liability, 165
  personal liability, 160
  termination, 165
Specifications, 143
Strategic planning, 90
Strategic triangle, 94
Strategy, 34, 88–101
  defined, 89
Strategy alternatives, 101
Strength and weakness, 30, 249
Structural work act, 181–183
Sun Tzu, *The Art of War*, 89

Tactics, 34
Threats, 31
Three C's, 93
Trade Shows, 59
  AEC, 59
  AIA, 59
  CSI, 59

Value of the architect's work, 104–105, 115–117

Word processing, 143

About the Authors

RONALD A. MCKENZIE is a licensed architect and manages McKenzie Marketing Group, Inc., Chicago, Illinois. He is a graduate of California Polytechnic State University, San Luis Obispo, California.

BRUCE SCHOUMACHER is a partner with the law firm of Querrey and Harrow, Ltd., Chicago, and is the author of *Engineers and the Law: An Overview*.